OKANAGAN COLLEGE LIBRARY

03793643

K

Heterosexual Masculinities

Contemporary Perspectives from
Psychoanalytic Gender Theory

D1707598

Edited by
Bruce Reis
Robert Grossmark

Routledge
Taylor & Francis Group
New York   London

Donnel B. Stern
Series Editor

When music is played in a new key, the melody does not change, but the notes that make up the composition do: change in the context of continuity, continuity that perseveres through change. "Psychoanalysis in a New Key" publishes books that share the aims psychoanalysts have always had, but that approach them differently. The books in the series are not expected to advance any particular theoretical agenda, although to this date most have been written by analysts from the Interpersonal and Relational orientations.

The most important contribution of a psychoanalytic book is the communication of something that nudges the reader's grasp of clinical theory and practice in an unexpected direction. "Psychoanalysis in a New Key" creates a deliberate focus on innovative and unsettling clinical thinking. Because that kind of thinking is encouraged by exploration of the sometimes surprising contributions to psychoanalysis of ideas and findings from other fields, "Psychoanalysis in a New Key" particularly encourages interdisciplinary studies. Books in the series have married psychoanalysis with dissociation, trauma theory, sociology, and criminology. The series is open to the consideration of studies examining the relationship between psychoanalysis and any other field—for instance, biology, literary and art criticism, philosophy, systems theory, anthropology, and political theory.

But innovation also takes place within the boundaries of psychoanalysis, and "Psychoanalysis in a New Key" therefore also presents work that reformulates thought and practice without leaving the precincts of the field. Books in the series focus, for example, on the significance of personal values in psychoanalytic practice, on the complex interrelationship between the analyst's clinical work and personal life, on the consequences for the clinical situation when patient and analyst are from different cultures, and on the need for psychoanalysts to accept the degree to which they knowingly satisfy their own wishes during treatment hours, often to the patient's detriment.

PSYCHOANALYSIS IN A NEW KEY BOOK SERIES

Donnel B. Stern
Series Editor

OKANAGAN COLLEGE
LIBRARY
BRITISH COLUMBIA

Heterosexual Masculinities

*Contemporary Perspectives from
Psychoanalytic Gender Theory*

Edited by
Bruce Reis
Robert Grossmark

Routledge
Taylor & Francis Group
New York   London

Routledge
Taylor & Francis Group
270 Madison Avenue
New York, NY 10016

Routledge
Taylor & Francis Group
27 Church Road
Hove, East Sussex BN3 2FA

© 2009 by Taylor & Francis Group, LLC
Routledge is an imprint of Taylor & Francis Group, an Informa business

Printed in the United States of America on acid-free paper
10 9 8 7 6 5 4 3 2 1

International Standard Book Number-13: 978-0-88163-502-7 (Softcover) 978-0-88163-501-0 (Hardcover)

Except as permitted under U.S. Copyright Law, no part of this book may be reprinted, reproduced, trans-mitted, or utilized in any form by any electronic, mechanical, or other means, now known or hereafter invented, including photocopying, microfilming, and recording, or in any information storage or retrieval system, without written permission from the publishers.

Trademark Notice: Product or corporate names may be trademarks or registered trademarks, and are used only for identification and explanation without intent to infringe.

Library of Congress Cataloging-in-Publication Data

Heterosexual masculinities : contemporary perspectives from psychoanalytic gender
    theory / [edited by] Bruce Reis, Robert Grossmark.
        p. cm. -- (Psychoanalysis in a new key book series ; 11)
    Includes bibliographical references and index.
    ISBN 978-0-88163-501-0 (hardcover) -- ISBN 978-0-88163-502-7 (pbk.) -- ISBN
    978-0-203-88831-5 (ebook)
        1. Masculinity. 2. Psychoanalysis. 3. Heterosexual men--Psychology. I. Reis,
Bruno Cardoso. II. Grossmark, Robert.

BF175.5.M37H48 2009
155.3'32--dc22   2008034677

Visit the Taylor & Francis Web site at
http://www.taylorandfrancis.com

and the Routledge Web site at
http://www.routledgementalhealth.com

Robert Grossmark:
For Carina, Tomas & Sophia

For Bruce Reis:
For Joanne and Olivia

Contents

Contributors

C. Jama Adams, Ph.D., is an associate professor of psychology in the Department of African American Studies at the John Jay College of Criminal Justice of the City University of New York. Dr. Adams has published in the areas of the psychology of migration, gender studies, and the self projects of working class African American men.

William F. Cornell, M.A., TSTA, studied behavioral psychology at Reed College in Portland, Oregon, and phenomenological psychology at Duquesne University in Pittsburgh, Pennsylvania, following his graduate studies with training in transactional analysis and body-centered psychotherapy. Dr. Cornell has published numerous journal articles and book chapters, many exploring the interface between transactional analysis, body-centered, and psychoanalytic modalities. He is editor of the ITAA *Script* newsletter and co-editor of the *Transactional Analysis Journal*. He is the editor of *The Healer's Bent: Solitude and Dialogue in the Clinical Encounter* (Analytic Press, 2005), a collection of the psychoanalytic writings of James McLaughlin, for which he wrote the introduction, and (with Helena Hargaden) is co-editor and author of *From Transactions to Relations: The Emergence of Relational Paradigms in Transactional Analysis* (Haddon Press, 2005). He maintains an independent private practice of therapy, consultation, and training in Pittsburgh and leads frequent training groups in Europe.

Michael J. Diamond, Ph.D., is a training and supervising analyst at the Los Angeles Institute for Psychoanalytic Studies, faculty and supervisor at the Wright Institute, Los Angeles, and an associate clinical professor of psychiatry at UCLA. He is a Fellow of the American Psychological Association and the International Psychoanalytic Association, and a diplomate of the American Board of Professional Psychology. He is the author of *My Father Before Me: How Fathers and Sons Influence Each Other Throughout Their*

Lives (W. W. Norton, 2007) as well as several publications on male gender, and is in private practice in Los Angeles.

Gerald I. Fogel, Ph.D., is a training and supervising analyst and former director of the Oregon Psychoanalytic Institute. He is on the editorial board of the *Journal of the American Psychoanalytic Association* and *Studies in Gender and Sexuality*. He co-edited *The Psychology of Men: New Psychoanalytic Perspectives* (Yale University Press, 1996) and *Perversions and Near-Perversions in Clinical Practice* (Yale University Press, 1991), and edited *The Work of Hans Loewald: An Introduction and Commentary* (Jason Aronson, 1991). He has written about masculinity, interiority and interior space in men, and a variety of other topics, and is in private practice in Portland, Oregon.

Robert Grossmark, Ph.D., is faculty at the National Institute for the Psychotherapies Training Program in Psychoanalysis, adjunct faculty in the doctoral program in Clinical Psychology at the Graduate Center of the City University of New York, and faculty in the subspecialty program in group psychoanalysis at the NYU Postdoctoral Program in Psychoanalysis and Psychotherapy.

Adrienne Harris, Ph.D., is a clinical associate professor at the New York University postdoctoral program in psychotherapy and psychoanalysis and a visiting scholar at the Psychoanalytic Institute of Northern California. She is an associate editor of *Psychoanalytic Dialogues*, and a consulting editor for *Studies in Gender and Sexuality*. She has co-edited *The Legacy of Sándor Ferenczi* (with Lewis Aron) and *Storms in Her Head: Freud and the Construction of Hysteria* (with Muriel Dimen), and is the author of *Gender as a Soft Assembly* (Analytic Press, 2005).

Irwin Hirsch, Ph.D., teaches and/or supervises at five psychoanalytic training programs and serves on four editorial boards. He has published over 60 psychoanalytic articles and reviews and is the author of *Coasting in the Countertransference: Conflicts of Self Interest between Analyst and Patient* (Analytic Press, 2008).

Emmanuel Kaftal, Ph.D., is a faculty member of the NYU postdoctoral program in psychotherapy and psychoanalysis as well as the Psychoanalytic Psychotherapy Study Center. Recently, he has become interested in the analyst's vulnerability, especially his/her vulnerability to physical illness understood in its social context.

Ethel S. Person, M.D., is professor of clinical psychiatry at the College of Physicians and Surgeons, Columbia University, and training and supervising analyst at the Columbia University Center for Psychoanalytic Training and Research. Dr. Person, along with Dr. Arnold Cooper and Dr. Glen Gabbard, edited *The APPI Textbook of Psychoanalysis*, published in 2005. She is the author of *Feeling Strong: The Achievement of Authentic Power*, *The Sexual Century* (William Morrow, 2002), and *By Force of Fantasy: How We Make Our Lives* (Penguin, 1996). She is privileged that, in 2006, American Psychiatric Publishing, Inc. reprinted her book *Dreams of Love and Fateful Encounters: The Power of Romantic Passion*. She has edited 11 other books and contributed over 100 papers to the psychiatric and psychoanalytic literature.

Bruce Reis, Ph.D., is on the relational faculty of the NYU postdoctoral program in psychotherapy and psychoanalysis and a contributing editor for *Studies in Gender and Sexuality*.

Louis Rothschild, Ph.D., is in independent practice in Providence, Rhode Island. Having completed a dissertation on psychological essentialism at the New School for Social Research, Dr. Rothschild worked as a postdoctoral fellow at Brown University's School of Medicine. Presently, he is the membership committee chair of the Division of Psychoanalysis (39) of the American Psychological Association and is the president of the Rhode Island Division 39 Local Chapter, the Rhode Island Association for Psychoanalytic Psychologies.

Eyal Rozmarin, Ph.D., is a candidate at the NYU postdoctoral program in psychotherapy and psychoanalysis and a psychologist in private practice in New York City. An Israeli who relocated to the United States, he is interested in the relations between subjectivity, history, and culture, and writes at the intersection of psychoanalysis, social theory, and philosophy.

Introduction

This book comes out of a fortuitous lunch that we had in 2006 in Greenwich Village. We started talking about our work as analysts, and in particular the many men whom we treat in our practices. Our conversation led to many shared issues in the treatment of these men and the overriding feeling that we were describing dynamics of these men and our experience of working with them that seemed beyond the bounds of existing psychoanalytic theory. It was almost by accident that our lunch conversation revealed a need for new thinking about clinical work with men at the turn of the 21st century and the whole issue of masculinity as it has been taken up within psychoanalysis. We also recognized that we were not alone in feeling this, and indeed since beginning this project many clinicians we have spoken with have echoed the need for revising the way that masculinity is theorized and encountered in psychoanalysis today.

Both of us grew up, analytically speaking, in a culture saturated with gender theory. Our education at the New York University postdoctoral program in psychotherapy and psychoanalysis introduced us to the central canon of psychoanalytic thinking as well as to feminist and queer theorists who were advancing psychoanalysis past its classical biases, bringing it into a world of constructed, fluid, and multiply gendered possibilities. We felt we had gained enormously in our clinical thinking from this work. As part of a new generation of analysts we attended analytic training alongside many women colleagues, queer peers and friends, and a few heterosexual men, and studied under feminist analysts who were at the forefront of rethinking gendered subjectivities. Yet what emerged in our conversation was the virtual absence of the application of such critical and generative thinking to the world of heterosexual masculinity. These analytic considerations dovetailed nicely with our membership in a generation that has comfortably, even eagerly, embraced the gender transgressions and provocations of the likes of David Bowie and glam rock and was situated at the center of social movements of liberation for women and homosexuals. Where, then, were the theories applicable to the men we were working with? And how would practice be changed by considering masculinity as a sex that is not one (Irigary, 1985)?

Perhaps it can be said that Freudian theory regarded women as damaged men, defined predominately by a lack. The feminist response to classical psychoanalysis righted this wrong, firmly establishing the importance of women as central figures in emerging developmental schemes and later as subjective centers of desire and power. This merged well with the rise of object relational approaches within psychoanalysis, which emphasized preoedipal dynamics, consequently shifting focus and power from issues of castration to the mother–child dyad. In this process, fathers began to recede from analytic view, appearing typically as absent or dangerous, generally as tertiary, beside the point. Fathers now were the ones who were lacking, by virtue of their absence, misattunement, and position outside of the dyad. In our discussion, we shared a discomfort with both positions— either devaluing women, or devaluing heterosexual men. Although it has been helpful to see the adverse effects of patriarchy and male hegemony on society, we felt that the men we see analytically deserved inclusion in the theoretical revolution around gender. This is not to say that we are naive to the oppressive history of patriarchal relations within psychoanalysis, nor do we wish to suggest that these forces are no longer with us. But we realized, by virtue of our training and our generational experiences, that the psychoanalysis we live with need not devalue women, homosexuals, or heterosexual men.

The advances of feminist and queer theory have given us many more theoretical avenues and perspectives with which to think critically, clinically, and theoretically about the subject. Heterosexual masculinity has yet to be approached from a view that understands gender as fluid, multiple, and emergent. Our work is an attempt to build on these 30 years of queer and feminist theory and to expand our understanding of heterosexuality and masculinity accordingly. In doing so, we hope to reposition heterosexual masculinity solidly within the larger field of gendered subjectivities, appreciating all the "essential contradictions," complexities, and multiplicities of the heterosexual masculine position.

Men are different now. We know from the consulting room that men's fantasies, sexual practices, desires, longings, excitements, fears, and anxieties are governed by more complex psychic and social coordinates than ever imagined possible within psychoanalysis. What to a previous generation would have appeared as pathological or defensive, we encounter now as forms of masculine subjectivity that include wishes for intimacy, receptivity, surrender, alongside ambition and the pleasures of phallic narcissism (Corbett, 2006). Psychoanalysis has always been about the interior life of an individual, yet considering the interior life of men anew opens the analyst up to courting surprise (Stern, 1990).

Out of our lunch conversation came a panel at Division 39 of the American Psychological Association in Toronto in 2007 where we presented companion papers, discussed by Adrienne Harris who had recently published *Gender as Soft Assembly* (2005), a book that had moved us greatly with its integration of nonlinear dynamic systems theory with a careful and sensitive clinical approach as applied to gender. There followed a groundswell of interest in our topic, confirming for us that there was a yearning for a more contemporary reading of heterosexual masculinity in the field. When we shared these papers with our reading group led by Donnel Stern, we were met with enthusiasm and the generous invitation by Donnel to explore this subject in an edited volume that he was excited to include in the Psychoanalysis in a New Key book series. We were delighted to have a book such as this one appear in a series titled "Psychoanalysis in a New Key" as we felt this book opens up a new register in relational analytic thinking around the topic of gender and clinical practice. This psychoanalysis is very different from the psychoanalysis that spawned the old gender theory. Like feminist and queer theory, it offers us new and exciting ways to conceive of life as gendered. Contemporary psychoanalytic ideas that emphasize the co-construction, contextualization, and emergent and unformulated nature of the unconscious lend themselves perfectly to understanding gender in its various forms and presentations, including heterosexual masculinity.

Our volume begins with two papers that set the stage. Ethel Spector Person outlines the vast differences and wide varieties of masculinities across cultures. Person engages the broad array of masculinities including the hetero- and homosexual and argues that the tendency to contrast masculinity with femininity obscures the many differences among men. She explores various "psychologies" of men as well as the cultural components that shape a society's ideas of what constitutes masculinity. Michael Diamond, perhaps more than any psychoanalyst writing on the subject of masculinity, reframes classical and ego psychological conceptions of masculinity in the language of contemporary clinical practice. In his chapter he does away with older developmental models of masculine growth. Male genitality, phallicism, and identification are all construed, as Diamond reworks the oedipal situation to emphasize what is gained rather than what is in danger of being lost.

In the next chapter, Bruce Reis addresses a cohort of men for whom traditional analytic constructions of masculinity fail to capture the variety of subjective experiences and desires. He situates heterosexual masculinities within multiple registers, drawing on clinical material from his practice and diverse figures from cultural life to illustrate the simultaneous hardness and softness, the emotional accessibility, and varied sexual excitations of post–baby boom heterosexual men. In the process he expands the scope of the erotic to include much more of the male body than solely the penis.

Robert Grossmark brings us into the clinical consulting room where heterosexual men openly talk and relate to one another in ways that defy old proscriptions of gendered masculine behavior. He presents detailed clinical notes of two sessions with two very different men, bringing the reader into the process of struggling with confusing and challenging forms of heterosexual masculine experience. As Grossmark engages these men, new forms of understanding and participation emerge from the clinical relationship.

Irwin Hirsch reexamines conventional assumptions about masculinity, morality, and the analyst's unquestioned judgments of what is proper for male sexuality and intimacy. Utilizing numerous clinical vignettes, he challenges his own and our ideas of health and success in relationships and in the process makes room for an increased variety of sexual practices and modes of relatedness in the lives of heterosexual men.

Emmanuel Kaftal reviews the transformation of classical theory of masculine development, revisiting the contributions of Freud, Rank, Sullivan, Greenson, and Stoller. Writing at a time when infant research was just beginning to influence psychoanalytic theory, Kaftal moves on to consider how men's past experience tends to militate against new interaffective experience, leaving men with a pervasive sense of otherness and consigning many of their nurturing capacities to the "not me" world of the feminine. Yet, in psychoanalytic treatment, Kaftal describes how men invite the analyst to breach their splendid isolation, and he recasts what had been previously regarded as "homosexual panic" as a new intimacy between men.

William Cornell, writing 16 years later, presents a moving illustration of the intimacy that Kaftal suggested was possible in the treatment relationship. He takes the unusual and brave step of presenting his own experience as a patient in analysis. He describes his experience of his analytic treatment, which included a potentially damaging enactment and its resolution in the acknowledgment of the difficulty of a loving relationship between men. In a blurring of the boundaries between hetero- and homosexual love, the most wished-for and most feared evocation of passionate attachment and desire between him and his analyst enabled both to come more fully to life with each other.

Eyal Rozmarin continues the theme of intimate attachments in examining two patients, one gay, one heterosexual, each of whom married during the course of their treatments. He mines his experience with these men to illustrate the social openings and constrictions facing each patient in their anxieties as they make their choices of partners. In the comparison of the two men's processes, Rozmarin reveals the surprising complexity of heterosexual marriage and commitment.

C. Jama Adams takes on the issue of poor African American men and their struggles to fully occupy various masculine positions. Illustrating how social elements at the macro level are always present, but are not absolute determinants of the individual's sense of self, he develops a theory that contrasts "reputational" and "respectable" masculinity. The variety of patients Adams introduces us to demonstrates the hopes, strengths, and challenges these men face while embedded in the larger web of socioeconomic relationships that both constrain and facilitate how they love and work, often in unacknowledged ways.

The subject of fathers and sons has been a main focus of the discussion of masculinity. Through a biographical vignette, Adrienne Harris brings us into the relation of fathers and daughters and ultimately into a new consideration of the masculine, extending the psychoanalytic view of fathers past the myth of their absence. Harris considers a multitude of fathers—the nurturant and the punishing—and views the father's sense of self and gender as permeable and co-constructed in the crucible of father–daughter relations.

Louis Rothschild, who through the Disney movie *Finding Nemo* highlights the doubts, anxieties, and needs for dependence of the father, revisits fathers and sons. Rothschild writes of his own experience as a father with an ill son, and tells of the feelings of helplessness and isolation that undermine traditional notions of hegemonic masculinity found in the classically strong oedipal father–son dyad. Rothschild recasts Herzog's "father hunger" to include the father's own hunger, and like Harris, opens the possibility of the father's development and growth through his relations with his children.

We close the volume with a prescient chapter, written 10 years ago by Gerald Fogel. He expands our ideas of masculinity by the inclusion of "receptivity," usually a mark of femininity, as an aspect of postoedipal maturity in men, rather than as passivity. The close examination of one case enables Fogel to introduce the idea that authentic "phallic" experience usually contains its "cloacal" counterpart as well: an internal space based on identification with the mother. Fogel reassesses classical developmental theory, illustrating how it cannot do justice to the actual ambiguities and complexities of emergent psychosexuality.

The discussion began with the two of us at lunch in Greenwich Village and has grown to include these varied voices. Considering the chapters together, what emerges is a very different man: present fathers whose gender is shaped and emerges in interaction with their daughters and sons; analysts who change a baby's diapers in session; men whose experience of sexual excitation and intimacy is broadened past antiquated conceptions of their constriction; and heterosexual analysts and patients who can love and play with desire between them in the analytic space, even as they find themselves socioculturally defined in ways that do not fully capture their relational potential. This new and different man is an emergent man, whose qualities continue to grow and change with each new examination of his multiple and fluid capacities. With the publication of this volume we invite the reader to join in the larger conversation begun here and consider heterosexual masculinities anew.

This book would not have been possible without the interest, support, and enthusiasm of Donnel Stern to whom we owe a tremendous debt of gratitude. We also thank all the members of our reading group with Donnel: Ghislaine Boulanger, Philip Blumberg, James Ogilvie, Betsy Hegeman, Steven Tublin, and Cleonie White who have been wonderful "Partners in Thought" (Stern, in press) over the past few years and who have miraculously always squeezed into a small office that expands to accommodate the intellectual breadth of our discussions.

References

Corbett, K. (2006, April 23). *Fantastic Phallicism: Recognition, Relation, and Phallic Narcissism*. Keynote address Division of Psychoanalysis of the American Psychological Association, Philadelphia, PA.

Harris, A. (2005). *Gender as Soft Assembly*. Mahwah, NJ: Analytic Press.

Irigaray, L. (1985). *This Sex which Is Not One*. Ithaca, NY: Cornell University Press.

Stern, D. (1990). Courting surprise: Unbidden perceptions in clinical practice. *Contemporary Psychoanalysis, 26*, 452–478.

Stern, D. (in press) *Partners in thought*. New York: Routledge.

1

Masculinities, Plural

Ethel Spector Person

> There is no realm in which theoretical controversy within psychoanalysis has more dramatically reflected larger intellectual currents than in the area of sexuality and gender.
>
> Mitchell & Black (1995, p. 218)

Masculinity cannot be regarded as a single entity. Both within Western culture and across cultures, a wide variety of masculinities are easily observable. Yet masculinity is so often contrasted with femininity that the many differences among men are at times obscured. To in part correct this deficiency, various "psychologies" of men are explored, as well as the cultural components that shape a society's ideas of what constitutes masculinity. Male heterosexuality and homosexuality are also examined, as are a number of the fantasies and fears that men typically experience. What cannot be left out of any exploration of male psychology are those sources of strength that permit so many men to fiercely protect their families and, when called upon, to fight their country's wars. Nonetheless, the differences between individual men are significant and can even be said to be vast.

Our field has undergone a sea change in how we think about the origins and development of femininity and masculinity. Freud fluctuated between two divergent theories about the sexes, centered on the nature-nurture controversy. He ultimately integrated them into what he called a "complemental series," which I take as an attempt to integrate masculinity and femininity, nature and nurture. Rivto pointed out that Freud's phrase, "a complemental series," was based on Goethe's insight that "[fate and chance] and not one or the other is decisive" (1990, p. 42).

We now know that in addition to nature and nurture, the culture in which we live plays an important role not only in our sexual practices but

1

also in the way we conceptualize gender. Our formulations about what is innate and what is learned (or socialized) can never be definitive or universal, if only because sexual mores and gender preconceptions are parsed differently in different cultures and centuries, sometimes even in different decades. To some degree, however, we have been so intent on distinguishing between men and women and masculinity and femininity that we have not systematically explored the wide variety of ways in which masculinity is expressed.

Before I discuss the different kinds of masculinities that can be observed, I want to call attention to how many differences there are among men. One comes to know men in different aspects of their lives, whether as sons, brothers, fathers, husbands, lovers, men of the clergy, scholars, businessmen, athletes, porters, conductors (whether of orchestras or trains), and on and on. Not only do we know men in different roles; we also know men of different religions and nationalities, who hold to different systems of belief regarding what constitutes optimal masculinity and what kind of relationship is to be sanctioned between men and women. What I am trying to get across is that I am not sure that as analysts we are in the best position to provide a fully comprehensive overview of the range of masculinities that exist. Nonetheless, in this chapter I have put together some thoughts about the varying range of what we call masculine.

Let me note from the start that masculinity is not the exclusive province of heterosexual men. Masculinity encompasses particular attitudes, behaviors, and self-identifications that are observed not only in the majority of heterosexual men but also in many homosexual men. Needless to say, men, both straight and gay, can display effeminate characteristics. Then, too, some women are perceived as masculine, among whom some self-identify as such (Person, 1999, pp. 296–315). To put it simply, what we generally think of as masculine is not restricted to men. However, my focus here is on masculinity in men.

Robert Stoller was one of the first psychoanalytic theorists to emphasize the innate biological contributions to primary masculinity and primary femininity. He described sex and sexual self-identification as determined by chromosomes, external genitalia, internal genitalia (for example, the uterus and the prostate), hormonal states, and secondary sex characteristics. He also emphasized that for men the penis is not the whole story. Stoller drew on the work of Spitz (1962), who had observed that before 8 to 10 months of age little boys do not play with their penises any more than with any other organ. Stoller's work is important on many levels, not the least of which is his acknowledgment of the importance of body and hormones along with early relationships.

Although the penis is not the whole story, it nonetheless is an important one. Tyson and Tyson (1990) have provided an excellent account of the boy's "discovery" of his penis, which they date as occurring in the second 6 months of life. They noticed at that time a conjunction in which intentional self-stimulation of the penis is paired with affectionate glances at the mother (p. 278). Clearly the boy takes pleasure in his penis from very early on, and it is one of the ongoing components in what we call masculinity. By the second year, the boy also takes pride in his urinary control.

Differences between masculinity versus femininity and differences among males are apparent relatively early in life. The first ejaculation, a key event in the male's sexual development, generally occurs between the ages of 10 and 16. In *Sexual Orientation and Psychoanalysis*, Friedman and Downey (2002) describe certain boyhood characteristics that are generally predictors of which boys will grow into the cultural norm for men. For those destined to be "masculine," their

> peer groups tend to be cohesive, bounded both from girls and from adults, and organized hierarchically. Dominance rank governs much behavior. In free play juvenile boys tend to be territorial, competitive, not accepting participation by girls and devaluing behavior deemed feminine or girl-like. Verbalizations tend to be confrontational and replete with challenges, mockery and bravado. ... Whereas girls gravitate to dyadic interactions and those between dyads and relatively small groups of peers, boys are drawn to groups of five to eight individuals or even more. (p. 209)

These male groups are more often than not hierarchically structured, with members organized around leaders. Friedman and Downey note that from early life not only boys, but also grown men, tend to negatively categorize boys who do not match the cultural male stereotype and who participate in girlish interests. I would add that the hierarchical structure among males endures into adult life and often becomes a defining feature of males' self-identity.

What later-life characteristics can be said to define masculinity? Gilmore (1991) observed that although androgynous cultures exist, they are relatively rare. She proposed that "in most societies ... three moral injunctions exist for men: to impregnate women, to protect dependents from danger, to provide resources for kin" (quoted in Friedman & Downey, 2002, p. 223). For Gilmore, ideologies of manhood always include a criterion of selfless generosity, even to the point of sacrifice. Again and again we find "real men" are those who give more than they take, they serve others. Real men are generous even to a fault. … Non-men are often stigmatized as stingy and unproductive. Manhood therefore is also a nurturing concept. … It is true that this male giving is different from and less demonstrative and more obscured than in the female. It is less direct, less immediate, more involved with the external; the "other" involved may be society in general rather than specific persons. (quoted in Friedman & Downey, 2002, p. 229)

My impression is that Gilmore emphasizes the best traits of masculinity, its protectiveness of others, traits that certainly exist in many men but not in all. In contrast to men supportive of women, there are those men who perceive women as weak and inferior, or overbearing, and a relatively small group of men who abuse women. Overall, each culture has standards for what constitutes masculinity, a construction that is generally internalized by the men and women who grow and develop in that culture (Friedman & Downey, 2002, p. 123).

Masculinity is undertheorized compared with femininity. Dimen and Goldner make this point explicitly: "Freud's idealization of phallic masculinity not only erased and debased femininity as a category and as a lived, embodied self experience. It also delayed the theorization of masculinity in all its specificity and multiplicity" (2005, p. 99). Clearly there is more than one kind of masculinity. A broad array of "masculinities" exist, not only within different cultures but also within any one culture, particularly in such a complex culture as our own. To put the matter simply, there are considerable individual differences in the way masculinity in defined (or understood), both in our own culture and in different cultures and subcultures.

I have a dictionary dating from 1858 that defines masculine as

1. having the qualities of a man; strong; robust; as a *masculine* body;
2. coarse as opposed to delicate or soft; as a masculine feature;
3. cold, brave; as a masculine spirit or courage;
4. in grammar the masculine gender of words is that which expresses a male, or something analogous to it; or it is the gender appropriated to males, though not always expressing the male sex.

The passage goes on to define masculinity in terms of the male's "coarseness of features, strength of body, boldness," and masculinity as "suitable to, or characteristic of, a man; virile, robust; sometimes, of a mannish woman." I find it striking that there is a reference to a mannish woman in a dictionary published so long ago.

As already noted, masculinity is not the sole propriety of heterosexual men. Because both heterosexuals and homosexuals may be masculine, masculinity is clearly not dependent on a man's sexual object choice. It is also important to note that there are both heterosexual and homosexual men who "fail" to conform to the cultural stereotype of what constitutes masculinity. We now understand masculinity and femininity as the construction of male and female gender role identities that develop fully only after the establishment of core gender identity. Masculinity and femininity incorporate identifications and fantasies of oneself as male or female. Although nearly all individuals self-identify as either masculine or feminine, what has been observed in analytic work is that there are subliminal thoughts and fantasies that suggest each of us internalize multiple identifications.

Gender Identity

For both boys and girls, a significant interest in their genital orgasm becomes evident somewhere between the years of 3 to 5, although, as I have noted, most boys begin to play with their penises beginning between 8 and 10 months of age. Endocrines play a large role in sexual behavior, particularly, it would seem, for men. If the testicles are removed before puberty, secondary sex characteristics do not develop, and there is little or no impulse toward sexual activity, whether masturbatory or interpersonal. This would suggest that libido may be not so much an inborn drive as a drive developed as a result of the mentalization and integration of bodily experience and its associated pleasure (Stoller, 1968, p. 11).* It appears that some of the typical behaviors and attitudes of boys are stoked by the presence of testosterone. In a sense, the brain acts as a computer that contextualizes messages from the body.

However, this is not the way gender was originally understood. For Freud, masculinity was the natural state for both sexes. He postulated that the girl retreats from masculinity into femininity upon the fateful and unhappy discovery that she has no penis (Freud, 1924, 1925, 1931, 1933; see Person, 2005). In sharp contrast, Horney (1924, 1926, 1932, 1933) and Jones (1948/1927, 1948/1933, 1948/1935) suggested that both femininity

---

* In contrast, the girl who is clitorectomized early in life may nonetheless engage in normal sexual activity with orgasm. Apparently, this is because minute amounts of androgens produced in the adrenals act to stoke pleasure.

and masculinity predate the phallic phase, and that each originates from an innate predisposition. In their view, both masculinity and femininity have preoedipal origins. Most contemporary theorists seem to hold the same opinion.

Although both biology and acculturation impact on core gender and gender identity, there is another factor attached to self-identification. In 1955 Money, Hampson, and Hampson published a study that established gender as distinct from sexuality. They demonstrated that the first and crucial step in gender differentiation was self-designation by the child as female or male in accordance with the sex of assignment and rearing. Designated as either male or female at birth, most of the children they studied came to self-identify as such in the first few years of life and to internalize behaviors consistent with their designated sex. There were, however, exceptions. A few individuals who had been sexually reassigned because of abnormalities of their genitals reverted to their biological sex. Self-definitions encompass both core gender identity and gender role identity. *Core gender identity* refers to one's self-identification as male or female. However, *gender role identity* refers to a self-identity that comprises behaviors and preferences referable to masculinity or femininity.

Gender role identity is believed to be shaped to a significant degree by gender identification with the same-sex parent, but this cannot be the whole story. A male raised solely by his mother may grow up with a strong sense of masculinity. Thus, both same-sex identifications and complementary identifications can be key in the formation of gender identity. In essence, a boy raised solely by his mother may acquire masculine characteristics through a complementary relationship to his mother. Moreover, he may identify with men other than his father. Similarly, a woman raised solely by her father may be entirely feminine. To put it simply, core gender identity depends primarily (although not exclusively) on one's self-identification as male or female.

Considerable evidence exists to support the idea that boys' doubts about their masculinity may first surface during the oedipal period, the result of the dual threats of castration anxiety and a sense of genital inferiority in comparison with their fathers. Beginning in adolescence and extending into adulthood, the male is constantly evaluating, critiquing, and enjoying his sense of maleness, the size of his penis, and his sexual longings and behavior. He is also comparing himself to his peers. Anxiety over performance and prowess is as basic to male sexuality as its reputed aggressive content, and it may well be the lingering result of feelings of the weakness and fear of inadequacy inevitably experienced in earliest life.

For some French theorists, particularly for McDougall (1980) and Chasseguet-Smirgel (1984), the boy is not only subject to castration anxiety, the result of fears that the father will retaliate for his son's competitive wishes, but he may suffer an even earlier blow to his sexual narcissism as a result of his inability to secure his mother's sexual love, his interpretation being that he does not have the genital endowment to compete.˙ He senses that his mother rejects him in favor of his father because his penis is too small. Those men who do not recover from a sense of genital inadequacy are often destined to suffer lifelong penis envy in any literal sense (Person, 1986). In part this is because the penis so often serves as a metaphor for power in the male world. Males' experience of themselves as more powerful than females (possessors of higher status, purveyors of greater knowledge) gets incorporated into their psyches very early in life. Although the Harry Potter novels—in which Harry has magical powers—appeal to both boys and girls, I would suggest that boys would be less likely to read the series if the main character was a girl.† It may be that penis envy in both sexes is more the metaphorical expression of the wish for power than for a penis, or for a bigger one.

Although it has long been argued that boys' fears about their own masculinity stem from castration anxiety vis-à-vis competition with the father, some theorists propose potential fault lines in the development of masculinity prior to the oedipal complex. Chasseguet-Smirgel (1984) argued that Freud's interpretation of femininity as the product of deficiency, that is, of the lack of a penis, might be better understood as a male's need to overcome feelings of helplessness in response to his mother's power. In her opinion, the power of the paternal phallus is invoked to put down the mother.

As early as 1928, Melanie Klein suggested that boys suffered from pre-oedipal envy of the female reproductive orgasm, what she called sites "of receptivity and bounty" (Klein, 1928, p. 180). Klein's idea has been discussed and reasserted by a number of contemporary women theorists, among them Dimen, Goldner, and Chodorow. They suggest that the boy's fear of his mother is engendered in the preoedipal period. To the degree that his fear does not diminish, it may be incorporated into a reaction formation, the visible evidence of which is the boy's punishment or

---

˙ Although Freud's theory clarified a wealth of material about what we now call gender, it was based primarily on oedipal and postoedipal development.

† It has been pointed out that the author only used her initials J. K. along with her surname Rowling because her publisher feared that if the author was known to be female, boys would be less likely to read the books.

denigration of his mother. Such a preoedipal dynamic may be the root of
the notorious woman hating observed in some men.

In complete antithesis to women-hating men, some men identify with
women or may even desire to be a woman, as is sometimes evident in their
mannerisms and sometimes even in fully acknowledged female identifications. One observes this in extreme form in a subgroup of cross-dressing
males, some of whom go so far as to disguise themselves as female prostitutes and position themselves near bridges and tunnels. Such a dynamic
may be understood as an identification with the powerful female aggres-
sor. In a much less dramatic enactment, some female self-identifications
can be observed in that subgroup of men whose verbalizations are arch,
facetious, sarcastic, or bitchy. Their barbs are often, but not invariably,
directed toward women. Some may inadvertently use a dropped wrist to
make a point. Such maneuvers express a superficial bravado that may be
campy or at the same time plead for recognition. These behaviors can be
observed in both straight men and gay men. Such "effeminate" behaviors
act to provide the man a sense of borrowed power, even though it may
diminish his sense of masculinity.

The Masculinities

What constitutes male gender role as defined by the masculinities? Many
observers have confirmed that female behavior and male behavior are dis-
crepant within the first years of life, before the child knows the sexual
difference. Because the roots of gender differentiation precede the phallic
phase, Freud's gender theory cannot be the whole story.

Stoller (1968) took a different tack from the conventional interpretation of gender, going so far as to claim femininity as the natural state.
He proposed that femininity was built into earliest unconsciousness in
both sexes, basing his theory of protofemininity on his work with male
transsexuals. But if one cannot demonstrate Stoller's contention that a
protofeminine state exists in men other than transsexuals, then one is not
justified in assuming that the natural state is feminine. I do not believe
there is substantial evidence to support a hypothetical protofeminine state
in males.

I would agree with Horney (1924, 1926, 1932, 1933) and Jones (1948/1927,
1948/1933, 1948/1935) that femininity and masculinity are parallel constructs. However, their contention that a masculine gender derives from
innate heterosexuality cannot be correct, inasmuch as both homosexuals

and heterosexuals may be masculine in feelings and in behavior. Moreover, effeminate characteristics can be observed among homosexuals and heterosexuals alike.

Most investigators agree that gender differentiation, observable by the end of the first year of life, is under normal circumstances immutable by the third (for the one major exception, see Imperato-McGinley, Peterson, Gautier, & Sturla, 1979). Core gender derives from nonconflictual learning experiences, not from conflict. Stoller made this point in his studies of primary femininity in women, but his argument that protofemininity occurs in both sexes clouded his contribution, in that it kept him from acknowledging "primary" masculinity in men.

Core gender identity, once established, locates the appropriate object for imitation and identification. Why core gender is of such crucial importance in organizing personality is still an open question. But because it does play a major organizing role in psychic structure, the question is often raised as to why only two gender possibilities exist. However, we do know that some bisexuals embrace both genders, perhaps constituting what might be called a "third" gender. Marlene Dietrich is perhaps a good example of such a dual identification, manifest in her dress and in her sexual interest in both men and women. Some men are also said to identify as belonging to a third gender, but they appear to be a small minority. The men I know who cross-dress may identify themselves as longing to be female but acknowledge themselves as male, and those who have conversion operations identify as female.

In the most usual patterns, early object relations are different in the two sexes, a fact that decisively shapes the attributes of femininity and masculinity. These object relations are operative in the preoedipal identification and fantasies that emerge as soon as the infant differentiates self from object. It is only by learning their gender and identifying with the "appropriate" parent that children are launched into the oedipal period.* However, to say that gender orders sexuality is only partly true. Prioritizing gender cannot detract from the autonomous qualities of sexuality, such as the intense pleasure of sexual stimulation from the interactions between sexuality and gender. True enough, gender, itself the result of postnatal

---

* I have added quotation marks to the word "appropriate" insofar as it is inadvertently restricted to heterosexual development. Boys who identify as feminine will identify more with the mother, resulting in a higher incidence of homosexual object choices, and girls who identify with a male figure will be more likely to be lesbians. But given this strong identification, one might say that gender precedes sexuality in development and organizes sexuality and not the reverse (Person, 1986).

events, frequently organizes object choice and sexual fantasies (Baker, 1980), but not always. As noted above, there are some homosexual men who are decidedly masculine, even hypermasculine, and some heterosexual men who appear effete.

In sum, there is no evidence that the original (or natural) gender state is masculine as proposed by Freud, feminine as proposed by Stoller, or innate as proposed by Horney and Jones. Typically, core gender identity arises from the sex of assignment and rearing. (I say typically but not inevitably; there are reports of male children reassigned to femaleness to conform with their genital appearance who reject the reassignment and choose to resume a masculine role, having never given up their identity.) Core gender is by and large nonconflictual and is cognitively and experientially constructed. With exceptions, gender role identity, both normal and "aberrant," is shaped by one's sexual identity, body structure, hormones, ego, socialization, and sex-discrepant object relations. Unlike core gender identity, gender role identity is a psychological achievement and may sometimes be fraught with psychological conflict.

The Cultural Component in Definitions of Masculinity

Men sometimes view women as receptacles (in Argentina, mothers are given a slipper charm upon the birth of a daughter) or as mere objects of desire. It is not easy to give up the cultural myth of phallic omnipotence and supremacy—sometimes, it seems, for women as well as men. The image of a "large, powerful, untiring phallus attached to a cool controlled male, long on experience, confident and knowledgeable enough to make women crazy with desire, has long-standing and very deep roots in our culture" (Zilbergeld, 1978, p. 23). Although this image is useful in building up self-esteem for some men, it leads others to feel unsure about their masculinity.

Moreover, what we define as masculine inevitably encompasses a cultural component and therefore changes over time. The film character James Bond exhibited what some would consider a feminine interest in appearance and style that would have been foreign to the film cowboy portrayed by John Wayne. As Neal Gabler says of Bond, "operating in the postwar *Playboy* ethos, Bond didn't need to divide his true masculine self from his urbane exterior. He was sophisticated and feral, soft and hard, smooth and rough, modern and traditional, intimate and bold, consumer and the producer all at the same time" (2002, p. 55). Masculinity is also perceived differently in different social classes, religions, places, and eras.

One need only think of the wigs and ornate costumes worn by men in 16th- and 17th-century Europe.

The hedonism and consumerism that Gabler describes, with its emphasis on male self-beautification, have recently come to haunt men in the same way that women's appearances so often preoccupy and haunt them. In part, men's emphasis on appearance may be a crossover from the male homosexual world, a world that has shaped many of our views of style and chic—not too surprisingly when we think of their important male homosexual influences in the worlds of fashion, hairdressing, and interior design. Then, too, it has become increasingly apparent that many gay men spend a lot of time and effort—at the gym and elsewhere—to maintain their attractive appearance. Not just the idea that thin is healthier but also the ideal of a taut body, already part of movie culture, has infiltrated the corridors of male heterosexual culture. What this demonstrates are the ways people of different sexes and sexual persuasions impact one another. Sometimes we borrow what we admire and envy without being completely aware of its source.

Male Fantasies and Fears

It was the feminists of the 1960s and 1970s who first took a long look at the psychology of men and who suggested that male sexuality is often infused with hostility, even sadism. In *Sexual Politics*, Kate Millet (1970) examined how an all-conquering male sexuality was depicted and celebrated to the detriment of those being conquered in some serious fiction (e.g., the works of Norman Mailer, Henry Miller, D. H. Lawrence, and Jean Genet). And in *Against Our Will: Men, Women and Rape*, Susan Brownmiller (1976) declared that

> throughout history, no theme grips the masculine imagination with greater constancy and less honor than the myth of the heroic rapist. As man conquered the world, so too he conquers the female. Down through the ages, imperial conquest, exploits of valor and expressions of love have gone hand in hand with violence to women in thought and in deed. (p. 320)

Although Millet and Brownmiller are brilliant analysts of the sociology involved, they fall short of a full understanding of the psychology of male sex and power. The operative word in Brownmiller's analysis of male sexuality must also take into account the more or less unconscious fears underlying men's conscious wishful fantasies, many of which are enacted.

Moreover, what Brownmiller leaves out are the kindnesses, protectiveness, and capacity for love that so many men display.

I, along with Nettie Terestman, Wayne Myers, Eugene Goldberg, and Carol Salvadori (1999), conducted interviews to compare male and female responses of 193 university students to questions about sexual experiences and fantasies. Although there were few significant gender differences in experiences, there were many differences in fantasies. As we concluded, "males fantasized about sex more [than women] and exhibited greater interest in partner variation and in the spectrum from domination to sadism. While male sexuality is often described as aggressive/sadistic and female sexuality as passive/masochistic, most men and women in our population did not report fantasies supporting such stereotypes." In our 3-month study, most fantasy items were mentioned with equal frequency by men and women, but a number were mentioned more frequently by men: "touching/kissing sensuously," "oral-genital sex," "seducing partner," "intercourse in unusual positions," "sex that lasts for hours," "watching partner undress" ($p < .01$); "sex in unusual locations," and "having partner masturbate you" ($p < .05$). Men also reported more fantasies involving "two or more lovers," "being involved in an orgy," "sex with famous persons," "sex with a virgin," and "masturbating your partner" ($p < .05$); and "watching partner masturbate," "anal intercourse," and "sex with a much older person" ($p < .05$). Of the fantasies considered relatively rare, most were endorsed by 10% significantly more often by males: "forcing partner to submit" and "sex experiences with a much younger partner" ($p < 1$); "whipping/beating a partner," "degrading sex partner," "torturing sex partner," and "being attracted to someone with a physical abnormality" ($p < .05$). "Dressing in the clothes of the opposite sex" was also more frequently endorsed by men ($p < .01$). Although our sample was extremely small, these results do show certain differences between the two sexes. It was clear that in men's descriptions of their experiences "masturbation by self or partner, watching pornography, mutual genital petting, and intercourse in unusual locations emerged with greater frequency than in women" (Person et al., 1999, p. 240). The male predilection for masturbation may simply imply a greater propensity for initiatory sexual behavior. It was apparent also that some male fantasies were designed so as to cover over, or deny, men's sexual fears, some of them pervasive. With regard to performance, men sometimes worry about getting it up, keeping it up, and satisfying their partners, because there is a fundamental difference in sex: a man cannot hide his failure to achieve an erection, whereas there is no certain way to gauge a woman's sexual arousal or orgasm. Thus, it is difficult for a man to be sure he is a good lover. That men frequently ask their partners "Did you come?" is evidence of this. Sexual anxiety is also manifest in the obsession some men have with their partner's past lover: "Was he better? Did you have more orgasms? Better orgasms?"

Some men fear sexual impotence, a fear that can itself lead to impotence. The popularity of Viagra suggests that the idea of the sexually ever-ready male is more myth (or fantasy) than reality. Experiences of sexual inadequacy may be more frequent now, when so much traditionally male turf is being ceded to women (for an early report of this trend, see Ginsberg, Frosch, & Shapiro, 1972).

Even men who are confident about their performance may be so intent on demonstrating their ability to gratify a woman that their own participation lacks spontaneity. Such men may feel comfortable pursuing their own pleasure only after they have brought the woman to orgasm; some may be able to attain full erection only when the woman is sated. Perhaps the most striking feature of the male's sense of sexual inadequacy is the belief that the other men truly possess the macho sexuality that he aspires to, making his own endowment and skills appear even more meager. The overestimation of other males' potency may have its deepest roots in the small boy's awe of his father's superior sexual endowment. Some men appear to suffer, too, because of their idealization of the male experience during adolescence, a time when perpetual readiness appeared to be the rule.

Masculinity and Sexual Object Choice: Heterosexual and Homosexual

Over time, our notions of what is innate and what is learned have changed. Whereas homosexuality was once interpreted as the outcome of growing up in a family in which some familial constellation predisposed the child to a homosexual adaptation, some professionals in our field (including me) now believe that most homosexuals are innate. Some male homosexuals are notable for their masculine, even hypermasculine, behaviors and preferences. For example, the actors Randolph Scott and Cary Grant, screen idols who played iconic masculine roles quite different from one another, were gay men who lived together for some time. (Grant may have been bisexual, as he married several times.) Some male homosexuals report that they were effeminate in earliest childhood, well before the oedipal phase. In other words, the effeminate boy may be effeminate by nature, not by nurture. This suggests that there may be some hardwiring or endocrine influence in establishing gender characteristics that may or may not be predictive of sexual object choice.

Some men who are anxious about performance, and who fear women's rejection or infidelity, resort to fantasies of power. In these fantasies, through utilizing denial and reversal, the penis emerges as all-powerful, performance as extraordinary, sexual partners as plentiful, and dominance and aggression as reparative themes, reversing what the fantasizer believes to be true. Such fantasies fuel their project of male dominance and the wish for female subordination.

Masculinity, as I have suggested, is not exclusively connected to sexual object choice. Although many gays are masculine in both appearance and behavior, there has always been a group of men in gay culture who appear hypermasculine. For example, look at all the Tom of Finland erotica, fantasies of bikers, truckers, cowboys, and police. In contemporary culture, many of these fantasies are enacted to become "reality." Here in New York these men are called "Chelsea Boys." They are exceptionally well built and work at it. I would venture to say that they view themselves as more masculine than the average heterosexual man. Some of them even view heterosexual intercourse as less than masculine, because it forces a man to have sex in a way that a "guy" does not want to have sex, that is, with "too many feminine strings attached." Steroids are a big part of this lifestyle, and boy image is extremely important. Although these men can sometimes be intimidating and seem to "have it all," other people, including some homosexual men, question whether the Chelsea Boys and their counterparts outside of New York have authentically internalized a healthy body image.

Aside from sexual object choice, heterosexual men and homosexual men share many characteristics. Members of both groups may agonize not just over their physical endowment but also over their performance. There is one significant difference: past adolescence, some heterosexuals feel threatened by the appearance of another man's erect penis, probably out of fear that some sexual innuendo must be involved. However, there are heterosexual men who enjoy having sex with a woman while a buddy is in the same room having sex with another woman. And some men who have sex with other men still self-identify as heterosexual if their contact is on the "DL," short for "the down low," which originally meant their contact was restricted to reaming the anus of another man, but has now been reinterpreted to express covert homosexuality (King, 2004). This phenomenon became evident with the onset of the AIDS epidemic, when HIV cases started appearing among presumably monogamous married men.

Differences in the expression of masculinity are the result of many diverse antecedents: biological differences, early life experiences, power relations, scripting, socialization, and sex-discrepant expectations that shape fantasies and cultural myths, as well as issues of genital awareness and oedipal dramas described in classical psychoanalytic theory. It appears that sexual preference and gender role are sometimes more discordant than we generally recognize. For example, such complexity is particularly evident in transvestites' sexual interest in women. On some level, the self-identity of a good number of transvestites seems to fluctuate somewhere between heterosexuality and self-identification as a female lesbian.

Issues of Narcissism and Humiliation

Before I discuss some fault lines in male psychology, I want to emphasize men's strengths. Men can be extremely good team players (in work and in sports), and they can be extremely nurturing to others. They protect their families, and they fight in wars. They can also be close friends with one another and with women. Many men hold to a sense of honor and are both protectors and nurturers of others. For all these reasons, it is hard to discuss masculinity fully within the context of a short essay.

Until recently, culture critics wrote more about changes in the female gender role than in the male gender role, holding to the notion that masculinity is essentially ahistorical—a strange parallel with Freud's dictum that man is born, but woman is made. But over the past 50 years our images of ideal masculinity have shifted, a shift that goes beyond Gabler's comparison of John Wayne and James Bond.

The same body hatred that so often infects women can today be seen to afflict men as well and is reflected in the varieties of body modification they are increasingly seeking. The number of men engaged in bodybuilding has increased dramatically in recent years. Some men also take steroids for muscle and strength enhancement. Many men feel that their penises are inadequate in either length or girth. Just as women may have breast enlargement to counteract their anxieties, some men are opting for penile enlargement, an increasingly booming business. Gary Rheinschild, a specialist in penis enlargement, reported that he performed more than 3,500 penile enlargements in a single year (cited in Bordo, 2001, p. 73).

Castration anxiety clearly plays a role in many men's preoccupation with the size of their penis. A man calling himself "Preacher" sent a letter to their editor of the men's magazine *Maxim* describing a "medical breakthrough":

> Now, about this penile enlargement surgery crap. I'm a biker—tattoo, bunch of broken bones, all that. When I was a young buck hanging around the Bay Area … I was introduced to a technique by a patch holder in a Bay Area club. … You take a padlock that weighs approx. six to eight ounces, put a fat rubber band on its shackle (the part that opens and closes), and wear it on your schlong. …You do it about 15 to 20 hours a week and you do this for a *couple of years*. I know other bikers who have told their sons about this when they hit puberty, and I sure as well woulda liked to be told about this by my father when I was that age. It can move your dick from being six and a half to about nine inches. Anyone, and probably at any age, can do this. It doesn't require some perseverance … but then so does anything worthwhile. (June, 1999)

Men's growing concern with their appearance was highlighted in the hit television show *Queer Eye for the Straight Guy*, on which gay men did makeovers on straights, including waxing body hair. When I was growing up, chest hair on men was considered sexy. No longer. But while men are to some degree being feminized, they have not given up the myth of phallic omnipotence and supremacy. I have quoted Zilbergeld's description of the "large, powerful, untiring phallus attached to a cool controlled male, long on experience, competent, and knowledgeable enough to make women crazy with desire," an image with "long-standing and very deep roots in our culture" (1978, p. 23). But this fantasy is more often the antidote to underlying feelings of inadequacy than evidence of real sexual self-assurance.

To compensate for such feelings, many men resort to power remedies in fantasy. (It should be noted that men are as interested in how they are compared to other men as their erotic and sexual successes. How a man is identified in terms of his work is a major marker of self-regard or its lack. Men's self-identity is connected to their performance in the world of work and their place in any hierarchy of which they are part.)

Michael Lewis (1990) underscored the link between power and sex in the male psyche in *Liar's Poker*, in which he reported that the most successful investment bankers are referred to as "big swinging dicks." For many men, however, the primary concern is professional success. In the lower economic realms, macho swagger and macho fantasies serve to compensate for men's feelings of subordination in the male economic hierarchy. Paradoxically, while a man's macho sexual fantasies are in some ways adaptive, insofar as they momentarily counteract underlying fears, they may also aggravate an already pervasive sexual anxiety by reinforcing the belief that other men are actually living what for him are only fantasies. At the extreme, some men enhance their self-esteem by dominating and sometimes brutalizing women.

Dimen and Goldner (2005) note that it took 50 years after Freud's work on what we now call gender for Chasseguet-Smirgel (1984) to coin the term *phallocentrism*, a fact highlighting how Freud's thesis posited and valorized a primitive unisex/gender system in which there is but one masculinity. Their intention is to establish "the rich variations in the way gender is experienced and performed *within* each sex as well as the commonalities that cross the boundary between them … [all] effaced by Freud's universalized, phallicized theory of a sexual difference" (p. 96). Though their concerns are somewhat different from those of Michael Lewis, they are making a similar point.

Freud's formulations on gender, as initially rendered, were a challenge not only to women's sense of their identity but also to that wide spectrum of men who did not conform to the cultural stereotype. This is why it is important to acknowledge and explore the range of masculinities. Gender is a term that must be understood to incorporate the variety of masculinities and femininities that in fact exist.

Men may live by the clock or by the cock. But they also draw on the strength of their joint connections with other men. We often overlook the power of bonding between men and dwell more on their hierarchical positions in work or war. But I do want to go back to my earlier comment on the hierarchical nature of male bonding, which I believe continues throughout life. This hierarchical structure is inevitable in corporate life and in the military, and issues in judgments of success or failure and in an ongoing competitiveness. Nonetheless, men often partner to good effect in the world of work, as seen in the joint creative synthesis of the two young men who jointly created Google. And men also bond in friendship. For my husband and his cronies, their bonding is ritualized in Monday night gin rummy games. If someone is missing from the game, the assumption is that he is out of town on business or sick enough that he cannot get out of bed. But they will check it out. These tough aging guys are both tender and intimate in their mutual caregiving, but their form of intimacy is less verbal as regards the discussion of their personal lives and more centered on talk of common interests and activities.

Conclusion

A truly credible theory of gender must go beyond Freud's emphasis on nature, nurture, and interpersonal relations, beyond any historical theory of people and society in order to give full due both to the hormonal development of early life and to the world in which we live, and to the impact the latter inevitably has on our ideas about the nature of masculinity and femininity, male and female sexuality, bisexuality, heterosexuality, and homosexuality. The line between male heterosexuality and bisexuality may not be as impenetrable—please forgive the pun—as one assumes. A classic example appears in Mario Vargas Llosa's (2003) *A Way to Paradise*. The painter Paul Gauguin is the novel's central character, living in Tahiti with a native woman and committed to heterosexuality. One day a woodcutter takes him on a walk to find balsa wood. As they plunge into a stream, Paul has an erection and feels the desire to abandon himself, "to surrender, to be loved and treated awfully like a woman by the woodcutter" (p. 63). The woodcutter senses this and inserts his penis into Gauguin's anus. For the woodcutter, this sexual act is a mere diversion, but Gauguin experiences it as euphoric, and it provided him a creative burst.

As cultural mores have led to a lowering of the repressive barrier, cross-gendered identifications and behaviors have surfaced more frequently. A growing number of individuals self-identify as bisexuals. A central question is whether the bisexual self-identifies as belonging to two sexes or, alternatively, of being sexually interested in both men and women. Over time I have come to believe that it is impossible to fully understand heterosexuality and homosexuality without theorizing bisexuality and acknowledging its varying incidence in different historical eras and in different geographical regions.

I do not believe it is possible to theorize male sexuality and masculinity on the basis of hormonal and genital difference and early development alone, without considering the cultural constructs of power and the inevitable hierarchical structures in the work and lives of most men. Among the contemporary threats to men we need to focus not only on masculine competition, but also on the loss of authority once ceded to men that has been brought about by the massive entry of women into the workforce and by women's more readily expressed sexual preferences and active participation in the unfolding of sexual encounters.

Given that sexuality first develops in the relatively dependent, helpless child, it is unlikely that it can ever be completely free of submission/dominance connotations. The limits to sexual liberation—meaning liberation from power contaminants—reside not in the biological nature of sexuality, or exclusively in cultural and political arrangements, and certainly not in the sex difference, but in the universal condition of infantile dependency. The consequences of that dependency and a lingering sense of powerlessness along with the need to overcome it through the enactment of one or another kind of power may form the substance of tragedy. Such a suspicion, of course, echoes Freud's pessimistic assessment of the human condition.

Like Freud, we should remain interdisciplinary. Sex is not purely instinctual or hormonal, nor is it exclusively grounded in object relations. We should be aware of universalizing our observations. Part of the glory of our sexuality, our gender, and our creative potential is their malleability in different circumstances and in different cultures. Looking back over the psychoanalytic literature, it is easy to see that much more was written about female psychology and male homosexuality than about male heterosexuality, except when the topic addressed was intended to differentiate between male and female. This is one of the reasons that *The Psychology of Men*, published in 1986 by Fogel, Lane, and Liebert, was one of the important turning points in the way we conceptualize masculinity. Chodorow's (1994) *Femininities, Masculinities, and Sexualities: Freud and Beyond* has also been influential in turning attention to masculinity.

Because our focus has so often been on the differences between male and female, we have tended to overlook the wide variety of differences among men. It is for this reason that this chapter on masculinities is so important. It allows us to discuss the different masculinities that can be observed, rather than compelling us to comment endlessly on the differences between men and women.

With ongoing social change and the new scientific findings that will surely emerge, our culture's notions of the spectrum of what constitutes masculinity will not remain the same. The shaping and enactment of our drives—the fundamental *materiel* of the Freudian unconscious—are reincarnated in different generations and locations into new configurations. Even our preconscious impulses and wishes incorporate subliminal attitudes and beliefs that permeate contemporary culture. The traffic among culture, psyche, and biology is always played out on a three-lane highway.

Acknowledgment

A version of this chapter originally appeared in the *Journal of the American Psychoanalytic Association, 54*(4), 1165–1186. Used with permission. © 2006 American Psychoanalytic Association. All rights reserved.

References

Baker, S. W. (1980). Biological influences on human sex and gender. In C. R. Stimpson & E. S. Person (Eds.), *Women, Sex, and Sexuality* (pp. 175–191). Chicago: University of Chicago Press.

Bordo, S. (2001). *The Male Body: A New Look at Men in Public and In Private.* New York: Farrar, Straus & Giroux.

Brownmiller, S. (1976). *Against Our Will: Men, Women and Rape.* New York: Bantam Books.

Chasseguet-Smirgel, J. (1984). *Creativity and Perversion.* New York: Norton.

Chodorow, N. (1994). *Femininities, Masculinities, and Sexualities: Freud and Beyond.* Lexington: University of Kentucky Press.

Dimen, M., & Goldner, V. (2005) Gender and sexuality. In E. S. Person, A. M. Cooper, & G. O. Gabbard (Eds.), *APPI Textbook of Psychoanalysis* (pp. 96–113). Washington, DC: American Psychiatric Press.

Fogel, G. I., Lane, F. M., & Liebert, R. S. (Eds.). (1986). *The Psychology of Men.* New York: Basic Books.

Freud, S. (1924). The dissolution of the Oedipus complex. *Standard Edition, 19,* 173–179.

Freud, S. (1925). Some psychical consequences of the anatomical distinction between the sexes. *Standard Edition, 19,* 238–258.

Freud, S. (1931). Female sexuality. *Standard Edition, 21,* 221–243.

Freud, S. (1933). Femininity. *Standard Edition, 21,* 112–135.

Friedman, R. C., & Downey, J. I. (2002). *Sexual Orientation and Psychoanalysis: Sexual Science and Clinical Practice.* New York: Columbia University Press.

Gabler, N. (2002, January–February). Male bonding: Why is James Bond so popular? He's a baby boomer writ large. *Modern Maturity,* 52–53.

Gilmore, D. D. (1991). *Manhood in the Making: Cultural Concepts of Masculinity.* New Haven, CT: Yale University Press.

Ginsberg, G., Frosch, W., & Shapiro, T. (1972). The new impotence. *Archives of General Psychiatry, 26,* 218–220.

Horney, K. (1924). On the genesis of the castration complex in women. *International Journal of Psycho-analysis, 5,* 50–65.

Horney, K. (1926). The flight from womanhood: The masculinity complex in women, as viewed by men and by women. *International Journal of Psycho-analysis, 7*, 324–339.

Horney, K. (1932). The dread of women: Observations on a specific difference in the dread felt by men and women respectively for the opposite sex. *International Journal of Psycho-analysis, 13*, 348–360.

Horney, K. (1933). The denial of the vagina: A contribution to the problem of the genital anxieties specific to women. *International Journal of Psycho-analysis, 14*, 57–70.

Imperato-McGinley, J., Peterson, R. E., Gautier, J., & Sturla, E. (1979). Androgens and the evolution of male gender identity among male pseudo-hermaphrodites with 5A-redutase deficiency. *New England Journal of Medicine, 300*, 1233–1237.

Jones, E. (1927). The early development of female sexuality. In *Papers on Psychoanalysis* (pp. 438–451). London: Balliere, Tindall, & Cox, 1948.

Jones, E. (1933). The phallic phase. In *Papers on Psychoanalysis* (pp. 452–484). London: Balliere, Tindall, & Cox, 1948.

Jones, E. (1935). Early female sexuality. In *Papers on Psychoanalysis* (pp. 485–495). London: Balliere, Tindall, & Cox, 1948.

King, J. L. (2004). *On the Down Low: A Journey into the Lives of "Straight" Black Men who Sleep with Men*. New York: Broadway Books.

Klein, M. (1928). Early stages: The Oedipus complex. *International Journal of Psycho-analysis, 9*, 168–180.

Lewis, M. (1990). *Liar's Poker*. New York: Penguin.

Llosa, M. V. (2003). *A Way to Paradise*. New York: Farrar, Straus, & Giroux.

McDougall, J. (1980). *Plea for a Measure of Abnormality*. New York: International Universities Press.

Millett, K. (1970). *Sexual Politics*. Garden City, NY: Doubleday.

Mitchell, S. A., & Black, M. J. (1995). *Freud and Beyond: A History of Modern Psychoanalytic Thought*. New York: Basic Books.

Money, J., Hampson, J. P., & Hampson, J. Y. (1955). An examination of some basic sexual concepts: The evidence of human hermaphrodism. *Bulletin of the Johns Hopkins Hospital, 97*, 305–315.

Person, E. S. (1986). The omni-available woman and lesbian sex: Two fantasy themes and their relationships to the male development experience. In G. Fogel, F. M. Lane, & R. S. Liebert (Eds.), *The Psychology of Men* (pp. 71–94). New York: Basic Books.

Person, E. S. (1999). Some mysteries of gender: Rethinking masculine identifications in heterosexual women. In *The Sexual Century: Selected Papers of Sex and Gender* (pp. 296–315). New Haven, CT: Yale University Press.

Person, E. S. (2005). As the wheel turns: A centennial reflection on Freud's *Three Essays on the Theory of Sexuality*. *Journal of the American Psychoanalytic Association, 54,* 1257–1282.

Person, E. S., Terestman, N., Myers, W., Goldberg, E., & Salvadori, C. (1999). Gender difference in sexual behaviors and fantasies in a college population. In E. S. Person, *The Sexual Century: Selected Papers of Sex and Gender* (pp. 230–242). New Haven, CT: Yale University Press.

Rivto, L. (1990). *Darwin's Influence on Freud: A Tale of Two Sciences.* New Haven, CT: Yale University Press.

Spitz, R. (1962). Autoeroticism re-examined: The role of early sexual behavior patterns and personality formations. *Psychoanalytic Study of the Child, 17,* 283–315.

Stoller, R. (1968). *Sex and Gender.* New York: Science House.

Tyson, P., & Tyson, R. (1990). *Psychoanalytic Theories of Development.* New Haven, CT: Yale University Press.

Zilbergeld, B. (1978). *Male Sexuality.* New York: Bantam Books.

2

Masculinity and Its Discontents
Making Room for the "Mother" Inside the Male—An Essential Achievement for Healthy Male Gender Identity

Michael J. Diamond

Although probably obvious, the landscape of psychoanalysis and gender abounds with conceptual, terminological, technical, and sociopolitical difficulties often characterized by identity politics. Not surprisingly, gender, with its basis in differentiation and an accompanying history of gender-based suffering and oppression, is a minefield where disturbance is to be expected (Benjamin, 1996; Harris, 1991). Yet today, much as when Freud started his psychosexual prospecting, there continues to be something about the terrain that draws us close to the heart of the mind-body-spirit interface. And happily, we now have an assortment of canvassing tools that Freud did *not*, including advances in early child–parent observation, the influence of feminist and postfeminist queer theorizing, the interdisciplinary, cross-culturally informed study of societies and ancient cultures, and the impact of the postmodern outlook to situate us in a position to reconsider our understanding of gender.[*]

---

[*] In integrating these advances, I believe that, along with many other analysts writing in this area, sophisticated psychoanalytic theory must be able to go beyond simply deconstructing gender dichotomies and, instead, strive to sustain the necessary dialectical tension between traditional, essentialist and, postmodern, constructionist perspectives. In every culture, gender polarity is internalized and, thus, each child is directed to develop qualities attributed to his or her own sex and, in some measure, to suppress or disavow qualities of the other sex (Young-Eisendrath, 1997). In listening to my patients, and hopefully to my colleagues, I consequently aim to maintain the dialectical tension between the dichotomous (or fixed) aspects of gender experience and the more integrated experience of gender, between gender *rigidity* and *fluidity,* and between (*core*) *gender identity* and the *gender multiplicity of the multigendered self.*

Today we are more likely to understand that gender identity development is *not* a linear, continuous trajectory, and that a boy's (and later, a man's) experience of the ambiguities of his gender are continually being reworked across differing developmental junctions. As I clarify in this chapter, gender identity develops from the early, preoedipal identifications with each parent. A healthy sense of masculinity requires incorporating the multitude of these early identifications (as well as subsequent ones) and inevitably demands a psychic achievement in the integrative-synthetic sphere.

Overview: Masculinity and Psychoanalysis

Until three decades ago, the psychoanalytic study of male development was essentially organized around Freud's oedipal theory and the idea that the boy wants to "have" his mother (Freud, 1923b, 1924, 1925). To overcome the castration anxieties aroused in competing with his father, the boy identifies with him and, in turn, constructs the sense of his own masculine identity.

Since then, attention has been redirected to the fact that before the boy wants to have his mother, he wants to be his mother, or at least be with what his mother provides (i.e., her maternal nurturance). Hence, the boy's preoedipal relationship with his mother and the actual involvement by the father in the early triadic environment are now seen as crucial to understanding male gender identity.

Analysts influenced by Margaret Mahler (Mahler, Pine, & Bergman, 1975) began to formulate a new way of understanding male psychology. Most significant were Ralph Greenson and Robert Stoller, two Los Angeles–based psychoanalysts who formulated what has become known as the disidentification hypothesis. This theory argues that in order to establish a normal, healthy sense of masculinity, the small boy must disidentify from his mother and counter-identify with his father. This supposition has been taken as the benchmark to explain the male's struggle to experience his gendered identity as "masculine." The theory happens to be congruent with a dubious though unconsciously widely held view in patriarchal cultures that masculinity is defined by its not being feminine. In other words, the most significant thing about being a man is not being a woman. This reductive and monolithic view has been unfortunate for both sexes but perhaps especially so for men, since gender identity, as long as it is based on the disavowal of whatever is construed as feminine, remains an unstable psychological achievement.*

More recent work by researchers and psychoanalytic gender theorists has furthered our understanding of boys' earliest and subsequent sense of masculinity (Axelrod, 1997; Benjamin, 1988, 1991; Fast, 1984, 1990, 1999; Hansell, 1998; Lax, 1997; Pollack, 1995, 1998). In my own work, I revise the disidentification model and provide a set of theoretical lenses to help us achieve a deeper, more complete understanding of our male patients (Diamond, 2004a, 2004b, 2006). I emphasize how both heterosexual and homosexual masculinity is forged from the boy's earliest wishes to be both his mother and father, and how these early identifications require adaptations and accommodations throughout the life span. I advocate that a male's gendered ego ideals and the sense of his masculinity as well as the ambiguities of his gender are continually being reworked throughout his life. Moreover, the phallic and genital features of a man's internal experience are best understood as coexisting positions in varying, discontinuous balances that shift as a man matures, rather than representing different developmental phases that supersede one another.

Terminology: Phallic and Genital Masculinity

A brief word on terminology is needed. In using the terms phallic and genital, I am referring to a specific orientation, typically manifest in a cluster of traits, which psychoanalysis views as originating from early psychosexual, libidinal development. From the classical psychosexual standpoint, the phallic phase refers to that pregenital period beginning at about 2 years of age and extending into the oedipal phase, during which the phallus is the primary erogenous zone. Freud describes this "infantile genital organization" as reflecting "a primacy of the *phallus*" rather than of the genitals (1923b, p. 142, original italics). The phase comprises two subphases: phallic narcissism (or, phallic exhibitionism), characterized by a self-satisfaction based on an overestimation of the penis, exhibitionistic desires to gain attention, and the primacy of dyadic relations; and the later phallic-oedipal phase proper, with its triangular configuration, idealization of oedipal objects promoting phallic omnipotence, and

---

* Reis (2008) argues persuasively that heterosexual men are for the most part constrained by the socially constrictive definition of male desire wherein an assumption of normativity creates an expectation of heterosexuality that is *not* in force for either femininity or the homosexualities.

heightened castration anxieties (Edgcumbe & Burgner, 1975; Greenspan, 1982; Jones, 1933; Schalin, 1989). Throughout the entire phallic phase, the high valuation of the penis is manifest in phallic pride with its associated desires and anxieties. Figuratively speaking, extending, thrusting, and penetrating become paramount along with the associated personality traits of assertiveness, aggression, strength, and potency in the realization of one's desire.

I hold that phallic ambitions, propensities, and energies are utilized, integrated, and transformed throughout a male's development, and that these phallic features of internal life will play an important role in his adaptively expressing and experiencing his masculinity. These healthy aspects of phallic masculinity are evident in the male's embracing of his desires and ambitions, pursuits, competitive yearnings, delights in bodily pleasures, and hierarchical relations, as well as his capacities for achievement, penetration, and dominance. A male's defensive phallicity, on the other hand, frequently reflects more transitory regressive tendencies in an otherwise healthy personality; alternatively, it may indicate more rigid characterological distortions based on primitive defensive operations employed to protect his fragile, inflexible masculine gender identity. In the latter case, the so-called phallic character is characterized by exhibitionistic self-display, haughty reserve, a regarding of the penis as an instrument of aggression (rather than love), recklessness, misogyny, and an excessive need to display one's potency. Such pathology can manifest at varying developmental junctures, although is traditionally understood as regressively based on oedipal-phase anxieties (Jones, 1933). This is evident in adult men who persist in defining themselves by conquest, sexual potency, and aggression when relational needs, a greater appreciation of otherness, and reflectivity might otherwise come to the fore.

The genital phase is considered the final stage in instinctual libidinal development, representing what has been called "genital primacy" (Freud, 1905). Genital primacy does *not* equate, however, with the mere capacity for orgastic functioning; "genital," taken beyond psychosexual theory, is used broadly to reflect the male's capacity to attach equal importance to his own and his partner's satisfaction. Thus, what becomes more primary are the male's relational needs and abilities to both develop and utilize his theory of mind (Fonagy & Target, 1996; Mayes & Cohen, 1992) in order to achieve connection to, and intimacy with, others.

In addition to, and of equal importance, there is an interiorized, culturally minimized dimension of genital masculinity pertaining to the inner body and testicles, the inner genital space, that reflects the more open, spatial, and receptive aspects of male psychic experience (Fogel, 1998; Friedman, 1996) as well as an expansion of bodily sensual pleasure, beyond that of the satisfactions associated with the penis, as reflected in the genital male's exploring his own visceral excitation (Bordo, 1999; Reis, 2008). In other words, as Reis (2008) proposes in his discussion of heterosexual men, men yearn not only for the pleasures of the penis-in-vagina, but also to enjoy being penetrated, having one's testicles stimulated, experiencing pleasure through the use of their mouths, and fantasizing as well as engaging in a variety of sexual practices that are too easily societally pathologized. In short, maturing, healthy genitality is characterized by the attenuation of the anxieties pertaining both to masculine inner space and to non-penis-dominated sensuality, as well as the lessening of anxieties associated with their psychical sensibilities. Penetration and receptivity, as well as intrusion and inclusion, are the hallmarks of genitality. Genital aims for connection and the recognition of others in their uniqueness and subjectivity (i.e., otherness) are a manifestation of this postambivalent integration of phallic propensities in the service of reality.

The term *genitality*, as I use it, involves adaptive assertion, aggression, and modulated phallicism, in which penetration in the service of mastery, potency, and authority is integrated with the needs for connection and attachment. Phallic urges are present and remain significant, but in their genital countenance, they are transformed into more aim-inhibited and object-recognizing forms. What I think of as both the hierarchical and the relational facets of each male become more fluidly part of his complex and yet more flexible psychic structure. In this respect, there is a strong resemblance between the analytic ideal of the genital character and both the Anglo Saxon prototype of a gentleman and the Judeo Hebraic exemplar of a *mensch*. Speaking psychosexually, the maturing man's genital features help him to become oriented more toward making love rather than simply fucking—although of course the impulse to fuck remains an important dimension of his masculinity and love making.

Thus, to paraphrase Freud, in order to truly understand "what men really want," we need to appreciate the challenges inherent in the varying developmental junctions over the course of a man's life. In this chapter I focus on how boys establish their earliest sense of masculinity and then reflect on the interplay between this initial sense of masculinity and the central developmental challenges that ensue. I will begin, however, by briefly considering the important roles played by both biology and culture.

Anatomy, Destiny, and Culture

Freud's famous dictum that "anatomy is destiny" is no longer the linchpin of psychoanalytic gender theorizing. Research on the masculinization of the brain or lack thereof demonstrates that several biological variables are related to specific gender-related traits, maturational challenges, and intra-psychic conflicts commonly experienced by males (e.g., Panksepp, 1998; see also Baron-Cohen, 2003). Nonetheless, on the basis of clinical evidence, the biological givens in gender identity formation are significantly counterbalanced by what psychoanalysis emphasizes: the early imprinting of the boy's actual interactions with his primary attachment figures; his internalized object relations; the prevailing sociocultural determinants; and most important, his unique psychodynamically determined reactions to each of these influences, particularly as they interact with his basic biological development (cf. Blos, 1984; Stoller, 1976). We might say therefore that with respect to biology, the destiny of a boy's masculinity is based on what he makes of his anatomy.

Contemporary thinking about gender, emerging over the past 30 years, has resulted in an influential critique, in large measure empirically based on Freud's phallocentric theories of male and female development (Dimen & Goldner, 2000). Freud, in collapsing the distinction between biological sex, sexuality, and gender, "made gender crudely derivative of the anatomical differences between the sexes" (Goldner, 2002, p. 63). Today's more complex gender-identity paradigm untangles gender per se from sex and sexuality. Consequently, masculine gender identity must be distinguished from core gender identity and from sexual (gender) object choice. Core gender identity refers to the sense of belonging to a biological sex and is established in the first year and a half of life (Stoller, 1968). It is the felt conviction of being biologically male (or female) and is what I refer to when discussing the boy's maleness. This stands in contrast to what this chapter largely addresses, namely, the boy's "gender identity" (which Stoller [1968] termed "non-core gender identity" and what Person and Ovesey [1983], as well as research psychologists, call "gender role identity"). This sense of masculinity or the male's self-image as a gendered being is far more complicated and ambiguous than maleness. It is fundamentally constructed out of the boy's early identifications with each of his parents and, as I suggest, is reworked throughout a man's life.

Gender, Masculinity, and Culture

The issue of gender is aptly regarded as an "essential contradiction" (Harris, 1991) and in its interface with one's sense of self is "softly assembled" (Harris, 1995). Moreover, large-scale intellectual currents are dramatically reflected in psychoanalytic theoretical controversies in the area of sexuality and gender (Mitchell & Black, 1995). As I noted earlier, contemporary psychoanalytical theory must be able to sustain the necessary dialectical tension between traditional essentialist (either/or thinking) and a postmodern, constructivist (both/and) perspective. This is a tension between biological givens, such as hormonally influenced brain and bodily masculinization, and the psychosocially created.

As cultural beings, we cannot so easily contain this tension. Anthropologists write about a ubiquitous sociocultural process that renders a splitting of gender traits so that aspects of human personality are distributed unequally between the sexes (Labouvie-Vief, 1994; Young-Eisendrath, 1997). In every culture, the individual internalizes a culturally shaped gender polarity that directs him or her to develop qualities attributed to his or her own sex and, in some measure, to suppress qualities of the other sex.* In Western societies, despite efforts to reduce this gender splitting, the underlying cultural images for masculinity generally continue to mean being rational, protective, aggressive, and dominating, while those for femininity mean being emotional, nurturing, receptive, and submissive (Benjamin, 1988). It becomes each individual's burden to keep the other gender's characteristics less developed within.

Fogel (2006) underscores that human beings are inherently psychologically bisexual. Fogel, much like Jungian theorists, speaks heuristically and metaphorically of masculine and feminine principles existing within each individual as a gender polarity and argues that dialectical balance between them is required for healthy maturation. The masculine is characterized by outwardness, boundaries, shapes, entities, definitions, penetration, deconstruction, differentiation, separation, space, and doing modes. In contrast, the feminine is represented by inwardness,

---

* This occurs even though hormonal influences on the fetal brain and genitalia demonstrate differences between the two genders. Regardless of how we define the concepts of masculine and feminine from a constitutional perspective, what is most serviceable in psychoanalysis stems from clinical observation that demonstrates that "in human beings pure masculinity or femininity is not to be found in either a psychological or a biological sense. Every individual on the contrary displays a mixture of the character-traits belonging to his own and to the opposite sex; and he shows a combination of activity and passivity whether or not these last character-traits tally with his biological ones" (Freud, 1905, p. 220n).

ambiguity or fluidity, receptivity, construction, creativity and synthesis, containment, groundedness, integration and unification, space, and being. In theorizing about men, psychoanalysis must comprehend the implications of the "lost feminine half," and consequently the metaphorical phallus as the sole organizer of higher mental functioning must be dispensed with and the "dark hole" in a man's inner genital must also be recognized (Fogel, 2006, pp. 1143–1144; see also Elise, 2001, in her discussion of "phallic supremacy").

Culture plays a pivotal role in interfacing with the psychodynamics of gender identity, and as Person (2006) observed, there are a wide variety of masculinities across cultures and even within Western societies, and masculinity is *not* the exclusive province of heterosexual men (as demonstrated in Harris' chapter in this volume). Moreover, as analysts, we focus largely on the parents in relation to their son and to one another. But sibling and peer relations that elaborate the lateral dimension of psychic life, specifically "boy culture" with its enforced male code that every boy encounters growing up, as well as the larger society that parses sexual mores and gender preconceptions, must be kept in mind as we try to understand each unique male patient.

Male Gender Identity Development

The internalization processes involved during a boy's unique struggle to differentiate from his mother profoundly affect his forming a sense of himself as a male. The boy's separation from the world of his mother is a complex process involving the interaction of biological and psychosocial factors. This is evident, for instance when, at around age 3, boys experience a momentous psychophysiological alteration caused by their body's maturation that drives newly intense genital sensations. This arrival of sexuality is quite disruptive, partially because it also represents the loss of innocence in his relationship with his mother. Bollas calls this "the death of infancy" (2000, p. 15), wherein the little boy experiences his own sexuality as destroying his own and his mother's innocence. The "mother-as-comforter" becomes the "mother-as-sex-object," and this loss results in considerable intrapsychic conflict, elaboration, and defense.

Regarding the formation of male gender identity, my ideas depart from Greenson's (1968) prevailing normative model, in which infant boys develop in a feminine direction (Diamond, 2004a, 2004b, 2006).* To achieve a secure masculine gender identity, according to Greenson (and Stoller), boys must disidentify with their mothers, repudiate their feminine identifications, and counter-identify with their fathers. In challenging this model, however, and drawing on Fast's (1984, 1990, 1999) seminal work, I argue that this forceful splitting is both theoretically and clinically problematic, as well as ultimately indicative of substantial psychopathology.

The Problem with Disidentification

There is abundant evidence that little boys do tend to move away physically from their mothers and toward their fathers (or surrogates) to establish themselves as "boys" among males (Abelin, 1975; Gilmore, 1990; Mahler et al., 1975; Stoller, 1965, 1966; see also Freud, 1921). How do we understand this psychoanalytically? Is this "moving away" a prerequisite for a male's psychological development (some cross-cultural data suggest otherwise)? More to the point, is it necessary for a boy to create a mental barrier against his desire to maintain closeness with his mother?

To answer these questions, let's consider masculinity in the clinical sphere where we frequently encounter patients with conflicted, fragile, damaged masculine self-images. Traditionally, these internal conditions are understood as expressions of "too little" or "too much" masculinity. Boys or men with too little masculinity are looked upon as passive, non-phallic characters largely under the sway of the negative Oedipus complex. In contrast, those with too much masculinity tend to be defensively counter-identified from their mothers, often evidencing a heightened phallic narcissism. However, when we look more closely at many of our male patients, we often see evidence of both too little masculinity in their overt passivity and inhibited aggression and too much masculinity in their phallic insistence on staving off emotional experience and in the terror of being penetrated (as for example, by other men's eyes in public urinals).

---

* It is noteworthy that Freud originally understood gender as stemming from the fact that masculinity was the natural state for both sexes. A girl retreated from masculinity into femininity upon discovering she had no penis, whereas a boy's masculinity is threatened during the oedipal period and, thus, masculine gender identity can only be firmly established through a successful identification with his father during this phase. In contrast, Greenson and Stoller proposed that boys are naturally protofeminine and must learn to renounce their femininity in order to achieve healthy gender identity. Today, there is no evidence to support such protofemininity, and most contemporary theorists view both masculinity and femininity *not* as innate but rather as having preoedipal origins in one's earliest relationships, identifications, and fantasies (Person, 2006; Brady, 2006).

In short, the clinical picture is far more muddied than prevailing clinical notions of masculinity might suggest.

It is noteworthy that Greenson's (1968; see also 1966) formulation emerged from his work with Stoller in studying transsexuals (Stoller, 1964, 1965, 1968). To support his thesis, Greenson used a case example of Lance, a "transsexual-transvestite five-and-a-half-year-old boy" whose mother hated and disrespected her husband and men in general, while his father "was absent … and had little if any pleasurable contact with the boy" (1968, pp. 371–372). Employing this clinical material, clearly reflective of a quite disturbed family system, Greenson generalized that Lance's "problems in disidentifying" were both developmentally normative and extremely meaningful in understanding "realistic gender identity" formation (p. 371). Soon thereafter, analysts eager to better understand men adopted the Greenson-Stoller hypothesis and made it the most important clinical application of preoedipal theorizing in treating men.

What Disidentification Actually Reflects

The pathological systems in which Lance was enmeshed are characteristic of families unable to triangulate successfully. Drawing from Abelin's (1971, 1975, 1980) observations and expanding on the ideas of Fast (1984, 1990) and Axelrod (1997), I would argue that such pathological forms of early triangulation are set in motion by:

1. Mothers who are severely misattuned to the individuation needs of their young sons;
2. Fathers who are either weak and unavailable or misogynist themselves;
3. A parental couple prone to splitting; and/or
4. The child's own biological constitution, temperament, and drive endowment, particularly with respect to what neuroscientists refer to as "brain and bodily masculinization" (Panksepp, 1998) and what psychoanalysts broadly term "merger proneness."

Under any or all of these circumstances, early gender identity development takes on the quality of a conflict or struggle, as Greenson suggests, and the little boy will tend to internalize the father's (and the mother's) contemptuous, devaluing attitude toward women. When this defensively based disidentification (and counter-identification) occurs, a pathological phallic rigidity commonly results. Thus, a kind of zero sum game operates in which masculinity requires that femininity be relinquished. Engaging in the defenses of denial and disavowal of maternal identifications, the young boy attempts to expel from consciousness early identifications typically grounded in more pathological triangular relations. What has been recently termed femiphobia—an unconscious hatred and dread of the part of the self that is experienced as feminine—often ensues (Ducat, 2004). In other words, the male's repudiation of his "feminine" self signals a failure in optimum development and is evident in a defensively phallic organization that denies a man's "procreative capacity and nurturing possibilities" (Fast, 1984, p. 73).

Revisioning Boys Turning Away From Their Mothers

In contrast, under "good enough" conditions, the boy's turning away from his mother is transitional (Diamond, 1998; Fast, 1999). This transitional turning away from the mother helps the boy to differentiate and separate from his primary external object. However, this is not the same as "disidentifying" from his internal maternal object. In fact, the boy's particular experience of loss actually facilitates his internalization of key aspects of his relationship with his mother.* Accordingly, these crucial and lasting early maternal identifications evolve directly from the separation-differentiation process; as Fonagy (2001) argues, in bringing attachment research into psychoanalytic focus, a boy's secure sense of masculine identity develops from the quality of the boy-to-mother attachment (not separation). Attachment theorists refer to this as attachment-individuation rather than separation-individuation (Lyons-Ruth, 1991).

Disidentification is a perplexing term, actually a misnomer, because early identifications are never simply removed nor repudiated in the unconscious once and for all (if they were, there would surely be less need for psychoanalysis). Rather, the boy's early identifications with his mother and father remain significant in his psychic structure; typically they become more accessible as he matures (Diamond, 2004a) and come to play a more active and conscious role.

---

* Identification, the most mature level of internalization central to the child's basic sense of self, occurs when there is a disruption to sufficiently gratifying emotional ties to a primary other (Loewald, 1962). Such internalization builds psychic structure as "the child reaches out to take back ... what has been removed from him" (Loewald, 1962, p. 496). Through the internalization process, renounced external objects, such as the mother who the boy turns away from, become internal objects as the internal relationship becomes substituted for an external one.

In healthier, more normative forms of early gender identity development, progressive differentiation, rather than opposition, predominates,
enabling masculinity to be founded upon a reciprocal identification with
an available father (or surrogate), a mother who is able to recognize and
affirm her son's maleness, and a parental couple who together are able to
acknowledge and love their son.

The Involved Father

Freud (1921) first observed that the father plays an important role in
the establishment of his son's gender identity within the early triadic
relationship. In the little boy's turning away from and experiencing loss
in relationship to his mother, an available, preoedipal father tempers his
son's more defensive tendencies to disengage forcefully from her while
providing a conventional focus for masculine identification (Diamond,
1998, 2004b). The boy who is able to achieve a reciprocal identification
with an available, loving father who possesses a body and genitalia like
his own is provided a foundation for a more secure and often more varied gendered expression of the self. This affirming, mutual bond with the
father—who is like the boy but who remains independent and outside
the boy's control—facilitates his integration of his maternal-feminine
identifications.

At around age 3, even as they turn toward the world of their fathers,
boys face another loss in relationship to their mother. As I have noted
earlier, they begin to experience her in a new way, in a sexual manner, in
addition to her accustomed role as maternal nurturer. Preoedipal splitting
occurs, and the boy feels he has two mothers (and two selves)—one that
is pregenital and one that is genital. Conflict then emerges as to which
mother he desires, the evocative sexual one or the comforting nurturer,
and temporary refuge from this conflict is sought. A way to achieve this
is by putting the conflict outside the mother–child relation, setting up the
father as "the second other" (Greenspan, 1982) and thus the one to blame.
By standing for sexuality in the boy's unconscious, the father is blamed
for breaking the bliss of ignorance and turning it into the sin of sexual
knowledge. The father is consequently called upon to accept this potentially adaptive projection and to bear his child's hatred toward the outside-
the-mother world that fathers represent (Bollas, 2000).

When a father fails to metabolize this projection and provide a healthy
preoedipal, "genital" object for identification, the little boy, in a "hysteric"

effort to resolve his conflict, inevitably seeks a return to the mother through desexualizing both the self and the mother. As Bollas observes, by idealizing her nonsexual characteristics, he turns her into a Madonna mother, and the self into a sexual innocent (i.e., "a perfect little boy"). Without the father's containing presence to keep him linked in the boy's mind to his mother, an opposition can form between love and sexuality that encourages the boy's viewing sexuality as a form of separation from maternal-like love.

Through the boy's relationship with a father (or father surrogate) whom he admires and who interacts with and mentors him in a caring way, in part through bearing such projections, the boy is able to internalize a paternal imago in which the active and penetrating and the receptive and caretaking qualities of the father's parenting become a foundation for healthy and fluid masculine gender identity. In other words, a father who represents genital masculinity, where his adaptive phallic strivings are integrated with his more relationally oriented, connected, and nurturing masculine qualities, helps to set the stage for his son's healthy sense of maleness.[*]

The Parental Couple

The boy's internalization of this healthy, genital father imago also depends on the nature of the father's relationship to the mother, and hers with the father.[†] As her son initially engages in differentiating from her, the "good enough" mother often continues to experience dramatic shifts in her own libidinal life. These libidinal changes typically begin during her pregnancy and persist early on, when her primary maternal preoccupation and

---

[*] A problematic legacy of classical Freudian oedipal theory is a tendency by some analysts to discuss the son's desire for his father primarily in "negative" oedipal terms—specifically as the "negative" or "inverted" oedipal constellation. This is a regrettable interpretation of Freud, who wrote of the boy's early love for his father and the ubiquity of psychic bisexuality (Freud, 1925). In furthering Freud's insights, several post-Freudian analysts have incisively conceptualized the dyadic, early father–son relationship and the triangular dynamics of the rapprochement phase wherein both parents need to contain and manage their own separation issues and competitive, envious feelings (Abelin, 1971, 1975, 1980; Benjamin, 1988, 1991; Blos, 1984).

[†] Although I focus on traditional heterosexual coupling, these triadic parenting issues also pertain to homosexual couples where the partner who is more of the "second" other is called upon to draw the primary nurturer back into the sexual liaison. Each partner's initial identifications with his or her own feminine and masculine caretakers play a significant role in these dynamics, as implied in my subsequent discussion pertaining to the "'father' in the 'mother'" (and vice versa). It is beyond the scope of this chapter, however, to discuss homosexual and single parenting in more detail.

attunement to her baby is dominant (Winnicott, 1956). For that reason, a father is frequently called upon to invite his wife to return to their conjugal relationship so that she learns to divide more of her focus between the maternal and spousal parts of herself. Herzog (2005b) contends that the mother may need her husband to maintain the sexual component of "spousing and caregiving," particularly in the face of her wishes that her husband remain "the nonsexual man who can entertain the child" (p. 66).

By drawing his wife back to him in the context of his engaged fathering, the father protects both the marriage's adult sexuality and intimacy and facilitates his son's efforts to differentiate from his primary object. Through firm yet sensitive efforts to restore the couple's suspended sexuality, the father uses his manliness to strengthen his connection with his wife and provide his son an object of identification able to locate maleness within the matrix of intimate relationship. Winnicott asserted that this sexual bond between parents provides the child "a rock to which he can cling and against which he can kick" (1964, p. 115).

In this fashion, a father helps his son recognize the link joining his parents together and thereby establishes "triangular space" (Britton, 1989). By being both a caring father to his son and an exciting lover to his wife, he offers each a dyadic relationship with him that is parallel to and competing with the mother–son unit (Campbell, 1995; Diamond, 1998). In reclaiming his wife and son, the relating man supplies a vital anchor for both his child and partner. Accordingly, the boy is better able to represent himself with his mother, his father, and with mother and father together. In being jointly regarded by his parents rather than individually appropriated by either for their unconscious need fulfillment, preoedipal triadic reality becomes a prerequisite for the favorable regulation of the oedipal phase (Herzog, 2005a).

In contrast, when the father is unable to join with his wife to facilitate his son's internalization of triadic reality, the boy's identification with his mother becomes problematic and negatively impacts his masculine gender identity. This is evident in some boys' more hysterical and perverse solutions to the prospect of separating from their mother; disavowing their own and their mother's sexuality, they unconsciously remain in the position of the little boy with his presexual mother. These boys manifest profoundly shame-based defensive configurations, reflecting their tenuous sense of masculinity.

The Attuned Mother

The significance of the boy's relationship to his mother needs to be underscored. A mother's recognition and affirmation of her son's maleness help him to progressively differentiate from her rather than to establish his sense of masculinity in violent opposition to her femaleness.

By recognition and affirmation of his maleness, I am referring to the mother's capacity to support her son's journey toward the world of his father—the world of males. A mother who is able to contain her own separation anxieties and fears of loss, as well as her envy of the budding son-to-father connection, is better able to support her dyadic relationship with her child. Needless to say, the mother's oedipal dynamics are crucial, for she has to be able to modulate her own competitive impulses as they emerge during this early period of triangulation.

A son who is not supported by his mother when he is turning outward from her tends to internalize a particular identification with her—one that in effect opposes his "phallic" forays toward his father and the external world. This problematic identification then operates to impede a boy's healthy aggression, competition, mastery, and authority, as if these qualities would themselves represent an attack on the mother. We see the outcome of a boy's unconscious identification with a competitive, envious, and possibly misandrist mother in our male patients who become attacking and even envious of their own healthy, assertive, more phallic-like qualities.

So to be more precise, a little boy especially identifies with the sense of his mother relating to him as a male person (of the opposite sex), and the ensuing internalizations continuously affect his felt masculinity. The mother's unconscious limitation in recognizing and sanctioning her boy's maleness, as well as her husband's fatherliness, a limitation evident in Greenson's (1968) case of Lance, establishes a more pathological maternal identification for her son.

The Little Boy's Maternal Identifications—
The "Father" in the "Mother"

The mother's endorsing her son as a male person tends to operate more unconsciously, and her boy identifies with these unconscious attitudes—what Ogden (1989) calls the paradox of "masculinity-in-femininity." In other words, a boy's elaboration of his masculinity (and triadic object relations) is deficient without a firmly established internal object father in the mother's unconscious. Because of her identification with her own securely established internal oedipal father, the mother is also able to bring the phallic/genital father to the emerging triadic relationship with her son. The unconscious father, or male, in the mother (or in the female analyst) is very much a part of her son's (or patient's) maternal identification. Mothers deficient in this internal object father place their sons in a precarious position from which to psychologically elaborate both their masculinity and Oedipus complex.

The boy's sense of masculinity is especially impacted by his mother's feelings about his physicality, sensuality, and temperament as well as by her endorsement of the father's paternal authority. Little boys lacking in this largely unconscious, intersubjective recognition of their maleness establish a highly conflictual internalization of their mothers. For these boys, particularly when their fathers are emotionally or physically absent, defensive phallicity or phallic narcissism becomes psychically urgent. In "narcissistically valorizing the penis" (Braunschweig & Fain, 1993), they tend to employ the phallus as a defense and compensate by relying on narcissistic pathology, often featuring perverse sexuality (Herzog, 2004).

When these problematic early identifications occur, a phallic ego ideal and more severe forms of gender splitting are relied on to manage the uncontained anxieties arising in such a relational matrix. Such arrested phallicism, marked by a partition in the bodily experience of the sensual from the sexual, operates to stave off intimacy (Bollas, 2000; Elise, 2001). One such patient of mine, a 30-something man, whose father abandoned the family and whose mother was "burdened" by her son's maleness, spent month after month in therapy recounting his daily sexual conquests while attributing his "successes" to the enormous size of his penis and his gigantic, Mensa-worthy mind. Interestingly, analytic work could truly deepen only when, to his great shock, he found himself romantically involved with a transsexual partner; at that point he was forced to examine his defensively constructed, highly fragile sense of masculinity. Indeed, it is characteristic of the phallocentric male to operate defensively, as if his phallus is all that he has to make him masculine.

The Gendered Nature of the Male's Ego Ideal

I have elsewhere asked the question how are we to understand the shaping of the boy's ego ideal along gendered lines, or to put it more colloquially, why is the "male ego" so important for men (Diamond, 2006)? In short, I believe that the gendered nature of the masculine ego ideal is founded on the boy's distinctive struggles during the initial stages of gender differentiation—a struggle requiring the little boy to adapt to a significant disruption in relation to his mother. It is the boy's gendered ego ideal that helps him to heal what he experiences as an abrupt, rather traumatic sense of loss during his struggle to separate from her.

How Do Boys Compare With Girls?

To better grasp this idea, I will briefly contrast boys with girls at the time of their initial gender differentiation during the second or third year. Young boys tend to be less mature cognitively and emotionally than little girls. There is typically another developmental asymmetry, in that little boys are pressured to renounce gender-inconsistent traits far more than young girls are. In fact, by age 6, boys experience considerably less gender constancy (i.e., feeling that one remains the same gender regardless of changes in appearance or behavior) than do little girls (Fast, 1984; Hansell, 1998).

Taboos against cross-gender behavior tend to be enforced much more brutally by parents, peers, and society generally when exhibited by boys (Maccoby, 1998). There are also greater prohibitions against early homoerotic attachments and homosexuality for boys; as they mature, boys show considerable inhibition against reexperiencing their early maternal erotic attachment (Wrye & Welles, 1994). Moreover, due to heightened shame associated with homoeroticism and father hunger, boys also have difficulty with their father-directed erotic desires. Unlike girls, boys are inescapably called upon to safely negotiate a passage through the dangers of this "traumatic discovery of otherness" (Ogden, 1989). Boys do not grow up experiencing themselves as masculine by dint of being male; masculinity has to be won and typically proven repeatedly.

The Boy's Separation "Trauma" and the Male's Sense of Shame

Psychoanalysts have cast the boy's experience of separating from his mother's world as his initial preoedipal crisis, or "trauma," conceptualizing it either along more traditional, metapsychological lines, emphasizing the loss of an ideal state of primary narcissism and unity with his primary object, or in relational terms that emphasize a primarily socially imposed interpersonal rupture resulting from the small boy's premature loss or repudiation of his sense of connection to his mother. However it is conceptualized, the boy must adapt to the loss just as he is realizing that he is sexually different from his mother. Thus, this loss occurs as he realizes that he can neither be the mother nor be of her female gender; Lax regards this as bedrock trauma for males, "a painful narcissistic mortification … that may have lifelong consequences" (1997, p. 118).

The boy not only loses a large part of his primary dyadic connection but is also pressured to repudiate what he has lost. Normative socialization for males relies heavily on the aversive power of shame to shape acceptable male behavior. The gender-related issue of being independent from his mother—rather than a "momma's boy," "tied to her apron strings," or a "pussy, sissy, or faggot"—reinforces his need to conform. Owing to this societal enforced separation from the mother-orbit, the young boy is culturally prohibited from knowing or valuing his loss and coerced to deny his need for his mother. He may feel emotionally abandoned without being aware of it (Pollack, 1998), while experiencing his identification with his mother as shameful. This is most often manifest in defensive efforts against neediness. As Elise (2001) contends, males can embody impenetrable citadels in an effort to stave off shame states that are not so easily metabolized. I advocate, however, that such "phallic" pathology only occurs when the male is *not* able to draw upon and integrate his varied identifications with his good enough involved father, attuned mother, and sexually linked parenting couple.

Phallic Narcissism and Maturing Masculinity

As Freud indicated, phallic narcissism begins as a natural, adaptive process to mitigate the small boy's experience of loss and envy. The boy's traumatic loss of the "paradise" of the earliest, highly gratifying relationship with his mother disposes him to create a phallic image of himself in relation to the world in order to regain control of the object now experienced as quite separate from his ego (Chasseguet-Smirgel, 1976, 1984, 1985; Manninen, 1992, 1993). In other words, the male's heroic quest commences as the little boy's phallic image provides him with an illusory way to win his mother's love, a victory that seems reflected in the gleam he is able to attain in mother's eyes.

The phallus partially represents the lost breast as his penis replaces the breast as the superior organ. In turn, the boy's breast envy is relegated to the deeper unconscious (Lax, 1997). The little boy omnipotently forms the adaptive and defensive illusion of "the supremacy of his own masculine equipment" (Manninen, 1992, p. 25), and the phallus, initially employed to assuage the boy's differentiation anxieties, becomes the symbol of invulnerability—a permanently erect monolith of masculine omnipotence (Ducat, 2004)—manically defending against the depressive dangers of an all-too separate but still needed maternal object. In short, phallic monism—the belief that the penis is the sexual organ—comes to guard against any recognition of lack or deficiency.

The masculine, phallic ego ideal is thus based on the boy's unconscious denial of differentiation in the service of his grandiose wish for maintaining the unlimited possibility inherent in the omnipotent, idealized union with his maternal object. The seminal issue for most men is how this early, preoedipal phallic narcissism and phallic omnipotence is integrated into an ongoing and evolving sense of masculinity (Diamond, 2004a, 2006). However, for some men without an opportunity for a maturing ego ideal that integrates the phallic ego ideal with the genital ego ideal (represented by the internalized "genital" father), phallicism in the form of a hypermasculine, phallic image of manhood becomes psychically urgent so as to achieve the missing psychic cohesion. Phallic behavior becomes largely compensatory and constitutes a narcissistic end in itself, for example, in the constant urge to assert oneself impressively, rather than serve more creative purposes (Schalin, 1989). In short, when things do go awry, the phallic ego ideal becomes needed in order to manage narcissistic anxieties arising in the complex reality of gender differentiation. True differentiation is denied, while penetration offers the promise of transcendence of vulnerability, limitation, and dependence. Under these circumstances, phallic masculinity is arrested, the phallic ego ideal dominates, and the sense of phallic urgency is paramount.

This arrested phallic narcissism or defensive phallicity (in contrast to the more adaptive phallicity with its suitable penile pride that fuels creative, purposeful activity in childhood and young adulthood) ultimately becomes a persistent obstacle to young adult as well as middle-life growth and development and is evident both in the fragmentation anxieties and the sense of shame that are evoked whenever a stable masculine identity *cannot* be maintained.*

Transforming Masculinity in the Course of Male Development

The relationship between these phallic facets and the genital features of a man's masculinity is continually being reworked, evoking distinct challenges at key developmental junctures. These challenges emerge particularly during the oedipal and latency phases, in adolescence and young adulthood, and again during mid- and later life. Although beyond the scope of this chapter to examine each of these critical junctures in depth, it is pertinent nonetheless to note the main gender identity–related factors operating throughout these other phases (Blos, 1978; Colarusso, 1995; Diamond, 1998, 2004a; Erikson, 1963; Freud, 1924; Levinson, Darrow, Klein, Levinson, & McKee, 1978; Schalin, 1983).

For example, during his oedipal phase and latency years, a boy's sense of his masculinity is especially impacted by his father's beneficial use of his paternal authority, emotional regulatory capacity (particularly in modulating aggression), and admirable skill in doing things. The boy's sense of his maleness, then, is directly related to his budding ability to express and modulate aggressive and competitive urges, acquire a sense of industry, and attenuate his adaptively needed, albeit illusionary, phallic omnipotence. In adolescence, as the boy differentiates from his family in seeking to develop his own identity, his masculinity is considerably influenced by his father's capacity to bear his son's moving away from him (as the boy did earlier with his mother) and constructively deal with the threats to his own narcissism, as well as by the teenage peer group's sanctioning of his masculine identity. Accordingly, by late adolescence and early adulthood, a

---

* In rethinking masculinity, I stress the importance of healthy, adaptive phallicism in contrast to arrested phallicism in the male's expression of self (Diamond, 1997, 1998, 2004a, 2006). Healthy phallicism is based primarily on what classical psychoanalysis refers to as neutralization, sublimation, and integration of the grandiose strivings of phallic narcissism or exhibitionism as well as phallic omnipotence during the oedipal phase (Edgcumbe & Burgner, 1975; Schalin, 1983). This phallic development occurs mainly because of involved, good enough fathering (or surrogate fathering) during a son's preoedipal, oedipal, and latency years. Other analysts have also distinguished the healthy, adaptive nature of phallic narcissism from the pathologically defensive type, especially by emphasizing the importance of the bodily component in the desire to penetrate (Corbett, 2003; Schalin, 1989).

young man's sense of manhood is directly tied to adult identity formation, especially influenced by his sexual prowess and ability to endure pain. In young adulthood, mentors are crucial as the young man embarks on his "heroic" journey to become his "own man" with lasting intimate relationships in the world outside his family. Thus, during his adult years, he is more likely to appraise his manhood in terms of his career success and ability to relate to and provide for his family. Finally, as I will discuss next, in his mid- and later life, undoubtedly related to the diminishment of testosterone, his manliness becomes more flexible, particularly in the course of evaluating the success of his generativity and, most likely, fatherliness.

The Maturing Male Ego Ideal

The adult man who is able to develop a maturing ego ideal that integrates the phallic ego ideal with the genital ego ideal (represented by the internalized, involved, and loving "genital" father) is freed from his reliance on the bifurcated, "phallicized" manhood that plays such an important, beneficial role in his childhood, youthful, and younger adult adaptations. Thus, the achievement of a mature sense of masculine identity is dependent on the adequate negotiation of a shifting balance between the phallic ego ideal and the genital ego ideal through the life cycle.

Reworking the Balance Between Phallic and Genital Ego Ideals in Aging

In early adulthood, men attempt to live up to idealized notions of what it is to be a man, notions that are reminiscent of the phallic little boy's view of his father. Thus, young adult men are typically dominated by the phallic ego ideal characterized by the "heroic illusion" (Levinson et al., 1978)—a variant of the boy's original phallic desire to win his mother's love. Nonetheless, young men increasingly need to call upon more of a genital ego ideal in striving to establish lasting, intimate relationships. If all goes well, there is an increased reality orientation as the pleasing of the self replaces the more unconsciously archaic wishes to win mother's love— thus, grandiosity lessens, a sense of otherness and empathy increases, and maturing adulthood is on course.

Developmental achievements in the area of work, intimacy, and fathering or mentoring typically precede the impact of aging in stimulating the reshaping of the masculine ego ideal. The maturing man's task then is to integrate the various phallic and genital aspects of his inner world in order to achieve what might be termed the "mature" or "true" genital position or genital masculinity where phallic propensities are utilized in the service of reality.

By midlife, a man's changing masculinity optimally weighs the perpetual male struggle along "genital" lines as, depending on the context, his divergent identifications can be adaptively and more flexibly activated (cf. Meissner, 2005). In brief, the pleasures of receptivity, being, experiencing, and understanding frequently come to take precedence over the excitement of striving and reaching, and priority is given to insight, connection, and nurturance. Unless a pathological upsurge of defensive phallicity occurs whereby the aging man persists in defining himself by conquest and aggression, this is a time when affiliation, a deepening of eros, and a greater appreciation of the preciousness of life can take center stage.

Masculinity in Mid- and Later Life

For most men, early and later middle age is the time when their nurturing and "feminine" sides are more fully integrated into their notion of mature masculinity. To illustrate how these dynamics may manifest in mature adulthood, I will briefly consider the gender identity crisis that men face during midlife and middle adulthood, as well as later life and aged adulthood—a time when a man differentiates from his more "youthful self" and fundamentally reworks his sense of his masculinity. I argue that the inevitable challenges to a man's identity at mid- and later life frequently help him to transform his gendered identity as a result of reconciling his masculine gender enigmas (Diamond, 2004a, 2006). Moreover, this is most likely for those men who have relied on more defensively phallic, less pluralistic constructions of their subjective sense of masculinity.

The Midlife Transition

Analysts writing about the man's midlife challenge, including Jung (1934/1954, 1936/1959), Erikson (1963), and Jacques (1965), argue that the aging man must come to terms with parts of his psyche that were necessarily renounced or repudiated earlier in order to establish a stable sense of identity. There is an awakening during life's second half, perhaps related to the attenuation of testosterone, in which the psyche becomes engaged in a process of descent—a propelling inward and downward in order to experience a sense of meaning beyond the mere facts of physical existence.

The midlife transition, signaled by the confrontation with one's personal death and its attendant anxieties, optimally leads to further transformations of the male ego ideal. Midlife development is arrested when the maturing man continues to call upon defensive phallicity to maintain his sense of masculinity, and he persists in defining himself by conquest and aggression within hierarchical-based relations. We see this all too often in the sad efforts of many men who tear apart their lives and families for a "trophy wife" or in their ruthless pursuit of achievement until their bodies grind them to a halt. These are the aging men who keep trying to prove their manhood when, primarily through their more conscious relational needs, they should be embracing their personhood.

The Male's Midlife Crisis

Men at midlife often experience a sense of ennui and a "depressive crisis" that reflects the pain inherent in having had to restrict oneself psychically in order to achieve sufficient mastery and a culturally sanctioned sense of manhood. This constriction in the self produces a developmental need both to reclaim the lost parts of the self and to come to terms with one's limitations.

This entails renewing his acquaintance with previously rejected gendered dimensions—particularly many of his early identifications and internalized objects set aside because of their seeming incompatibility with his more constricted, rigidly ossified, phallic sense of masculinity. Midlife individuation, or what Colarusso (1997) terms "the fourth individuation," consequently takes place through attempts to come to terms with those parts of himself that were disowned largely out of fear of being deprived of his masculine gender identity. The middle age man, as Jung (1936/1959) suggested, must make room within for the internal feminine to animate himself while his biological fires dwindle.

The Male's Late-Life Crisis

As men move beyond their middle age, the losses of aging mount, particularly with respect to one's physical and bodily changes. Consequently, a man's opportunities for ongoing later-life development depend upon his healthy midlife gender identity integration as well as on his capacity both for generativity and successful mourning.

In considering late-life masculine gender identity, potential mortifications and narcissistic crises characterized by shame, indignity, and humiliation are likely to occur as a result of the challenges inherent to acknowledging physical disintegration, separation and loss, dependency, and the "inevitability of time" as a fact of life. Indeed, fantasies of omnipotence are severely challenged if not brought to a complete halt. For example, Schafer (1968) noted how the reality of old age forces one to give up the fantasies of undying objects and abandon the hunt for an ideal object. Manic, phallic-narcissistic defense mechanisms tend to lose their power, and growing acceptance replaces the manic search for the ideal.

Teising (2007) contends that old age itself becomes particularly mortifying for men whose gender identity tends to remain distinctively phallic narcissistic. In these cases, the illusory venture of the phallic conquest of the world is often pursued up to the end of life, and feelings of helplessness, need, and despair are disavowed, while grandiose, omnipotent fantasies and actions attempt to preserve the illusion of control over the fundamentally out-of-control nature of aging and dying. I observe that the successful transformation of the phallic-narcissistic elements of the male ego ideal during midlife helps to establish the elderly male's later life course. Regardless, late life provides an additional opportunity for achieving a more integrated, gendered identity. Parent–child roles are reversed and the old become dependent on the care of the young (Diamond, 2007).

For the aging man, physical frailty and dependence as well as the inevitability of death are more easily acknowledged when he can integrate into his own identity the requirement to receive care or as Teising describes it, "an internal space representing the female—formerly experienced within the maternal other" (2007, p. 1337). As I have suggested in this chapter when discussing the formation of the genital object, this comforting internal object initially develops from the care provided by an attuned mother as well as an involved and loving father. A comforting, caring internal object is therefore available when external objects are lost and, as a result, helps to provide sufficient containment within relationships that can help the aged male to master the crisis of physical aging (Kaplan, 1994). Teising (2008) notes that for some men, it is only in old age that the object dependence of human existence, "the first fact of life," is no longer denied, while the illusory Western attitude of autonomous individuality is finally overcome and our fundamental relational nature fully embraced.

The Transformation of the Male Ego Ideal:
An Integrative Psychic Achievement

In terms of the ego ideal, the "phallic" ego ideal's dominance is waning for biological and psychological reasons, and the aging man is forced to deal with "the necessity of growing small" (Manninen, 1992, p. 23)—less grandiose, omnipotent, phallic—in order to become "whole." As a result, the ego ideal can become less sharply gendered at midlife and beyond— a more balanced, yet fluid masculinity is attained—and the ideals previously associated with becoming a man give way to those associated with becoming a person.

However, this is often no picnic since male certitude is dismantled, most forcibly in the arena of gender identity, and the anguish or "purgatory" of midlife (Jacques, 1965) reflects the breakdown in the structure of a man's identity. For example, an analytic patient who experienced an anxious, shame-dominated "midlife crisis" was able to draw upon and eventually make use of his previously repudiated maternal identifications. Thus, in achieving the ability to enjoy being a man without disavowing identifications with women, this patient developed and reconciled his new definition of what it means to be a man with the more rigid notion of masculinity that he had formed years ago (Diamond, 2004a).

Conclusion

By reworking the relationship between the phallic and genital features of his masculinity through life experiences or through the psychoanalytic treatment process, many men are able to achieve a new experience of their masculinity. Another patient in our very last session together after 9 years of intensive analytic therapy was recounting what he had taken from our work. Although not versed in psychoanalytic jargon and with no conscious knowledge of my own writings in the field, he stated: "You've really been like a father to me … a father surrogate I suppose and as a result, you've helped me to find a mother inside!" I asked him what he meant by "a mother inside" and he replied, "Well, it's like now I have a kind of mother inside me that lets me just be with my feelings. I don't have to do something or try to get rid of them but rather just kind of hang with them now."

In maturing adulthood, the fully becoming man who has largely transcended the need for a clearly defined, well-bounded masculinity is freed from his reliance on the bifurcated, "phallicized" manhood that may have been particularly adaptive earlier in life. This transformed male ego ideal can be heard in Walt Whitman's timeless ode to the fluid interiority of a more fully realized manhood:

> I am of old and young, of the foolish as much as the wise,
> Regardless of others, ever regardful of others,
> Maternal as well as paternal, a child as well as a man.

—*Leaves of Grass* (1855/1986, p. 40)

Acknowledgment

Portions of this chapter originally appeared in the *Journal of the American Psychoanalytic Association, 54*(4), 1099–1130. Used with permission. © 2006 American Psychoanalytic Association. All rights reserved.

References

Abelin, E. L. (1971). The role of the father in the separation-individuation process. In J. B. McDevitt & C. F. Settlage (Eds.), *Separation-Individuation* (pp. 229–252). New York: International Universities Press.

Abelin, E. L. (1975). Some further observations and comments on the earliest role of the father. *International Journal of Psycho-analysis, 56*, 293–302.

Abelin, E. L. (1980). Triangulation, the role of the father and the origins of core gender identity during the rapprochement subphase. In R. F. Lax, S. Bach, & J. A. Burland (Eds.), *Rapprochement* (pp. 151–170). New York: Jason Aronson.

Axelrod, S. D. (1997). Developmental pathways to masculinity: A reconsideration of Greenson's "Disidentifying from mother." *Issues in Psychoanalytic Psychology, 19*, 101–115.

Baron-Cohen, S. (2003). *The Essential Difference: The Truth about the Male and Female Brain*. New York: Basic Books.

Benjamin, J. (1988). *The Bonds of Love*. New York: Pantheon Books.

Benjamin, J. (1991). Father and daughter: Identification with a difference—A contribution to gender heterodoxy. *Psychoanalytic Dialogues, 1*, 277–299.

Benjamin, J. (1996). In defense of gender ambiguity. *Gender and Psychoanalysis, 1*, 27–43.

Blos, P. (1978). *The Adolescent Passage*. New York: International University Press.

Blos, P. (1984). Son and father. *Journal of the American Psychoanalytic Association, 32*, 301–324.

Bollas, C. (2000). *Hysteria*. New York: Routledge.

Bordo, S. (1999). *The Male Body*. New York: Farrar, Straus, & Giroux.

Brady, M. T. (2006). The riddle of masculinity. *Journal of the American Psychoanalytic Association, 4*, 1195–1206.

Braunschweig, D., & Fain, M. (1993). The phallic shadow. In D. Breen (Ed.), *The Gender Conundrum* (pp. 130–144). London: Routledge.

Britton, R. (1989). The missing link: Parental sexuality in the Oedipus complex. In J. Steiner (Ed.), *The Oedipus Complex Today* (pp. 83–102). London: Karnac.

Campbell, D. (1995). The role of the father in a pre-suicide state. *International Journal of Psycho-analysis, 76*, 315–323.

Chasseguet-Smirgel, J. (1976). Freud and female sexuality: The consideration of some blind spots in the exploration of the "dark continent." *International Journal of Psycho-analysis, 57*, 275–286.

Chasseguet-Smirgel, J. (1984). *Creativity and Perversion*. New York: Norton.

Chasseguet-Smirgel, J. (1985). *The Ego Ideal*. New York: Norton.

Colarusso, C. A. (1995). Traversing young adulthood: The male journey from 20 to 40. *Psychoanalytic Inquiry, 15*, 75–91.

Colarusso, C. A. (1997). Separation-individuation processes in middle adulthood: The fourth individuation. In S. Akhtar & S. Kramer (Eds.), *The Seasons of Life: Separation-Individuation Perspectives* (pp. 73–94). Northvale, NJ: Aronson.

Corbett, K. (2003, April). "Pride/Power/Penis." Paper presented at the spring meeting of the Division of Psychoanalysis (39) of the American Psychological Association, Minneapolis, MN.

Diamond, M. J. (1997). Boys to men: The maturing of masculine gender identity through paternal watchful protectiveness. *Gender and Psychoanalysis, 2*, 443–468.

Diamond, M. J. (1998). Fathers with sons: Psychoanalytic perspectives on "good enough" fathering throughout the life cycle. *Gender and Psychoanalysis, 3*, 243–299.

Diamond, M. J. (2004a). Accessing the multitude within: A psychoanalytic perspective on the transformation of masculinity at mid-life. *International Journal of Psycho-analysis, 85*, 45–64.

Diamond, M. J. (2004b). The shaping of masculinity: Revisioning boys turning away from their mothers to construct male gender identity. *International Journal of Psycho-analysis, 85*, 359–380.

Diamond, M. J. (2006). Masculinity unraveled: The roots of male gender identity and the shifting of male ego ideals throughout life. *Journal of the American Psychoanalytic Association, 4*, 1099–1130.

Diamond, M. J. (2007). *My Father Before Me: How Fathers and Sons Influence Each Other Throughout Their Lives*. New York: Norton.

Dimen, M., & Goldner, V. (Eds.). (2000). *Gender in Psychoanalytic Space: Between Clinic and Culture*. New York: Other Press.

Ducat, S. J. (2004). *The Wimp Factor: Gender Gaps, Holy Wars, and the Politics of Anxious Masculinity*. Boston: Beacon Press.

Edgcumbe, R., & Burgner, M. (1975). The phallic-narcissistic phase. *The Psychoanalytic Study of the Child, 30,* 161–180.

Elise, D. (2001). Unlawful entry: Male fears of psychic penetration. *Psychoanalytic Dialogues, 11,* 499–531.

Erikson, E. H. (1963). *Childhood and Society.* 2nd ed. New York: Norton.

Fast, I. (1984). *Gender Identity.* Hillsdale, NJ: Analytic Press.

Fast, I. (1990). Aspects of early gender development: Toward a reformulation. *Psychoanalytic Psychology, 7*(Suppl.), 105–117.

Fast, I. (1999). Aspects of core gender identity. *Psychoanalytic Dialogues, 9,* 633–661.

Fogel, G. I. (1998). Interiority and inner genital space in men: What else can be lost in castration? *Psychoanalytic Quarterly, 67,* 662–697.

Fogel, G. I. (2006). Riddles of masculinity: Gender, bisexuality, and thirdness. *Journal of the American Psychoanalytic Association, 4,* 1139–1163.

Fonagy, P. (2001). *Attachment Theory and Psychoanalysis.* New York: Other Press.

Fonagy, P., & Target, M. (1996). Playing with reality: I. Theory of mind and the normal development of psychic reality. *International Journal of Psycho-analysis, 77,* 217–233.

Freud, S. (1905). Three essays on the theory of sexuality. *Standard Edition, 7,* 125–243.

Freud, S. (1921). Group psychology and the analysis of the ego. *Standard Edition, 18,* 69–143.

Freud, S. (1923a). The ego and the id. *Standard Edition, 19,* 12–62.

Freud, S. (1923b). The infantile genital organization: An interpolation into the theory of sexuality. *Standard Edition, 19,* 140–145.

Freud, S. (1924). The dissolution of the Oedipus complex. *Standard Edition, 19,* 173–179.

Freud, S. (1925). Some psychological consequences of the anatomical differences between the sexes. *Standard Edition, 19,* 248–258.

Friedman, R. (1996). The role of the testicles in male psychological development. *Journal of the American Psychoanalytic Association, 44,* 201–253.

Gilmore, D. D. (1990). *Manhood in the Making.* New Haven, CT: Yale University Press.

Goldner, V. (2002). Toward a critical relational theory of gender. In M. Dimen & V. Goldner (Eds.), *Gender in Psychoanalytic Space* (pp. 63–90). New York: Other Press.

Greenson, R. R. (1966). A transsexual boy and a hypothesis. *International Journal of Psycho-analysis, 47,* 396–403.

Greenson, R. R. (1968). Disidentifying from mother: Its special importance for the boy. *International Journal of Psycho-analysis, 49,* 370–374.

Greenspan, S. I. (1982). "The second other": The role of the father in early personality formation and the dyadic-phallic phase of development. In S. H. Cath, A. R. Gurwitt, & J. M. Ross (Eds.), *Father and Child: Developmental and Clinical Perspectives* (pp. 123–138). Boston: Little, Brown and Co.

Hansell, J. H. (1998). Gender anxiety, gender melancholia, gender perversion. *Psychoanalytic Dialogues, 8*, 337–351.

Harris, A. (1991). Gender as contradiction. *Psychoanalytic Dialogues, 1*, 197–224.

Harris, A. (1995). *Gender as Soft Assembly*. Hillsdale, NJ: Analytic Press.

Herzog, J. M. (2001). *Father Hunger*. Hillsdale, NJ: Analytic Press.

Herzog, J. M. (2004). Father hunger and narcissistic deformation. *Psychoanalytic Quarterly, 73*, 893–914.

Herzog, J. M. (2005a). Triadic reality and the capacity to love. *Psychoanalytic Quarterly, 74*, 1029–1052.

Herzog, J. M. (2005b). What fathers do and how they do it. In S. F. Brown (Ed.), *What Do Mothers Want?* (pp. 55–68). Hillsdale, NJ: Analytic Press.

Jacques, E. (1965). Death and the mid-life crisis. *International Journal of Psycho-analysis, 46*, 502–514.

Jones, E. (1933). The phallic phase. *International Journal of Psycho-analysis, 14*, 1–33.

Jung, C. G. (1954). The development of personality. In *Collected Works* (Vol. 17, pp. 167–186). Princeton, NJ: Princeton University Press. (Originally published in 1934)

Jung, C. G. (1959). Concerning the archetypes, with special reference to the anima concept. In *Collected Works* (Vol. 9, Pt. I, pp. 54–72). Princeton, NJ: Princeton University Press. (Originally published in 1936)

Kaplan, A. H. (1994). Experiencing aging: Separation and loss. In G. H. Pollock (Ed.), *How Psychiatrists Look at Aging* (Vol. 2, pp. 27–44). Guilford, CT: International Universities Press.

LaBouvie-Vief, G. (1994). *Psyche and Eros: Mind and Gender in the Life Course*. Cambridge, UK: Cambridge University Press.

Lax, R. F. (1997). Boys' envy of mother and the consequences of this narcissistic mortification. *Psychoanalytic Study of the Child, 52*, 118–139.

Levinson, D. J., Darrow, C. N., Klein, E. B., Levinson, M. H., & McKee, B. (1978). *The Seasons of a Man's Life*. New York: Knopf.

Loewald, H. W. (1962). Internalization, separation, mourning, and the superego. *Psychoanalytic Quarterly, 31*, 483–504.

Lyons-Ruth, K. (1991). Rapprochement or approchement: Mahler's theory reconsidered from the vantage point of recent research in early attachment relationships. *Psychoanalytic Psychology, 8*, 1–23.

Maccoby, E. E. (1998). *The Two Sexes: Growing Apart, Coming Together*. Cambridge, MA: Harvard University Press.

Mahler, M. S., Pine, F., & Bergman, A. (1975). *The Psychological Birth of the Human Infant: Symbiosis and Individuation*. New York: Basic Books.

Manninen, V. (1992). The ultimate masculine striving: Reflexions on the psychology of two polar explorers. *Scandinavian Psychoanalytic Review, 15*, 1–26.

Manninen, V. (1993). For the sake of eternity: On the narcissism of fatherhood and the father-son relationship. *Scandinavian Psychoanalytic Review, 16*, 35–46.

Mayes, L. C., & Cohen, D. J. (1992). The development of a capacity for imagination in early childhood. *Psychoanalytic Study of the Child, 47,* 23–47.

Meissner, S. J. (2005). Gender identity and the self: I. Gender formation in general and in masculinity. *Psychoanalytic Review, 92,* 1–27.

Mitchell, S. A., & Black, M. J. (1995). *Freud and Beyond: A History of Modern Psychoanalytic Thought.* New York: Basic Books.

Ogden, T. H. (1989). *The Primitive Edge of Experience.* Northvale, NJ: Jason Aronson.

Panksepp, J. (1998). *Affective Neuroscience: The Foundations of Human and Animal Emotions.* New York: Oxford University Press.

Person, E. S. (2006). Masculinities, plural. *Journal of the American Psychoanalytic Association, 4,* 1165–1186.

Person, E. S., & Ovesey, L. (1983). Psychoanalytic theories of gender identity. *Journal of the American Academy of Psychoanalysis, 11,* 203–226.

Pollack, W. S. (1995). Deconstructing dis-identification: Rethinking psychoanalytic concepts of male development. *Psychoanalysis and Psychotherapy, 12,* 30–45.

Pollack, W. S. (1998). *Real Boys: Rescuing Our Sons from the Myths of Boyhood.* New York: Random House.

Reichbart, R. (2003). On men's crying: Lear's agony. *Journal of the American Psychoanalytic Association, 4,* 1067–1098.

Sandler, J. (1976). Countertransference and role-responsiveness. *International Review of Psychoanalysis, 3,* 43–47.

Schafer, R. (1968). *Aspects of Internalization.* New York: International Universities Press.

Schalin, L. J. (1983). Phallic integration and male identity development: Aspects on the importance of the father relation to boys in the latency period. *Scandinavian Psychoanalytic Review, 6,* 21–42.

Schalin, L. J. (1989). On phallicism: Developmental aspects, neutralization, sublimation and defensive phallicism. *Scandinavian Psychoanalytic Review, 12,* 38–57.

Stoller, R. (1964). A contribution to the study of gender identity. *International Journal of Psycho-analysis, 45,* 220–226.

Stoller, R. (1965). The sense of maleness. *Psychoanalytic Quarterly, 34,* 207–218.

Stoller, R. (1968). *Sex and Gender,* Vol. 1: *The Development of Masculinity and Femininity.* London: Hogarth Press.

Stoller, R. (1976). Primary femininity. *Journal of the American Psychoanalytic Association, 24,* 59–78.

Stoller, R. (2008). *At life's end: Between narcissistic denial and the facts of life.* Unpublished manuscript.

Teising, M. (2007). Narcissistic mortification of ageing men. *International Journal of Psycho-analysis, 88,* 1329–1344.

Whitman, W. (1986). *Leaves of Grass.* New York: Penguin. (Originally published in 1855)

Winnicott, D. W. (1956). Primary maternal preoccupation. In *Collected Papers: Through Pediatrics to Psycho-Analysis* (pp. 300–305). New York: Basic Books, 1958.

Winnicott, D. W. (1964). *The Child, the Family and the Outside World*. New York: Penguin Books.

Wrye, H. K., & Welles, J. K. (1994). *The Narration of Desire: Erotic Transferences and Countertransferences*. Hillsdale, NJ: Analytic Press.

Young-Eisendrath, P. (1997). Gender and contrasexuality: Jung's contribution and beyond. In P. Young-Eisendrath & T. Dawson (Eds.), *The Cambridge Companion to Jung* (pp. 223–239). Cambridge, UK: Cambridge University Press.

3

Names of the Father

Bruce Reis

Not long ago, a few analyst friends and I were talking. We were talking about another analyst of whom we all are very fond, when one of the analysts said that she liked this colleague because of the feeling she got when she was with her. "Some people," she said, in a flattering manner, "are just more gender-y than others." We all shook our heads in acknowledgment and later said our goodbyes. I didn't think of our discussion until sometime afterward, when I wondered about my friend's statement that some people are more gender-y than other people. When I thought about it more, I was not sure exactly what would lead someone to make an attribution like "more gender-y" of someone else; who would get to be called "more gender-y," and on what basis? More gender-y than whom? Then I wondered if anyone would ever use that description for me, and that is when something struck me: white, heterosexual men, such as myself, are not described in terms of gender. We are not included as a gender in the new paradigm of gender studies. Instead, our gendered existence is rendered through a doubling—a simultaneous absence and fullness of gender. We are at once the standard (of) gender, and its nonappearance. Since we are constructed as *the* gender, there has been no need to name us.

In discussing the ways issues of race inform the clinical, Adrienne Harris (2005), following on work in critical race theory and the analytic investigations of race by colleagues (Altman, 2006; Suchet, 2004), has recently written of the "unmarked" quality of whiteness that allows its color to appear colorless. Just as whiteness has been thought of as the absence of color, I would suggest, as others outside of psychoanalysis have begun to do (Kimmel, 1987, 1996), that male heterosexuality has been thought of as the absence of gender.

Since the 1980s masculinity studies have begun to complicate this absence in the category "masculine" by attending to its shaping in and through historical circumstances and social discourses (e.g., Adams & Savran, 2002; Connell, 1995; Di Piero, 2002; Gardiner, 2002; Haywood & Mac an Ghaill, 2003; Segal, 1990; Whitehead, 2002; Whitehead & Barrett, 2001). Many of these investigations have emphasized how the masculine is contingent upon intersecting social conditions and always driven by issues of race, class, gender, and sexuality. As the editors of *Constructing Masculinity* (Berger, Wallis, & Watson, 1995) observed, "Masculinity, the asymmetrical pendant to the more critically investigated femininity, is a vexed term, variously inflected, multiply defined, not limited to straight-forward descriptions of maleness" (p. 2). In large part, although with notable exceptions (e.g., Frosh, 1994), masculinity studies have not made their way into psychoanalytic gender discourse, as feminist and queer theory have, leaving psychoanalysts with a univalent notion of masculinity grounded in classical analytic theory.

Over the past 40 years feminist theorists and activists have advanced women's rights through challenging a tradition of male privilege. Within psychoanalysis, feminist theorists have challenged Freud's conceptions of femininity as a damaged masculinity, in the process rewriting, as well as more radically jettisoning, the very idea of normative developmental lines (Benjamin, 1995; Coates, 1997; Corbett, 2001; Harris, 2005; Horney, 1926). Contemporaneously, gay and lesbian presence in academia resulted in the creation of a queer theory that has rethought and reshaped intellectual discourse on gender, power, and privilege. By now these traditions have become familiar to many psychoanalysts. Indeed, within relational psychoanalysis, feminist and queer theorists continue to place on center stage the issues of gender, sex, and power.

Feminist and queer analytic approaches to the subject of masculinity have produced very similar descriptions of heterosexual men. By observing two of these descriptions my intent is to illustrate the terms by which the male heterosexual has been constructed. In doing so, I hope to demonstrate that male heterosexuality is not accorded the fluidity or multiplicity granted femininity or queer sexuality. Nor do these constructions evidence the complex "essential contradictions" that Harris has rightly applied to gendered positions. Viewing heterosexuality as monolithic leads to an essentialist conceptualization of male heterosexuality, even as the fluid, antiessentialist, and pluralistic nature of other sexualities are being recognized as socially constructed. It is my intent to dismantle this monolithic representation of masculinity to make room for a multiplicity of masculine gendered representations.

To be clear, I am not intending to argue that masculinity does not continue to occupy a hegemonic cultural position. Yet today's masculinity can and has been decentered from its hegemonic status. Traditionally, masculinity has been viewed as the most privileged subject position within society, and the power associated with masculinity has become a taken-for-granted aspect of its subject position. Yet, as I will argue throughout this chapter, social change, both positive as well as negative, has redefined power relations between men and women, rendering previous critiques of patriarchal power less relevant. For instance, in an article titled "The Decline of Patriarchy," Barbara Ehrenreich (1995) trenchantly argues traditional patriarchal power relations of men over women "is over," that it is "a memory, a thing of the past" (pp. 284–285). Ehrenreich notes both positive as well as negative changes in traditional family structure that have helped to bring about the decline of patriarchy, such as the rise in "female headed" households; declining interest on the part of men in supporting women as wives and full-time homemakers; and a diminishing sense in our culture that women need "protection." Ehrenreich considers a number of factors for these changes in recent American culture, including that men are no longer dependent on women for physical survival and that men have been embraced by the consumer culture. Men, according to Ehrenreich, no longer *need* women to prepare their meals or wash their shirts; and neither do men require women to express their economic status. But the most decisive factor cited by Ehrenreich for the decline of patriarchy has been the decline of male wages:

> In fact, one of the reasons for the fact that women have been catching up in earnings is not that women have done so much better, but that male wages have dropped. Patriarchal power based on breadwinning is now an option for very wealthy men, and this is a striking change. Men of color have long been paid too little to support a family, but this is no longer a "minority" problem. Young white males saw their wages decline by 20 percent in real terms in the twenty years from 1971 to 1991. (p. 288)

Coming to terms with these striking social shifts has meant a reexamination of changed masculine behavior and role expectations. Within psychoanalysis, that reexamination is only now beginning. I do agree with Dimen and Goldner (2005) that "Freud's idealization of phallic masculinity not only erased and debased femininity as a category of lived, embodied self experience. It also delayed the theorization of masculinity in all its specificity and multiplicity" (p. 102). But I would add that while feminists and queer theorists have spent the better part of 40 years challenging

Freud's views on women and homosexuals, they have continued to work within the Freudian paradigm—not rejecting Freudian theory, but reversing its developmental schemes (e.g., Benjamin, 1995; Chodorow, 1992).

Surely Lacan's pronouncements associating the masculine with the symbolic, his elevation of the phallus, if you will, into the foundation of the law that underlies culture itself provided decades worth of challenge for what indeed is described as a patriarchal and monolithic gender organization. Feminists and queer theorists have challenged the "psychic implications of gender's regulatory regime" (Goldner, 2003), but the supposed edifice of regulatory masculine power has remained largely undertheorized. Theorists such as Irigaray and Cixous, for instance, demonstrate the fluidity and multiplicity of the sex that is not One, but in the process reify Lacan's monolithic version of masculinity. Irigaray (1999) demonstrates how the female is "plural" by counting the avenues of pleasure, or self-touching, available to a woman. But the man remains limited, she writes, to the crude use of his hand on his penis, or his use of the female as a masturbatory object—for her, these are the sole sources of his pleasure. Leaving aside the heterogeneity of male heterosexuality, which I will return to shortly, we already know that this is an incomplete version of masculinity. If psychoanalysis is really ready to take seriously homosexuality as a masculinity, then Irigaray's vision of masculine pleasure fails to encompass a sex that is also, clearly, not one. Moreover, the idea that heterosexual men derive their pleasure solely from the penis-in-vagina (Dimen, 2003) variety of sex, to which Irigaray limits them, is simply not reflective of clinical and lived reality. In my practice, straight men yearn to be penetrated, they enjoy the stimulation of their testicles as sexual excitement, they use their mouths for pleasure, and engage in a wide variety of sexual practices that society, and our profession, does not allow them access to without the recrimination of diagnosis (Dimen, 2002). This brings me to an important point: heterosexual men are so fenced in by the socially constructed/socially constrictive definition of their own desire that any variation from that narrow band of behavior cannot be thought of as heterosexual. The "perversions" are an example of the types of behaviors that heterosexual men cannot engage in without being transformed from heterosexual man to pervert. I dare say that heterosexual women may enjoy same sex desire, and homosexual men may make sadomasochistic practice a regular part of their sexual behavior and not suffer the redefinition of their very gender orientation. This illustrates the cost to heterosexuality of its own supposed normativity. The assumption of normativity creates a regulative expectation of heterosexuality that is not in force for femininity or homosexualities. My point is that assumptions around heterosexual masculinity are such as to rigidly maintain the narrative of its monolithic structure within a 21st-century gender theory that emphasizes the fluidity, multiplicity, and essential contradictions of gendered positions. The following two examples will help to make this point.

In an article titled "Maleness and Masculinity" a gay analyst (Blechner, 1998) takes up the difficulties of definition of the term "masculine," interrogating the term, and finding a variety of queer identifications and practices that make claim to the designation "masculine." But when discussing heterosexuality in particular, the author concentrates only on homophobia and the straight man's dread of anal penetration. In other words, heterosexual maleness is discussed solely in terms of its fear of and defenses against homosexuality.

Penetration and the fear of being penetrated also play a central role in Elise's (2001) understanding of masculine identity. For Elise, the boy's fearful disidentification from the mother and defensive counter-identification with the father form a fragile foundation for the sense of self, gender identity, and sexual orientation. According to Elise, penetration is a threat not only to men's heterosexual identity and to their sense of masculinity, but also "to their very sense of personhood, to a separated and individuated identity" (p. 499). Elise conceives of heterosexual masculinity as something like a defensive reaction to maternal separation resulting in the compensatory phallicism of what she terms "the Citadel Complex," or, the "reliance on being the one to penetrate and an avoidance at all costs of the experience of being penetrated" (p. 518). Extending her ideas to critique, and yet at the same time upholding the Lacanian function of the father as a third to the maternal dyad, who brings separation and introduces difference, Elise remarks, with a mixture of blame and denigration:

> A father's emphasis on difference may be in the service of his narcissistic needs regarding sexual access to the mother and phallic supremacy. He may exert control over the children by ensuring their "separation" from the mother, by inducting the daughter into male-dominant heterosexuality (sometimes literally, with himself, in committing incest with the daughter) and by insisting that, to be a male, the boy has to follow suit in a most unnatural emotional act. (p. 515)

Both feminist and queer theory critiques of masculinity have engaged hyperbolic argumentation, what Butler (1995) described as "a hyperbolic theory, a logic in drag, as it were, that overstates the case, but overstates it for a reason" (p. 179). Although this rhetoric has been remarkably successful in making its case, it has had the unintended effect of collapsing differences by the force of its brio. Like a projective identification, these constructions of heterosexual men find their correspondences in the very real and all too frequent phenomena of male sexual and physical violence toward women and children and men's abandonment of their children and families. But also like a projective identification, these constructions tend to stultify and reduce, to lock their recipients into roles in a preordained script. Paternal presence becomes reduced to paternal function, which in turn becomes conflated with patriarchal power structure; and male heterosexuality becomes conflated with heteronormativity. Thus to be a straight man and a father is to force upon women and children, at best, an oppressive and at worst an incestuous introduction to what Elise terms "phallic supremacy."

There are many problems with this approach, not the least of which is that it necessarily leaves straight white men out of consideration for the same type of reclamation of a devalued social construction of their experience of gender. Kaftal (2001), in a thoughtful discussion of Elise's work, notes that her treatment of masculinity "does not take into account the paradoxes and contradictions inherent in concepts of gender and in the experience of sexuality"; and further observes that "having defined penetration as a binary concept, [Elise] forms her picture of men and women in the language of absolute difference" (p. 544). Kaftal's critique illustrates how Elise's proposed "Citadel Complex" universalizes and essentializes the male fear of penetration (qua maleness), re-creating a gender complementarity she supposedly seeks to transcend.

The cultural construction that fixes men's positions as unproblematic and unmarked represents a stultifying condition—not only for women, gays, and lesbians, but also for the men who are subject to its restriction. As long as men and heterosexual masculinity are homogenized as the oppressive and dominant creators of hegemonic regulatory norms, against which heterosexual women, gays, and lesbians can claim their difference, masculinity cannot forfeit its unmarked quality of taken-for-grantedness, and men are foreclosed from beginning to rethink the very boundaries that shape and define what it means to be a man. As cultural studies theorist George Yudice (1995) observed:

> Precisely because straight white men are perceived by progressives within identity politics and multiculturalism as the center of the dominant culture, they are not permitted to claim their own difference. There is irony here, for the very objective of progressive politics today—to dismantle privilege—ends up keeping

in place in our imaginary an ever greater monolith of power. Difference, which functions as the grounds for a politics of recognition, is only for the oppressed. What, then, are progressive, straight, white, men permitted to do in this context? (p. 280)

Recently Corbett (2006) has also observed that within psychoanalytic theorizing around gender, heterosexual men have experienced the same reduction that denies their difference. Corbett wrote that, "Fathers and paternal figures … are configured as off the path, locked in relations with their sons that are seen to enact and promote domination, the subjugation of women, and the perpetuation of masculinities that are determined by the quest for idealized phallic authority" (p. 18). For Corbett these flat descriptions of men are seen to support a theory of fragile masculinity based on maternal separations that are perilously defended against lest the experience of femininity should enter and dissolve any sense of identity. There is a problem that Corbett is pointing to here, and it is a familiar problem that has deep roots within psychoanalysis. The problem is that this approach threatens to do to heterosexual masculinity what psychoanalysis has historically done to femininity and homosexuality—that is, to negatively define a group in relation to what it is not. Heterosexual men, it would seem, are caught between a rather one-dimensional view of masculinity as oppressive and abusive and a supposed definition of their lack (of intimacy, of a desire for "penetration"), a lack presumably not experienced by women or homosexual men.

Corbett (1993, 2001, 2006) has advanced a compelling argument that psychoanalytic theory has positioned men as a-relational. In his observation regarding masculine identity, Corbett (2006) sees contemporary visions of masculinity as based on a problematic developmental scheme that forces the young boy to repudiate any feminine identification. The disidentification/counter-identification theory advanced by Greenson (1968) and Stoller (1964, 1965, 1968) and later utilized by Chodorow (1978) held that in order to achieve a masculine gender identity, boys must dissolve the "primary femininity" established through a "primitive symbiotic identification" with their mothers.

A number of excellent critiques of the disidentification/counter-identification theory have been advanced. In a series of papers Diamond (1997, 1998, 2004a, 2004b) has illustrated the "desirability and unavoidability of the boys' earliest preoedipal identifications with both parents" (2004b, p. 360). Although remaining in a more traditionally classical analytic paradigm, Diamond has suggested that normative masculine identity

formation may involve degrees of turning away from, rather than repudiation of, the feminine. It would seem that even within more traditional analytic circles, the disidentification/counter-identification theory is showing
its limited utility. Person (2006), representing an ego psychological vantage point, writes that "gender role identity is believed to be shaped to a
significant degree by gender identification with the same-sex parent, but
(that) this cannot be the whole story. A male raised solely by his mother,"
she writes, "may grow up with a strong sense of masculinity" (p. 1170). If
dual identifications are maintained, if identifications are not normatively
repudiated or refused, I wonder then if perhaps melancholy does not *typically* underlie the gendered subject (Butler, 1995)? Or to say it another way,
an index of health may be the individual's capacity to draw on the variety of identifications available to him, and melancholy would indicate a
disruption of the identificatory process, rather than its normal operation.
Gender does not have to be melancholic if it is not a fixed entity, but is
conceived instead as a series of ongoing experiences of self with other that
become represented over time.

Samuels (1993) goes even further than Diamond and most others in a
persuasive critique of the disidentification/counter-identification theory.
Samuels questions the assumptions upon which the theory is supposed to
operate. He disputes the existence of the originary fusional state between
mother and infant, citing infancy research that by this point has clearly
established no such fusion to occur. In the absence of this state, Samuels
clearly reasons, the proposed role of the father in separating the child from
the mother, in the terms by which psychoanalysts such as Elise continue
to speak of such a separation, is simply unnecessary: "there is nothing
that needs breaking up by the father" (p. 140). Although not explicitly
challenging the issue of the boy's supposed primary femininity, Samuels
questions the preferred narrative, the well-worn psychoanalytic trope that
has vanquished the preoedipal father from our exclusive focus on mother
and child, and narrated his first contact of a significantly emotional kind
with his child to be one of deprivation. Samuels takes seriously Diamond's
observations about the desirability and unavoidability of the boys' earliest
preoedipal identifications with both parents and illustrates how psychoanalytic theory has relegated the father to the status of the *other* parent.
What Samuels does is to open psychoanalysis to a subversive and radical
account of the father—one that recognizes his positive, direct, physical,
affirming, erotic, and playfully yet educationally aggressive presence in
the life of the infant. With this presence accepted, the boy no longer needs
associate nurturance solely with the feminine, and the issue of repudiation

becomes that much more problematized. Thinking about fathers and about sons in this way is a very different way than that proposed by most feminist or queer approaches.

There is no monolithic masculinity under threat here, no fragile foundation of anxiety against femininity or homosexuality. My practice is filled with men who are not inherently misogynistic or homophobic. They enjoy sex with women, their sexual practices vary with their multiple partners, and most certainly include a delicious array of polymorphously diverse experiences. Characterological and generational contributions of my patients' experiences of masculinity never fail to take me by surprise in the consulting room, and I often find the assumptions of what Layton (2002) would rightly call my heterosexist unconscious served up to me, just as the interpretation leaves my mouth. Many of my patients take for granted their ability to draw on multiple identifications, and at times I find myself at a disadvantage from having learned a psychoanalytic theory of masculinity based on repudiation of the feminine. For many of these men feminine identifications are matter-of-fact aspects of their varied and fluid internal worlds.

My therapeutic work with Ian comes to mind as an example. Ian can be a tough and exacting man in his work—but essential contradiction is built right into his expression of masculinity. A 20-something, rising star entertainment lawyer, Ian epitomizes a masculinity I often see clinically in post–baby boom young men. Ian recently broke up with a borderline woman, whom he had dated for 2 years; and he continues to live in the apartment that they had shared in Astoria, Queens. Astoria is something of a refuge for the 20-something professional class who shun the more trendy and more expensive Brooklyn neighborhoods. Although the relationship had been quite damaging to Ian, he clung to it for the considerable narcissistic supplies it offered. Ian and I had been discussing this implicit arrangement with his ex-girlfriend in his sessions as he ventured back into the world of dating, more conscious of this key vulnerability. Ian is a patient who uses the couch. He came in one morning and began: "So it's been an eventful few days. I saw the receptionist on Wednesday and I had a date with tall girl on Friday." The receptionist was a young and reportedly beautiful woman from his office, who narcissistically supplied Ian in a different way than his ex-girlfriend had. The receptionist enjoyed fellating my patient at every opportunity—at the holiday party, in a bathroom stall at the office, and even in more pedestrian locations like her apartment. By contrast, Tall Girl, as he called her, was a woman from a similar cultural background to Ian whom he works with professionally.

She is highly ambitious and a somewhat more settled and conventional person. "The date went fine," he continued, "nothing was wrong, I took her out to dinner, and she bought me a drink at a bar afterwards. We were standing on the corner after that and she said 'which way are you going?' and I said 'To Astoria,' and she said 'That's a drag.' I said 'Yeah,' and we found her a cab." Ian talked about whether he should have tried to kiss Tall Girl, and why he did not feel compelled to follow what sounded like her subtle invitation. "I don't know, she just wasn't very exciting to me." At this point I offered an interpretation, based on my thought that Ian was again delighting in being deliciously "done to" while rejecting a suitable woman, a woman perhaps like his mother, a retired scientist who he experiences as alternately dry, technical, and smothering, but *not* exciting. "Maybe she was too familiar," I offered. Ian takes up the interpretation, but not as I expected: "maybe too familiar to *me*," he says, "she's Jewish, from the suburbs, she's a lawyer, she was normal, not like these other girls I've been seeing, not like the receptionist." While I had interpreted that Ian drew away from Tall Girl because of the similarity to his mother, Ian used the interpretation to illustrate his own identification with Tall Girl and the problems that that caused for him.

"The receptionist came over on Wednesday," he continued, "and we were making out and everything, and then she said she couldn't have sex with me because she made a bet with her friend that she couldn't have sex for the entire month of January."

"It's February," I said, naively.

"It was the 31st! But I said to her, we had sex two weeks ago; and she said that didn't count, because it was in Queens. I said okay, so tonight won't count either ... but she said no. By this time we had already gone down on each other, which apparently was outside of the parameters of the bet. So I was frustrated, but like, okay, whatever. It's just that the Jewish girl didn't do much for me, where the receptionist I was really excited about, but I don't want to be with a girl who is going to cause me to suffer."

"Yeah, right," I say.

The inclusion of this vignette is meant to be purposively illustrative. A feminist reading of this vignette might well put the emphasis on Ian's exploitation of a woman lower down the office hierarchy. Her social class and ethnicity would serve as the ground of Ian's sexual pleasure as experienced through his power position vis-à-vis the receptionist. Yet how would it change matters to consider that Ian's excitement stemmed in large part from the receptionist's sexual aggressivity, that his attraction to her "was her attraction to me"? Indeed Ian's experience of sexual pleasure was largely conditioned through the receptionist's conferral of *her* power: "She would drag me into the bathroom and blow me." While not rejecting the feminist reading of this vignette, Ian's experience of pleasure makes it more difficult to determine just who is doing what to whom.

Ian's experience of masculinity does not inherently repudiate the feminine, but continues nevertheless to include the experience of struggle, anxiety, and conflict around his gendered selfhood. What is often striking is that men such as Ian sometimes feel quite syntonically identified with the feminine and often feel emboldened by their masculinity too. Their experience of gender is multiple and it is fluid, changing with context. Ian told me just recently for instance that he is a tremendous fan of the *Oprah Winfrey* show. He loves the topics and the guests and finds Oprah's advice to be helpful to him in his life. He records the shows so that he can watch them on the weekends and catch up. For Ian there is a fluid sense of continuity in being an emotionally open man who also enjoys pursuing sex with women. This "essential contradiction" is built right into his own sense of being a heterosexual man. When he told me that he discusses Oprah's shows as a way to get emotionally close to the girlfriends of his best friends, I asked if he was "dishing" with them in order to form even closer attachments to them, to which he replied, "Dude, you don't have to make it sound so gay!" I asked him, "You mean homosexual?" "Yeah," he said, "just because I talk about Oprah with a girl doesn't mean I don't want to sleep with her. But I protect myself, I don't talk Oprah to someone I just met, but with Tara, Scott's fiancée, I could sit on the couch and just cry watching Oprah with her."

Ian, and many like him, stands in opposition to the essentialist picture portrayed by Elise of the impenetrable, walled-off Citadel of masculinity. Indeed, when I read descriptions of heterosexual men such as Elise's I strain to recognize the people they are supposed to apply to. It is not that my practice does not contain men who are walled off emotionally or have difficulties with intimacy, it does. But Elise's description is too static to reflect the dynamic and contextual quality of men's emotional lives. Such monolithic descriptions fail to recognize that men can be hard and soft, and that these qualities together form an essential contradiction of masculine gender. The capacity to enjoy being a man without repudiating identifications with women (Layton, 1999) is in fact a common feature of heterosexual masculine experience that stands alongside, *and indeed interpenetrates*, more traditional constructions of masculine "hardness."

What should be most interesting to us as psychoanalysts, then, is not a sociological explanation of cultural prohibitions against men's emotional expression, but the psychological occlusions of these expressions by a culture that constructs men devoid of emotion or relatedness. Consider the 1994 *Time* magazine article, titled "Annals of Blubbering," which detailed the "surprising" fact that George H. W. Bush is "a frequent weeper." Barbara Bush is quoted as revealing that "touching and poignant things" bring "tears to the eyes" of the now former president. Surely the "surprise" that *Time* magazine links with the president's crying is an expression of the cultural pull toward a monolithic masculinity that prohibits the public display of emotion. But as Chapman and Hendler (1999) most importantly note in regard to this revelation: "There is space in American public life for sentimental men: big boys do cry, even when they become president" (p. 1). That American presidents have remarkable precedents for the public display of sentiment and relatedness is illustrated by the speech given in 1783 by George Washington as he resigned his military command. Both speaker and audience were in tears, the affective moment captured by Walt Whitman in "The Sleepers" when he wrote that Washington "cannot repress the weeping drops" while he "encircles [his officers'] necks with his arm and kisses them on the cheek, / He kisses lightly the wet cheeks one after another." Thus, Chapman and Hendler (1999) observe "one of America's foundational national moments, reproduced in one of its canonical literary texts, involves a fluid affective exchange between men" (p. 2).

But heterosexual men have suffered from the clumsy ways in which they have presented themselves as lacking in sophistication. The stereotypical characterizations that have followed are one dimensional and at times dehumanizing. There is the man/dog equation, so popular that a recent *New York Times* editorial lauded the praises of "training" a husband by the use of the same techniques as one would train a dog. And then there is the simplistic "metrosexual," a designation apparently meant to reify the strict regulatory constraints governing straight men's behavior. These atomistic characterizations have obviously failed to convey the fluidity and complexity of masculine sexuality and emotional life. Perhaps the epitome of the one-note characterization is the cultural trope of the bumbling father. Rendered harmless by producing children, Father's bumbling protects against a host of fears associated with the masculine (Jason Kruk, personal communication). But what would it take to reopen the possibility of erotizing the father and the father's body; to think about the father as sexual, and as sexy; to create a tension in psychoanalytic space where there is now only panic? It would mean imagining a role not dominated by prohibition, but rather open to delight and pleasure, a position not simply of restriction and transgression, but of visceral excitement and indulgence. Is that too dangerous for us to imagine?

After seeing the newest James Bond film, Paul, a 30-something, married man told me of a scene in which the actor Daniel Craig emerges from the sea in a small bathing suit: "I got goose bumps!" he exclaimed. "I mean, WOW!" he said. Paul was both admiring of and attracted to Craig's physical appearance, and had little trouble acknowledging as much. In examining the issue further, as it had to do with his own sexuality, Paul explained that he grew up with gay friends who were "out" and that while antigay sentiment was not foreign to his suburban childhood environment, his culture was such that gay men and women were visible presences in his youth. He associated gay men with having more "style" than straight men and valued this quality. Paul was not threatened by the existence of homosexuals and did not feel the need to violently repudiate his own same sex attractions, but most importantly, he felt quite securely identified as a heterosexual man and did not feel these qualities made him any less so.

Three years into treatment Paul was not just saying these words, he was saying these words to me. Our therapeutic relationship was not that of two walled-off men, unable to share internal experiences. Instead, Paul found in me an active receptivity and responded in kind with an openness of his own.

At the time he was speaking, he and I both had rings on our left hands, which at that moment in America clearly signified that we were both heterosexual men. I lift weights at the gym and keep a photograph of my daughter on my desk at work. Paul had seen the motorcycle helmet in my office, not displayed, but not hidden. So there was no anonymity of address, Paul knew I was a middle-aged daddy, obviously trying to rethink the "normative" path so many middle-aged daddies seem locked into.

Our dyad, shaped by this regulatory ideal, and yet also skating its perimeter, created space for Paul some months later to remark to his analyst, to another heterosexual man, his sexual excitement in viewing a man's body. Let me draw your attention to the register in which Paul's excitement was experienced—goose bumps (Jill Salberg, personal communication). How do we "read" this embodied libidinal excitation? In a culture that encourages men to think of themselves as their penises and gives men little encouragement to explore the rest of their bodies (Bordo, 1999), Paul's goose bumps were the visceral disclosure of an excitation that has been traditionally excluded from the male heterosexual register. His fleshy reaction implicitly challenges Irigaray who wrote that "woman has sex organs just about everywhere" but limited men's embodied pleasure to the penis, his *one* avenue of pleasure. Here Paul reveals to us the literal pleasure of the flesh and the pleasure of erotic spectatorship—the pleasure of looking.

In describing his attraction to the actor who played Bond emerging from the sea in a small bathing suit, muscled and lean, Paul consciously or not was reacting to the latest iteration of what has become a repetition in Bond cinema. In the earlier version of that scene, a version a generation earlier, Ursula Andress emerged from the sea in a small bathing suit, almost unbearably curvy, wet, and blonde. Now Daniel Craig was the object of the male gaze, in a scene meant to evoke the very complexity of modern heterosexuality—Bond as the ultra cool guy that Paul and I want to be, Bond as the guy who seduces and, in this film, falls in love with a beautiful and dangerous woman, and Bond the "hottie."

In interrogating the plurality of masculinities Person (2006) noted that the Bond character represents a different cultural model of heterosexual masculinity than that portrayed in films by John Wayne; a model "that exhibited what some would consider a feminine interest in appearance and style." She quotes the film professor Neal Gabler, who considered "Bond didn't need to divide his true masculine self from his urbane exterior. He was sophisticated and feral, soft and hard, smooth and rough, modern and traditional, intimate and bold, the consumer and the producer all at the same time." Those of us who grew up watching Bond—and I remember eagerly going to the theater to see the movies as a young boy—had, as Gabler observed, "the opportunity to identify with him in ways that [we] were increasingly unable to identify with more conventional, basically antihedonistic heroic types like the Wayne image" (quoted in Person, p. 1175).

I would go much further to suggest that straight men of my generation who grew up listening to glam rock albums, who, like me, snuck into the theater to hear Brando mutter the words, "Get the butter," who recited verbatim the cross-dressing Monty Python scripts in a geeky falsetto, who saw our mothers go to work and our classmates "come out of the closet" as young men and women, are men who are infrequently described in our analytic literature.

I remember as a preteen listening to the Kinks new song "Lola" and soon singing along to the story about a young man who has just moved away from home and who has never, ever kissed a woman before. When he meets Lola, there is only attraction, and no sense at all of its being a same sex attraction. And as Archer (2002) puts it:

> when he finds out Lola's a man, after a short (four-line) crisis, he looks at her, she at him, and in the space between stanzas six and seven, our narrator's world

> view changes. From not understanding how someone can look like a woman but talk like a man, the narrator ends up singing that boys will be girls and girls will be boys and happily jumps right in. (p. 53)

As kids we sang this song, and singing the song shaped our understanding of what it was we understood about the song. We sang affects of surprise and delight in identification with the song's narrator, and by the time the song ends with the words "But I know what I am, and I'm glad I'm a man, and so is Lola," we *got* the double meaning of the lyric and what it proposed about the subject of desire.

A common assumption is that straight men have somehow not been affected by the feminist and queer movements, that they have remained untouched by societal changes and continued on in a 1940s version of masculinity that continues to phobically repudiate femininity and homosexuality. I am sure this is true, especially of some more remote geographical or religiously influenced sectors, but it has certainly underestimated the degree to which straight men, influenced by changes made by their female partners and queer allies, have interrogated constructions of their straightness and made critical interventions into the institutional reproduction of the heterosexual norm (Thomas, 1999).

We live in times of rapid and sweeping sociocultural change. And I would suggest that the degrees to which our received notions of heterosexuality are being challenged and changed is quite substantial, and little noticed. Although the full effect of these changes may not have been noticed yet in psychoanalysis, they have been noticed in the popular culture. Archer (2004) makes the case that in the popular imagination the concept of heterosexual identity is rapidly being eroded. Archer points to Hollywood films like *Chasing Amy* and to moments in situation comedies such as *Friends*, *Roseanne*, *The Drew Carey Show*, and the teenage drama *Dawson's Creek* to illustrate wide changes in sexual culture, particularly among the post–baby boom generation. Contentiously, Archer argues that it is popular representations of heterosexuality, not homosexuality, that are dissolving more easily, the former taking on a more fluid cultural representation, the latter being increasingly ossified in rigid and stereotypic media representations.

Now this is not to say that all heterosexual men feel this way, and that some in fact would repudiate a sensation of attraction at that scene that Paul found provocatively exciting. But the other one of the two points I wish to make by this example is that certainly not all heterosexual men would, and talking about all heterosexual men as if they were the same is an egregious mistake. If the regulatory fictions of sex and gender are themselves multiple contested sites of meaning, as Butler (1999, p. 274) has suggested, then surely her conclusion is correct that the very multiplicity of their construction holds out the possibility of a disruption of their univocal posturing. Given the diversity of avenues leading toward this heterogeneous condition that we have agreed to call masculinity, it hardly makes sense to think masculinity as the sex that is "one." The men I describe here are involved in what Butler has called a "subversive repetition" of masculinity, which calls into question the regulatory practice of identity itself.

References

Adams, R., & Savran, D. (2002). *The Masculinity Studies Reader*. Malden, MA: Blackwell.

Altman, N. (2006). Whiteness. *Psychoanalytic Quarterly, 75*, 45–72.

Archer, B. (2004). *The End of Gay: And the Death of Heterosexuality*. New York: Thunder's Mouth Press.

Benjamin, J. (1995). *Like Subjects, Love Objects*. New Haven, CT: Yale University Press.

Berger M., Wallis B., & Watson, S. (Eds.), *Constructing Masculinity*. New York: Routledge.

Blechner, M. J. (1998). Maleness and masculinity. *Contemporary Psychoanalysis, 34*, 597–613.

Bordo, S. (1999). *The Male Body*. New York: Farrar, Straus, & Giroux.

Butler, J. (1995). Melancholy gender—refused indentification. *Psychoanalytic Dialogues, 5*, pp. 165-180.

Butler, J. (1999). Subjects of sex/gender/desire. In A. Elliott (Ed.), *The Blackwell Reader in Contemporary Social Theory* (pp. 270–276). Malden, MA: Blackwell.

Chapman, M., & Hendler, G. (1999). *Sentimental Men: Masculinity and the Politics of Affect in American Culture*. Berkeley: University of California Press.

Chodorow, N. (1978). *The Reproduction of Mothering: Psychoanalysis and the Sociology of Gender*. Berkeley: University of California Press.

Chodorow, N. (1992). Heterosexuality as a compromise formation: Reflections on the psychoanalytic theory of sexual development. *Psychoanalysis and Contemporary Thought, 15*, 267–304.

Coates, S. (1997). Is it time to jettison the concept of developmental lines? Commentary on de Marneffe's paper "Bodies and words." *Gender and Psychoanalysis, 2*, 36–54.

Connell, R. W. (1995). *Masculinities*. Berkeley: University of California Press.

Corbett, K. (1993). The mystery of homosexuality. *Psychoanalytic Psychology, 10*, 345–357.

Corbett, K. (2001). Faggot = loser. *Studies in Gender and Sexuality, 2*, 3–28.

Corbett, K. (2006, April). *Fantastic Phallicism: Recognition, Relation and Phallic Narcissism*. Keynote address, Division 39 spring meeting, Philadelphia.

Diamond, M. (1997). Boys to men: The maturing of masculine gender identity through paternal watchful protectiveness. *Gender and Psychoanalysis, 2*, 443–468.

Diamond, M. (1998). Fathers with sons: Psychoanalytic perspectives on "good enough" fathering throughout the life cycles. *Gender and Psychoanalysis, 3*, 243–299.

Diamond, M. (2004a). Accessing the multitude within: A psychoanalytic perspective on the transformation of masculinity at mid-life. *International Journal of Psycho-analysis, 85*, 45–64.

Diamond, M. (2004b). The shaping of masculinity: Revisioning boys turning away from their mothers to construct male gender identity. *International Journal of Psycho-analysis, 85*, 359–380.

Dimen, M. (2002). Perversion is us? Eight notes. *Psychoanalytic Dialogues, 11*, 825–860.

Dimen, M. (2003). *Sexuality, Intimacy, Power*. Hillsdale, NJ: Analytic Press.

Dimen, M., & Goldner, V. (2005). Gender and sexuality. In A. Cooper, G. Gabbard, & E. Person (Eds.), *American Psychiatric Association Publishing Textbook of Psychoanalysis* (pp. 93–114). Washington, DC: American Psychiatric Association Publishing.

Di Piero, T. (2002). *White Men Aren't*. Durham, NC: Duke University Press.

Ehrenreich, B. (1995). The decline of patriarchy. In M. Berger, B. Wallis, & S. Watson (Eds.), *Constructing Masculinity* (pp. 284–290). Routledge: New York.

Elise, D. (2001). Unlawful entry: Male fears of psychic penetration. *Psychoanalytic Dialogues, 11*, 499–531.

Flax, J. (2006). Masculinity and its discontents: Commentary on Reichbart and Diamond. *Journal of the American Psychoanalytic Association, 54*(4), 1131–1138.

Frosh, S. (1994). *Sexual Difference: Masculinity and Psychoanalysis*. New York: Routledge.

Gardiner, J. K. (2002). *Masculinity Studies and Feminist Theory*. New York: Columbia University Press.

Goldner, V. (2003). Ironic gender/authentic sex. *Studies in Gender and Sexuality, 4*, 113–139.

Greenson, R. R. (1968). Disidentifying from mother: Its special importance for the boy. *International Journal of Psycho-analysis, 49*, 370–374.

Harris, A. (2005). *Gender as Soft Assembly*. Hillsdale, NJ: Analytic Press.

Haywood, C., & Mac an Ghaill, M. (2003). *Men and Masculinities: Theory, Research and Social Practice*. Philadelphia: Open University Press.

Horney, K. (1926). The flight from womanhood: The masculinity complex in women, as viewed by men and by women. *International Journal of Psycho-Analysis, 7*, 324–339.

Irigaray, L. (1999). This sex which is not one. In A. Elliott (Ed.), *The Blackwell Reader in Contemporary Social Theory* (pp. 263–269). Malden, MA: Blackwell.

Kaftal, E. (2001). Outside in: Commentary on paper by Dianne Elise. *Psychoanalytic Dialogues, 11*, 541–548.

Kimmel, M. (1987). *Changing Men: New Directions in Research on Men and Masculinity*. Newbury Park, CA: Sage.

Kimmel, M. (1996). *Manhood in America: A Cultural History*. New York: Free Press.

Layton, L. (1999). What is a man? Postmodern challenges to clinical practice. In *Who's that Girl? Who's that Boy?* (pp. 169–191). Northvale, NJ: Jason Aronson, .

Layton, L. (2002). Cultural hierarchies, splitting and the heterosexist unconscious. In S. Fairfield, L. Layton, & C. Stack (Eds.), *Bringing the Plague: Toward a Postmodern Psychoanalysis* (pp. 195–223). New York: Other Press.

Person, E. (2006). Masculinities, plural. *Journal of the American Psychoanalytic Association, 54*(4), 1166–1186.

Samuels, A. (1993). *The Political Psyche*. New York: Routledge.

Segal, L. (1990). *Slow Motion: Changing Masculinities, Changing Men*. New Brunswick, NJ: Rutgers University Press.

Stoller, R. (1964). A contribution to the study of gender identity. *International Journal of Psycho-analysis, 45*, 220–226.

Stoller, R. (1965). The sense of maleness. *Psychoanalytic Quarterly, 34*, 207–218.

Stoller, R. (1968). *Sex and Gender,* Vol. 1: *The Development of Masculinity and Femininity*. London: Hogarth Press.

Suchet, M. (2004). A relational encounter with race. *Psychoanalytic Dialogues, 14*, 423–438.

Thomas, C. (1999). *Straight with a Twist: Queer Theory and the Subject of Heterosexuality*. Chicago: University of Illinois Press.

Whitehead, S. M. (2002). *Men and Masculinities: Key Themes and New Directions*. Malden, MA: Blackwell.

Whitehead, S. M., & Barrett, F. (2001). *The Masculinities Reader*. Malden, MA: Blackwell.

Whitman, W. (1993). The sleepers. In *Leaves of Grass*. New York: Barnes and Noble. (Originally published in 1855)

Yudice, G. (1995). What's a straight white man to do? In M. Berger, B. Wallis, & S. Watson (Eds.), *Constructing Masculinity* (pp. 267–283). New York: Routledge.

4

Two Men Talking
The Emergence of Multiple Masculinities in Psychoanalytic Treatment

Robert Grossmark

We behold not one story but many.

Adrienne Harris (2005, p. 162)

In this chapter I discuss the many ways in which heterosexual men can experience their maleness, their heterosexuality, and their masculinity and the conflicts that are evoked and emerge as the different conceptions and configurations of heterosexuality and masculinity collide and shift in the context of psychoanalytic work with a male heterosexual analyst. Taking a position that views masculinity and heterosexuality as continually constructed and transformed in relationships, I will focus on detailed descriptions of my psychoanalytic work with two very different heterosexual men and will give some detailed session notes so as to examine the complexity and density of the struggle as new configurations of heterosexual masculinity emerge in the analytic work.

The background to this work, and indeed the rest of this volume, is located in the growth of interest in the multiplicity of masculinity and heterosexuality. In the psychoanalytic field, Harris (2005) and Person (Chapter 1, this volume), for example, have noted that the masculine and heterosexual have tended to be seen as unproblematic and unremarkable, have been flattened out, and are often seen as unitary, in essence, a given. Gender theorists Kimmel (1996) and Connell (2005) have drawn attention to the multiple configurations of masculinity, and Person urges us to consider many masculinities. Until recently little attention has been given to the many configurations and constructions of masculinity as lived by heterosexual men. As both Kimmel and Connell have noted, the heterosexual male can often become invisible in the gender dialogue.

Put simply, heterosexual masculinity can be said to be no monolith and, as Reis describes in Chapter 3, any one man's heterosexuality can contain so many experiences, fantasies, conflicts, and desires. From a relational perspective, this also goes for the heterosexual male analyst himself. To describe an analytic couple as "two heterosexual men" says something, but that something can have many meanings. In the intersubjective matrix of the analytic setting where there is—and need be—interpenetration of affect and fantasy, the co-construction of transitional space and thirdness, and the emergence of the unformulated and unknowable, the analyst's heterosexuality is also emerging and shifting along with that of the analysand. To deeply engage with a patient is to allow ingress to that patient's world in many ways that sometimes we as analysts can hardly comprehend for ourselves. We all know we are changed by our work with patients, and I think that the many different male and heterosexual and polysexual self states that are evoked within us as we work with patients highlight this in a particularly poignant way.

For instance, Ogden (1989) talks of the masculinity-in-femininity, the mother's identification with her father, that later allows the son to find and internalize a male identification within his relationship with the mother. This is, from Ogden's viewpoint, helpful in the resolution of oedipal and male issues with the father. By extension, I would suggest that children find in their fathers, and analysands find in their male analysts, the mother-in-the-father that allows for nourishment, feeding, and a sense of maternal holding. I would suggest that it is an everyday experience for male analysts to be in touch themselves with the mothers within them, and that this is an everyday part of the heterosexual, masculine experience, although rarely articulated as such.

It is my hope that the analytic work with two patients discussed in this chapter will illustrate the multiplicity of the male heterosexual experience and being, both for the patient and analyst. From the language of nonlinear dynamic systems theory (following Harris, 2005) we will see the deep and shallow attractors of each man's heterosexuality become perturbed in ways that will lead to a phase shift that destabilizes the whole system of the person and of the therapeutic dyad, and augurs a deepening of analytic and personal work. In the first we will see the emergence in a dream of the issues of heterosexuality, manhood, and fatherhood, which had yet to be formulated by the patient. In the second example the patient is one for whom gender identification, maleness, and sexuality have been front and center from the beginning of treatment, and in the session we will see an enactment out of which previously unformulated aspects of maleness and his experience of himself emerge.

Both of these heterosexual men are fathers, as am I, and both of these clinical vignettes revolve, in part, around the issues and conflicts that come with fatherhood. All three of us had become fathers within the past decade. The focus here is on the foregrounding of issues of heterosexual masculinity as they arise in the context of this transition and as these issues emerge within the analytic work, in dreams and in enactment.

Brian

Brian first came to see me 2 years ago. His neat and elegant appearance was matched only by his neat and elegant description of his life. He initially painted a picture of a happy marriage with two wonderful little girls. His interest was in exploring his work situation. Brian, in his late 30s, owned a chain of dry cleaning businesses that was moderately successful. This is a business his father had begun with his brother after the family's emigration, with so many other mercantile Jews, from Eastern Europe. The business had grown and become quite successful. After the uncle's death, the father had decided to retire, and Brian had bought the business out. Some years later his father himself had died. Brian was unsure exactly what he wished to address about this situation, but knew that he felt troubled and depressed when he thought about the business.

He took to the idea of therapy with a growing eagerness, talking with insight that surprised him about the ambivalence he felt in regard to the business and his family. He related how as a young man out of college he had wanted to pursue the study of literature, and that his mother and older sisters had sat him down and impressed on him that he should go into the family business; after all, why had Dad slaved away so intensely all these years? We revisited this moment many times during those first few months. He began to wonder about how his family functioned, the fact that it was his mother, not his father, who insisted on the business for him, and the lack of consideration for his point of view and his aspirations.

At first images of his family life centered around a bustling and noisy family where he and his sisters liked nothing more than to sit with their parents and engage in spirited games and conversation. As we talked, darker and more ominous tones entered these happy images: his parents always ate alone after the children had been fed, his father generally returned from work with a scowl on his face, seemingly burdened in ways the young Brian could not understand, but that filled him with fear and dread. The father would retire to his study, and Brian would enter with fear and trembling when told by his mother to ask his father for help with homework or to convey some message. The father would generally appear irritated and impatient with Brian, and Brian would often have to fight to not cry when in his father's forbidding presence. This ogre-father was contrasted with the proud and praising father who would love to be entertained by the young Brian who was gifted with wit and verbal sharpness. At family gatherings no one could make his family, and especially his father, laugh like he could. Relating these moments, Brian was filled with conflicting and painful emotions; the loss of an adoring father and a sense of specialness, along with the sense that he, Brian, had needed a little too much effort to turn on these charming and praise-inducing performances.

His perception of his mother shifted as well. First described as a creative and loving woman who fit the stereotype of the dutiful wife supporting the father's dedication to the business and mothering the children, the image of her later included an almost fanatical devotion to whatever cause she took on and an aggressive rigidity that tolerated little difference of opinion. One is either with her or against her. This has helped Brian understand his unique and alienated feelings as a boy.

As for so many who lack the recognition and mirroring that help consolidate self, identity, and desire, he developed as a somewhat solitary and self-styled boy. He made some close friends but avoided team sports and physical exertion. There were no memories of his father engaging in any male bonding activities such as little league or playing with Brian at all. Not until college did he realize that he liked inhabiting his body and discovered a facility for tennis and other racquet sports as well as skiing and swimming—all individual endeavors. As an adolescent he refused to wear the trendy contemporary fashions, styling himself as a hippie/punk mix. There are traces of this adolescent rebellion to this day: he will comment that "there's no way in hell that I'm going to wear khakis: I mean everyone wears khakis in the summer." Individuality has to be held on to at all costs when there has been little or no mirroring and partnering in development and conformity is the only way to take up one's place in the family.

He began to articulate that he felt he had been forced into a presumption of who he would be, the son who would take over the family business and who would be devoted to the family and its tradition. He seemed moved in a distant and controlled way by much of our discussions and expressed some thanks for the opportunity to get these things out in the open. His expression that "Ah, now I see what therapy is all about!" felt genuine, yet slightly ingratiating; perhaps a way to evoke the sense of specialness and temporary safety he had experienced when entertaining his father and family.

The issue of his masculinity and heterosexuality was not front and center. It came into view most in relation to the growing questions about who his father really was as a man. Confusing the image of the terror-inducing ogre, there was the perplexing image of the father as unable to confront Brian, of a man who asked his wife to do what Brian saw as the difficult work, such as laying down the law when it came to business versus literature. Furthermore, since taking over the business, Brian has repeatedly discovered evidence of his father's bad business sense. The purchase of needlessly expensive office furniture and fittings, costly small business consultations, and a health care plan for the employees that was crippling the business financially were just a few examples of what coalesced into an image of a man driven by narcissistic and grandiose ideas of himself, rather than sound business sense.

He also talked at times of his discomfort with many men, which contrasted with the growing comfort and ease that emerged between him and me. For instance, describing a business trip to look at new technology at a dry cleaning convention, he told me of his frustration socializing with the other men (they were all men), their limited artistic interests (he would always prefer an art movie to an action thriller), and their macho posturing (he would often feel almost embarrassed to admit that he actually loved his wife and was not interested in stories of affairs, prostitutes, and the like). The implication was that we—he and I—were not like them.

The following session occurred as we approached the 2-year mark in the treatment. Brian came in, dispensed with any of his customary introductory remarks, and the following discussion ensued.

"I had a dream about Julie [his second daughter who was 4 at this time] and it's really weird." He conveyed some surprise; he rarely reported a dream and certainly not one that he would call weird, or that seemed uncomfortable to him. The dream: "Julie had lobster legs. Coming out in addition to her legs, beneath her vagina. Like from her inner thigh. I think Oh, it's okay, she's healthy, she doesn't seem to be bothered by them, and in the event, we can probably get them removed. It looked like old daguerreotypes of people born with extra sets of legs."

Brian exhaled and shook his head and said "Such a potent dream."

I say: "Yes. What do you think?"

He goes on. "Julie is so much more aggressive than Stephanie [her older sister who is 7]. It's consistently like that. I worry that Stephanie's reluctance and shyness would keep her back from doing things; she'd be so concerned about others' feelings. Stephanie's matured. She's quirky and different. Now she's taking rock climbing and the cello. She's quirky. Julie is terrifying. I fear she has no sense of caution. She's so great. Lovely. That feeling of confident abandon. To be able to push herself to things more and more."

"It was below her vagina, below her waist; like it could protect her vagina, like a manifestation of her personality that you can't see. Julie's sensitive and loving, but she's out there with both fists. People always see her as so sweet, so lovely."

Here Brian pauses. I say: "Lobster legs?"

Brian: "I've never eaten lobster; a kosher thing. I've never eaten any shellfish except oysters. It definitely comes from my upbringing. My father always ate shellfish, but out of the house only. I eat bacon. It doesn't bother me at all."

He pauses. I say: "Lobster legs on Julie—like some kind of penises?"

He goes on: "Julie, when she was little, I don't know, around 2, 3 or so, was into the idea that she had a penis. She'll still pretend she has a penis."

I ask: "Like how so?"

Brian: "Like she'll take a towel after her shower and twist it and put it between her legs and walk around the apartment and posture and say stuff, like she's saying look I've got a penis. Stephanie never did anything like that. I've talked about it with Linda [his wife]. You know, I used to feel it was important we be natural and naked around the house. You know, when the girls were little, they'd see me naked around the house. Not any more. It's not appropriate at all."

There's a pause.

He continues: "You know, Julie has a page-boy haircut. She looks great."

Another pause: "I never wanted a boy."

I ask: "How come?"

Brian: "The idea of a boy freaked me out a bit. I'm not into sports. I mean I have no connection to the baseball scores. The guys go immediately to the sports pages. We had dinner with some friends and this guy is talking on and on about his son's avid following of the baseball scores and statistics."

He pauses, and I am aware that we are in new and emotionally real territory. He looks deeply thoughtful in a way that I have rarely seen him. I feel strongly that I must leave him the space to just let whatever thoughts might come.

He says, slowly now: "But now, talking to you, the thought of having a boy; it's sad. I was playing with my friend's boy. You know what? I called him 'son.' It just came out. My dad called me 'son.' His dad called him 'son.' I mean, who's going to inherit my cuff links? I know it sounds trivial."

I say: "But it's something …"

He goes on: "I have a sweater of my dad's that I can't throw out."

Again I wait and he is deep in thought.

He says: "I'd like to teach a son how to tie a tie. I mean maleness. It's all such a parody. Thank god you don't have 'Iron John' on your bookshelf. You know Julie's name is Julie Paula. She's named for him; his name was Julius and in Hebrew it was Pincus. So she's Julie for Julius and Paula for Pincus."

I reflect and process this information realizing that Julie was born some while after his father had died: I say: "Julie was named for your father."

It is a rich and complicated moment for me as I am feeling strongly how much he wanted a son, and thoughts of my own little boy come into my mind. I feel a depth of love for my son and a tender connection to Brian. I see my son's face and think of how much I enjoy having both a little boy and a little girl. I feel some guilt, some fear, something grave, and something moving.

He says after a while: "The truth is, I was intimidated by the idea of having a son. I thought of a teenager looking for his identity. The clothes. The stuff. I don't know: the whole question: how to be a male."

I say: "It's been so intimidating and confusing; your family's ideas of maleness."

He says: "Driving home, after one of our sessions, I was thinking: Who am I? Is it just a series of events that I react to? To go through life, raise kids. I know; it sounds like that EST bullshit. But I wonder: what are my values? What's at the core? In life I'm so reactive, always reacting, dealing. Do I exemplify any inner set of beliefs? Okay, there's the business, my girls, my core with my wife. But go inside a bit. What are my core beliefs? Maleness. Fathering. Having a son. It's all related, isn't it? I don't think it's just about measuring up. It's more. It was a scary moment thinking, who am I, genuinely. My whole experience has been fairly reactive. This is the right thing to do; this is what I'm told to do. And I've done that. But I don't know what my own very specific set of beliefs would be. Or are you no more than who your father makes you and what he tells you to do?"

This was a moving session and was followed by a deepening in the treatment. We continued with the themes of this session and do so to this day.

He is now considering coming more times per week, and I have raised the issue of the couch, which both scared and interested him. The reason I wanted to present the material to you as it unfolded—and there is much here that is beyond the scope of this chapter—is to illustrate, for the purpose of this chapter, the complex dilemma of being a heterosexual male and how the issue of heterosexual masculinity and its vicissitudes was core to Brian's very being, and certainly to the treatment as it unfolded. Brian's heterosexuality and masculinity were softly assembled in a way that contained and neutralized many of the problematic and mysterious aspects of his and his family's dynamics. The dream was disturbing, "weird" to him. This complicated, alluring, and terrifying image of Julie's genitalia signified the beginning of a phase shift from the deep valley of disavowal to the shallow basin of confusion and questioning: what does it mean to be a man, a father, and indeed what does it mean to be himself? The questions are inseparable.

One of the interpretations of the dream that we talked about subsequently was that Julie and her lobster legs protecting her vagina illustrated his ambivalence and fears about his heterosexuality and masculinity; his outward bravado and "nonkosher" yearnings in life masked his more receptive and interior longings. He had thus lived with the conviction that he was not man enough to be the father of a boy and had suppressed his longing for a boy child. He was not the man he was brought up to be. He had disfigured himself and his own gender, covering over his own interior spaces. In the session itself he moved from his self-statement that he never wanted a boy, to the beginning of some mourning for the boy he did not have, the boy he was never able to be, and for the father who could not teach him how to be a man. The dream heralded the appearance of his own transgressive desires to be a man unlike his father and unlike the expectations of him, and furthered the long process of mourning his father. He revealed his own nonkosher lobster legs. In some ways his heterosexual masculinity had required a disavowal of softness and receptivity: recall his comment about "Iron John." Interestingly as he has been increasingly able to let treatment come into him and his life, his suppressed sense of his own agency and authority has come out into the open, rather than be transfigured and displaced. This has nowhere been more clear than in his work, where he has worked extremely hard and thoughtfully and has transformed the business, focusing more on growth and acquisition such that his income has substantially increased and his actual work activities are much more to his liking. It no longer feels to him like his father's business; indeed it has been totally transformed.

The dream also illustrated the manner in which the parents' unconscious fantasies of the child they would desire affect the genderedness of the child they actually have. The heterosexuality his parents imagined for him, as the only boy in this traditional male, business-oriented family, was different from the heterosexuality he felt would be true for him. Similarly the unconscious wish that Julie be "Julius" had resided within him and then in Julie's body and character. Indeed, in the dream, it is Julie's body that is the site for the rendition of his conflicts about his masculinity, and he later related the lobster legs of the dream to the pretend towel-penis that Julie would parade at home; a performance of masculinity rather than something organic. Other more classical interpretations of the dream, including the fear of his own incestuous desires for his daughter and his fear of a woman's genitalia as dangerous and animal-like, were given some thought, but did not register in the same way as the work related to his masculinity. Most prominently the dream opened up these issues about his masculinity, and as he was able to articulate them and follow their many meanings it seems that a greater ease developed in his relationship with both his daughters, and Stephanie, the older daughter, seems to have become more assertive and comfortable within herself.

Certainly, there is much more to be said about this case and this dream. But for the moment let us leave Brian and say that to me, it certainly seems to bring into focus the multiplicity and complexity of heterosexuality, the embeddedness of heterosexuality in the particular context of one's development, the fluidity of heterosexuality, the way that gender can bind the manifold unconscious conflicts that fill a life, and the unique opportunity that the intersubjective treatment space can offer for the reassemblage of softly assembled heterosexuality. He had been unable to feel comfortable being a man in his own way. His maleness had been assembled around appeasing and displaying adherence to a family fantasy. We see the opportunity for a more integrated and personal maleness emerge as both he and I find greater access to wider and deeper expressions of our masculinities together.

Nick

As a contrast, I will now describe Nick, who has suffered with much more severe psychopathology. Nick has brought the issue of gender into the treatment from the very beginning. Nick is a white American man in his early 30s with an MBA who works in information technology. Arriving in my office 6 years ago, he was an enraged ball of fury. His rage was directed at almost all authority and symbols of power. His superiors at work, the U.S. government, and anyone who did not see the world as he did were contemptuously derided. Those who stood up and fought the great evil were idealized and lauded, none more so than the 9/11 bombers and other suicide bombers. I figured I had better just stay steady and try to create a safe space within which I could find out who this man was. I was aware though that the issues of disgust, repulsion, and violence would be important and present in this treatment. His hair and clothes were always unkempt and disorderly. They seemed to speak of a neglect and abandonment. Over time he calmed down and articulated his difficulties with managing his emotions, his profound self-doubts, and the overwhelming rage that could leave him totally beside himself. The most comforting thing for him and for me in those first months of treatment was his dedication and devotion to his long-term girlfriend, who he described as a reliable and stable partner for him. Indeed, he also became dedicated to his treatment despite many periods of intense ambivalence and struggle.

He described his upbringing with a mix of pride and puzzlement. His parents had left Chicago with their small children for the isolated regions of Oregon where they boldly built their own house miles from the nearest habitation and supplies and lived a terrifically hard life. Nick and his older sister grew up with inefficient water and sewage at the end of a half-mile driveway that was often impassable in the rigorous winters. To myself I questioned the sanity of his parents. He viewed his father as a pioneering dreamer type, a man among men. He idealized the men of his father's side of the family as strong, rugged, and real men. His rage was mainly kept for his mother. She had left the home when he was 5 and had moved in with a sequence of men and women lovers. He and his sister lived an almost itinerant life, spending some time at the family house in the woods with their father and otherwise living in various households with the mother's lovers, her lovers' roommates, and sometimes with people he simply could not place. He described how on one occasion he went alone to stay with another "aunt" friend of the family, whom he barely knew, for some days at around 8 years old and packed his own bag for the visit. He arrived with a bag filled with nothing but tube socks. He was dumb-stuck when I suggested that he was neglected. It had never occurred to him.

His body and his sexuality were as chaotic as his rage. He believed for some of his teenage years that he was gay, tried to have sex with a close boy friend, was promiscuous and hyperstimulated with young girlfriends, and became fascinated with anuses and feces. We discussed the issue of sexual abuse and thought about possible suspects, mostly focusing on some local boys who later became juvenile criminals, and an uncle who has always seemed dangerous to him. He cannot recall anything specifically, but explicit sexual dreams involve his sister, his friends, some of his caretakers, and so on. Like his body and his presentation, his mind and his memory were an evacuative mess of out of control images and stimulation. He was grounded and also traumatized by an obsession with child pornography. He was excited more than anything by the image of an innocent little girl who looks to be getting pleasure as she is sexually or violently abused. His descriptions of some of the web sites that he would visit have at times been difficult for me to think about. Those explicitly involving screams, terror, and torture have caused me pain. I assume I am experiencing some part of his experience. The thing is, they all cause him immense pain too.

He has done much work in the treatment, and I should say that I have developed an affection and admiration for Nick. The guts it takes for him to confront and talk about these living repetitive traumas is very compelling. He now can see that his child pornography obsession is a form of retraumatization and self-assault and has greatly decreased the involvement with the pornography, yet the compulsion still holds a real sway over him and he dreams frequently of sexual activities with young prepubescent girls, as young as 4 or 5. The dreams are extremely stimulating to him. He lives in a kind of hell. Sometimes being with him is a kind of hell for me too. There are periods when the experience of our therapeutic inquiry collapses into a concrete world where his body and mind integrity are severely challenged. There have been explosions of rage while with me, and regressions where his talk has disintegrated into word-salad-like ramblings and paranoid ideation. Once out of these states he has been able to reorganize his mind and has thanked me for my calm and caring during these episodes.

Over time he has responded to the holding and containment I have tried to steadily provide and has opened up questions about who he really is. He now questions many beliefs he has taken on obsessively and passionately in his lifetime, including his antiauthoritarianism and his flirtation with homosexuality, among others. He has worked hard to have a relationship with both of his parents, who are accepting and understanding of who they are and were, while not avoiding anger and hurt that still linger. He has advanced in his career and most powerfully he married his girl friend and they have a baby boy who was 8 months old at the time of the session described below.

As we have worked together he has become involved with who I am and who I might be to him. He has predominantly seen me as a strong masculine heterosexual man. For example, he commented on the sound of the "strong sturdy flow of urine" he heard as I urinated in the bathroom before our session. (I should add that this was in my new office only a day or so after I had moved in, and it was news to me that my ablutions were broadcast so clearly in the waiting room.) He assumed a large and potent penis that would produce such a solid urination. He comments on the workman-like aspect of the office, when I have papers and open books on my desk. He has commented on the "precision" of what I have to say and the "solidity" of the boundary of time and space that he appreciates. His hair has become less wild, and he now sports a closely cut beard somewhat like my own. He has been pleased to find some convergence in our book collections and has borrowed and read some psychoanalytic literature. These aspects of the treatment have felt like a meaningful form of "object probing," to use Emmanuel Ghent's phrase, and I think that we have worked together to create a space where all of his thoughts and states can be tolerated and experienced.

With a patient like Nick, therapeutic change will begin in the realm of enactment and the world of doing and sensing, and I hope the following vignette captures the emergence of a different way of being a man that happened between us in the session. One day he did not arrive on time for his session. He called after a time to say that the babysitter had not shown up due to sickness and that he had Billy, his 8-month-old son, and was stuck in traffic. He was not going to make it on time. I told him that I had a free hour some time later. He was happy and gratefully agreed to come then. He entered the office carrying Billy in the snuggly, and I helped him into the office with his book bag, his baby bag, his coat, and so on. First things first: Billy needed a change. Whether he requested my help or whether I simply began to assist, I do not know, but we worked together like a cohesive couple. Laying out the changing mat, changing the dirty diaper, I took on the role of assistant, removing the soiled diaper and wipes and helping him to locate this and that. I produced some toys and *Sesame Street* characters that I keep in my office closet. The room was filled with the sweet and shitty smell of baby poop. My office was transformed: furniture moved, smells, sights, and sounds swirling around. All the while Nick cooed and played with Billy and I could not resist a coo or two myself, becoming wrapped into the world of babyhood, which I had experienced fully only a couple of years prior with my young children. I had not realized how much I missed it until now. Nick settled Billy into his lap and fed him as we settled into the session. Two men talking.

Nick told me a dream. The switch from the nurturing environment we had constructed to the tortured abusive world of Nick's dream world was jarring and unsettling for me. No doubt another enactment of shock and abuse: in the nursery, no less. Nick recounted another dream in which he found himself in potential sexual encounters with hyperstimulating and seductive women whom he viewed as inappropriate and undesirable partners for him. The environment was soiled by excrement and vermin. He was, however, encouraged by the dream because in this dream he repeatedly recoiled from the women and refused to go along with the sex, thinking how wrong it felt.

During the session there were intervals of tending to Billy. Both Nick and I played with the *Sesame Street* characters with Billy, and at one point kidded around with Elmo and Big Bird ourselves and enjoyed a chuckle together. At the end of the session he settled Billy back into his snuggly and I gathered the toys and put my office back together.

There is an enormous amount we could discuss about Nick, the chaos of his inner world, his constant dance with retraumatization, the relationship between shit, shame, and defilement, the evacuative quality of thinking itself, and his search for containment and boundaries, which, to some degree he finds in the snuggly and the transitional play space of the treatment.

However, the issue I wanted to draw our attention to is the emergent manifold experience of manhood and heterosexuality that infuses this session and the way in which different aspects of each of our heterosexual masculinity emerge as the session progressed. The session began with a shifting of boundaries; I rescheduled the session there and then. When I received Nick's call that he was with Billy and running late, I switched immediately into a mode of fellow father. I was in touch with that parent zone where surrender to the exigencies of care for young children simply overrides all else. I was able to be flexible and responsive even at some slight inconvenience to my own schedule and plan for the day. I think this is a kind of "making do" that parents engage in all the time. It is not the strict and rigid father of determination-at-all-costs that saw Nick's father build a house in a wilderness, yet not a passive I'll-do-whatever-you-want father who neglects and avoids the issue of boundaries. Perhaps we could say that I embodied the preoedipal father (Samuels, 1993) that he had never had access to. We worked together to clean and accommodate a baby. We were male moms together. We were partners. For me to share this kind of intimacy with Nick was very touching and enjoyable. I like babies and their care, and I think he was learning to. I like this kind of intimacy with men, and it introduced a new register of intimacy and shared masculinity into our relationship. What seemed to emerge was a new space between us where we could play with this new and rare identity. And play we did, and with dolls, no less. This is a male heterosexual zone that is new for him: one where joint nurturing of a baby enhances rather than detracts from the sense of masculinity. Nick, I believe, has longed for intimacy with men, but this longing was collapsed into the rigidity of the hetero-homo binary when he was younger and was a part of his experimentation with sexual involvement with men. Between his father's rigid and driven "phallic narcissism" and his mother's difficult journey to her homosexuality (she had eventually settled into a lesbian life), he was left with little room to find his own particular heterosexuality and to enjoy it. In nonlinear dynamic terms, the introduction of Billy, comothering, cofathering, play, and laughter into the treatment space all combined to disequilibrate the rigid attractor state of his heterosexuality and his image of me, based on ideas of hypermasculinity and bolstered by violent and hyperstimulating sexuality and the trapping of desire in grotesque and painful abuse. We entered the edge of chaos and instituted a phase shift to a more expansive and inclusive heterosexuality that changed our therapeutic dyad profoundly.

I have subsequently felt freer to nurture and protect Nick. I found myself worrying about the illegality of his Internet child pornography involvement and the risks to his career and life that any kind of legal incident could bring. I had not had that, perhaps obvious, thought before. Some sessions after this one I raised the question with Nick. "Was he concerned about getting caught or stung in some on-line police operation?" In the past he had been paranoid and rageful, as I mentioned before, when I would intrude too much. This time he was very touched and thoughtful. He told me that he felt really parented and talked more about the neglect that he experienced growing up. As a kid he was always at risk and never protected. I do not think I could have brought in this kind of concern— and perhaps would not have even thought it—prior to the session with Billy. In subsequent sessions, the sense of intimacy lingered, and Nick has expressed gratitude and affection for me and the work that we are doing.

Conclusion

In conclusion, I hope that these two clinical moments illustrate the multiplicity and fluidity of heterosexual masculinity and the journey that each man makes to establish, find, and enjoy his own heterosexuality and masculinity. I think they illustrate how male heterosexuality is so far from monolithic, is in fact manifold and surprising. Heterosexual masculinity is made, perhaps even won, is fluid, and constructed. They describe a clinical environment wherein both analyst and patient shift and expand the boundaries of their heterosexual masculinity, and where both can reside with increasing comfort and generativity in an emergent and sometimes surprising heterosexual intersubjectivity and intimacy. As they talked with me, Nick's and Brian's heterosexual masculinity is, you might say, "under construction," giving a new and nuanced meaning to the term "Men at Work."

References

Connell, R. W. (2005). *Masculinities*, 2nd ed. Berkeley: University of California Press.
Harris, A. (2005). *Gender as Soft Assembly*. Hillsdale, NJ: Analytic Press.
Kimmel, M. (1996). *Manhood in America: A Cultural History*. New York: Free Press.
Ogden, T. (1989). *The Primitive Edge of Experience*. Northvale, NJ: Jason Aronson.
Samuels, A. (1993). *The Political Psyche*. New York: Routledge.

5

Imperfect Love, Imperfect Lives
Making Love, Making Sex,
Making Moral Judgments

Irwin Hirsch

Prologue: An Analyst Learns

I have always learned best from my failures, and a number of years ago I became a more educated analyst at the expense of a very smart, handsome, likable, and mostly heterosexual man. Although he had a serious girlfriend, Z. engaged in cross-dressing flirtations with other cross-dressing men in cyberspace and at bars, and occasionally had one-night-stands with women. I believed that Z. would have a good life with this girlfriend and thought that she would help him settle into the hard work of his demanding profession as well as help him actualize what I felt would be his considerable potential as a loving father to his yet unborn children. I associated his cross-dressing as well as his infidelity largely to his identification with and his desire to over-come his infantilizing mother and his early life as her soft and overweight momma's boy. As he grew into adolescence Z. fled from this humiliating identification into sports (a very strong interest of my own), and he became an excellent athlete. Charming and flirtatious, throughout his late teens and 20s he had a very prodigious heterosexual sex life. He entered analysis in his early 30s ostensibly because his career was faltering. He was very bright and had excellent academic credentials, but balked at the grueling work required to advance his career, and he kept losing jobs. It took some time before he informed me, with some shame, of his by now long-time interest in cross-dressing, much of this recent activity occurring on the Internet during his long hours at the office. At no point did Z. indicate to me that he clearly wished to stop cross-dressing. He actually hoped that he might integrate this into his sex life with his accepting current girlfriend, although he feared informing her about of his cyberspace and bar contacts that stopped just short of hands-on sex with men.

In my misguided zeal to help Z. actualize his career and to solidify his relationship with his girlfriend, my interpretive schema accented the immaturity of his sexual interests, maintaining his archaic girly-boy identification with his mother and avoiding the "stronger" and more masculine emphasis on career and commitment to this, in my mind, wonderfully flexible young woman. Even if I had been largely on target with my insight in linking history to present, the more salient message this sensitive man heard from me was to control his cross-dressing distractions and to settle down to a promising career and a monogamous relationship with this girlfriend, with whom I was so taken. In his charming and seductive way Z. quit therapy for "practical" reasons, never challenging me for my egregiously unwarranted impositions on elements of a life that he desired. He probably even knew that it was not his cross-dressing per se that was blocking his career and his relationship, and that I was too threatened personally by his sexual tastes and his feminine sides to help him adequately integrate this into his love life and work life. I suspect that Z. even knew that the sports metaphors we so frequently spoke in and my interest in his career were reassuring to my own counter-identifications with my own infantilizing mother, and that my ambitions for him were as much countertransference based as anything else. I did Z. a great disservice and benefited a great deal more from him than he did from me. Z. helped teach me how self-serving it usually is to make so-called clinical judgments about others' nonnormative sexuality, including the moral value of monogamy and sexual fidelity as a universal ideal for all individuals.

Love, Sex, and Infidelity: Thesis and Clinical Illustrations

By way of overview of my thesis, I suggest that we not assume that all of our patients wish to optimize their potentials for love and for work in the ways Freud originally seemed to mean this. Everyone does not want lasting love relationships and/or intense intimacy, and everyone does not want monogamy. Also, everyone does not strive for a single relationship that integrates love and sexual fulfillment, as much as this is an ideal for many. From most accounts and surveys (e.g., Glass & Wright, 1992), sexual infidelity in marriage is statistically normal for both genders (as is divorce), and, as opined, the more options one has in life, the more likely infidelity is exercised. Infidelity per se cannot be subsumed under any rubric of psychopathology any more than are the multiple variations of missionary position heterosexual sex, many of which were formerly considered "perversions" by respected analytic colleagues. There is certainly no universal motivation for infidelity, or, for that matter, for fidelity; does fidelity result from—to name the extremes—very strong values or fear of infidelity's potential consequences? By the same token, infidelity's multiple motives may make trouble or they may be largely adaptive. They should therefore be explored or understood analytically, just as analysts should examine motivations for monogamy. There are many ways to have meaningful relationships and satisfying lives, and psychoanalysts' ideals about such matters are best personally reflected upon and minimally imposed on patients. Likewise, sexual fidelity can be hard to define. For example, how do we characterize kissing and fondling at the office Christmas party; or engaging in the increasingly popular recreation of lap dancing, in all its variants; or talking "dirty" on the Internet; or masturbating to the widening array of pornographic stimuli?

Y.

A trim, well-dressed, and vivacious man (Y.), 67 years old when we began analysis, viewed himself as my mentor in the ways of sex and family life. He perceived me (some dozen years younger than he) as conservative and cautious and was inclined to share with me the wisdom accumulated from an adventurous and interesting, "rags-to-riches" life. Brilliant and manically driven in all dimensions of life, he had accumulated a fortune through myriad businesses, had ambitions directed toward high elected office, enjoyed a wide range of avocations, contributed enormous sums philanthropically, and was very involved with his large family—wife, three children, and numerous grandchildren. His wife, who felt at her wits' end after catching him in yet another of his many sexual infidelities, remanded him to analysis. When young they had had a passionate sexual relationship, but for some time Y.'s interest was gone. He claimed to love and deeply admire his wife, and as well, he now enjoyed a close relationship with his large family. He had been a disengaged and preoccupied father, but had become a deeply involved grandfather and spent considerable time with this close-knit group of children and grandchildren.

I initially felt like I was engaging in a grand deception—Y. placated his wife by visiting me, but would rather "be buried" than abandon his sexual exploits. However, not too long after beginning treatment, Y. ran into certain problems with his businesses and became quite anxious and somewhat depressed at various limits that were being forced upon him. At this point I began to feel that his reasons for coming to see me were more legitimate—more internally driven. He alternated between speaking quite openly about his fear that his life would revert to the feelings of dependence, weakness, and oppression that characterized his early years, and enthusiastically informing me of his most recent sexual exploits, or the latest honor bestowed upon him by some charitable organization. I never experienced this as a crude boasting; indeed, I always perceived Y. as a refined man, soft spoken, genteel, and elegant in his manner. He spoke of his achievements with a richness and pleasure that felt almost sensual. It was in this latter mode when Y. situated himself as my father/teacher, sharing with me what he believed was a wisdom that would enrich my own pedestrian life. Certainly there was an element of dominance-submission here, and I was quite capable of feeling small in contrast to this larger-than-life, characteristically charged, and energetic man. In addition, having lacked a father who was strong and accomplished, I believe I was receptive to engaging with Y. in this configuration. On the other hand, his sense that he had power in relation to me helped him share his fears with me.

Since he was pushed by his wife to see me in order to cure him of his sexual infidelities, much of the wisdom Y. shared with me focused on the absurdity of my engaging him in such an endeavor. He spoke of sex and love as two entirely distinct phenomena, mocking the broadly applied term, "making love," as simply, "fucking the same person whom you love." He reported that he knew one person, a golfing buddy roughly his age, who still thoroughly enjoyed having sex with his wife—the woman he also loved. This was hard for Y. to comprehend, although he did reflect that he sometimes envied this man, his ability to be satisfied with what he had in life, and his capacity to be more tranquil and less driven than he. Y. claimed to regret hurting his wife by not responding to her sexual desires and by philandering relentlessly even though she was aware of it, although not enough to resist sexual opportunity with the attractive and much younger women available to him. On the other hand, he underscored the unnatural and counter-intuitive property of desiring only one sexual partner, stating that usually the only people who adhere to monogamy are those without opportunity (with a subtext that I might be among those). He argued that his wife should have accepted this fact long ago, and that if she had had sexual liaisons of her own, she might have been less hurt and angry with him. He further lectured that in no other culture are men in particular, especially powerful men like him, expected to remain monogamous.

I saw Y. into his early 70s, when, even barely able to be erect with the aid of Viagra, he was still shamelessly seducing much younger women with reasonable frequency; much of this sex consisted of his receiving oral and manual stimulation to orgasm. By this time Y.'s wife preferred to believe he was too old and impotent for even this, and she caused little stir. I believe that our analytic efforts helped Y. get beyond his overt fears that he would some day lose his esteemed and powerful place in society and once again be the castrated little boy of his early years, but there remained covert anxieties and angers that still fueled his driven ways. Y. did indeed cause considerable pain to his wife, and his marital con-figuration undoubtedly had repercussions with his children, although each of them developed into highly functioning individuals. However, by the time treatment had ended his marital strife had ceased and he seemed to me to be a largely constructive force in his family. He even often felt helpful toward the women with whom he was having sex. From Y.'s accounting, they all fully knew it was "just sex," and took from it whatever benefit they may have received: gifts, help in opening up career opportunities, or simply association with a charming, attractive, and charismatic older man. Of course it is possible that some of these women felt cheapened, or expected more from Y. and were hurt by the experi-ence, but Y. did not speak of these eventualities. By the time we stopped our work together, Y. was more vigorous and satisfied with his life than are the vast majority of men in his age range, and from my perspective, he met most of Freud's original criteria regarding work and love: a rich and involved career, a vital and involved, although ambivalently loving contemporary relationship with his wife, an affectionate and generous connection to his children and grandchildren, and a contribution to society (in the form of extensive philanthropy). Y. affirmed what others in the psychoanalytic literature have suggested (e.g., Freud, 1912; Eagle, 2003) and are currently arguing with greater frequency: the relation-ship between sexual desire and love is complicated, and for better or for worse, the two feelings are often poorly correlated and difficult to integrate.

X.

Another, briefer example will underscore this point. X. initially consulted me with his wife because of her complaints about their awful sex life. She seemed to have no clue that he was gay, and actually rather effeminate in manner. After this became clear to her they decided to remain married, and I worked individually with X. They stopped trying to have sex with each other, he pursuing bathroom blow-jobs and other anonymous encounters, and she, as I later learned from her analyst after my work with X. had ceased, both short-term and more serious affairs with male colleagues. Both parties seemed to have looked the other way. From X.'s descriptions and from what I saw from his wife originally in couple's therapy, these two people loved each other dearly and deeply—indeed, in a way more profound than do most heterosexual married people I have met in and out of my professional context. Once the tension of sex was removed, they were deeply intimate friends, powerfully loving like brother and sister: they shared a multitude of interests and values, enjoyed being together to the point of exuberance, and "fit together," as compatible— except for sex—as virtually any couple I know. X.'s reports of his wife's loyalty, tenderness, and caring over the long period of his tragic and grueling struggle with AIDS, which would end in his death, remain among the most moving experiences I have encountered in my work.

W.

I certainly do not intend to argue that long-term love relationships cannot include a strong monogamous sexual relationship, although so far I have attempted to illustrate, with these true but hyperbolic illustrations, that the pleasures of sex and of long-term love can readily operate on different tracks (Freud, 1912). Sexual infidelity may be designed to end love relationships, or have that consequence even if not intended, but this sort of transformation is not inherent. If one does not think in traditional moral or in idealistic terms, there are many mundane illustrations of long-term relationships surviving in part because infidelity serves as a compromise. While I suggest here (particularly later in this chapter) that such compromises are more common for men, women are by no means foreign to engaging in extramarital sex as a means of adapting to and attempting to preserve imperfect marriages. For example, W. consulted me because of postaffair anxiety. Her affair consisted of sex with a male business associate about whom she had long had intensely erotic, often masturbatory, fantasies. Although he too was married, she worried that she would become too enamored with him and no longer be able to function with her husband in her marriage. She claimed to love her husband and their family configuration (two small children), and she hoped to remain married to him. W. had chosen to marry a man whom she could control and who would not impede her independence and her demanding career pursuits. From her reports, she was the dominant party in the marital dyad (e.g., the primary breadwinner and decision maker), had much affection toward but only a modest sexual interest in her reportedly very good-looking husband, and was the recipient of his complaints about dispassionate sex. Although she had consciously planned to not marry someone too strong for fear of winding up the submissive masochist that her mother was, her sexual passions inclined her toward powerful older men (most of them, as she described, not nearly as physically attractive as her husband). Over the course of our work together W. became frightened of her attraction to me and began to fear that our involvement would render her marriage insignificant. She felt submissive toward me and feared that I had significant influence and power over her. This configuration closely paralleled what she had seen in her parents' relationship and what she had always resolved to avoid. These transferential feelings were explicated, although perhaps because I found this relational configuration comfortable, they never shifted very much. However, the intensity of her dependent and submissive transference of feelings led her to further appreciate both her marital configuration and her preference for remaining the dominant figure in it. Her ultimate compromise and adaptation were to remain in her comfortable marriage, yet feel less anxiety when she engaged in periodic sexual trysts with lovers to whom she no longer worried about submitting in ways beyond the immediately erotic. From the perspective suggested earlier in this chapter W.'s compromise may be seen from outside of traditional moral or idealistic terms as an adaptive meeting of her wish for preserving the gratification derived within her imperfect marriage while pursuing erotic desires that W. felt were not able to be met within the context of that marriage.

V.

A serious professional man, religiously committed, and reportedly deeply in love with a wife toward whom he was quite sexually attracted, V. was anxious, guilt-ridden, and depressed that he found it irresistible to, in his words, "sexually cheat." Despite a reported active and hearty sexual attraction to his wife, he claimed to be nearly addicted to Internet pornography, obsessed with locating and sometimes visiting prostitutes found originally through this medium, and unable to control lap dancing involvements when traveling on business. He noted that a high percentage of his male colleagues either saw prostitutes or lap danced when traveling, although it "tore him up" emotionally more than it did most of them. V.'s preoccupation with pornography started in adolescence, originally as an attempt to master humiliation at the hands of a seductive, emotionally volatile, and overbearing mother. He became aware that his secret sexual life seemed to give him some sense of autonomy from her, and over the course of analysis it became clear that he feared being dependent on and at the whim of his strong-willed wife, and of me, as his mother in the transference. On the other hand, V. literally asked me to be a strong father to him, to back him up in his effort to finally abandon his childhood fears and what he felt was his moral weakness in response to these fears. Actually, he wished for me to actively prohibit all extramarital sex, and as well, to be a male presence who would counter the power of his wife and of his internalized mother. Though I did not literally accept the role of a prohibitive religious force, I felt quite comfortable with V. in the phallic role as a ballast. V. and I worked together for some time, and indeed, he eventually became far less obsessed and preoccupied with pornography and with the exciting pursuit of prostitutes. When at home, he was relatively present, and his marital sex life produced significant pleasure. He reported feeling stronger and less threatened by female irrationality. When he traveled professionally, which he did a few times each year, he indulged himself with lap dancers. This took up minimal emotional space for V., and although he claimed to be still striving to resist this type of infidelity, at the time of termination of our work together, he had not. Indeed, he reported that this sexual compromise, for the time being, helped him feel independent and sexually potent in the context of his marriage.

Discussion: Imperfect Love, Imperfect Lives

In each of my clinical illustrations sexual infidelity occurred in the context of reported love toward a spouse and the strong desire to preserve the marital dyad. Infidelity, however, is also often designed to hurt the other, to exact revenge for emotional injuries, and/or to destroy a relationship.

Indeed, destructiveness and revenge were among all of my patients' multiple motives. However, if one thinks in terms of adaptation or compromise, infidelity sometimes provides an emotional spacing that may allow imperfect love, sex, and family relationships to persist or endure over time. I do not offer this as a professional recommendation, but as a response to the risk of analysts creating ideals that patients do not really wish to meet, and that we analysts in our own personal lives may not approach. It feels crucial to me that we analysts infer from the imperfections in our own lives the likelihood that our patients too will not emerge from analysis as ideal lovers and/or ideal workers. In an article that portrays psychoanalysts as sexually nonnormative as the rest of the population, Dimen (2002) pointedly illustrates the hypocrisy of analysts' moralism in the context of living sexual lives every bit as idiosyncratic as our patients. Freud himself did not work and love optimally, and biographers (e.g., Jones, 1955) have suggested the total absence of sex from a very young age in their own marriages. Many analysts today still fail to acknowledge how rare it is for anyone to function on all or on most cylinders in the realms of work and love and sexual pleasure. It is both a cultural and an analytic ideal to achieve an integration of love and sexual fulfillment in a long-term relationship, although in reality I think that this is an ideal state only reached by a small minority of couples. In my clinical work and in conversation with friends, I observe that minimal sex or no sex at all characterizes a higher percentage of long-term marriages than does sexual ecstasy. Infidelity in all its forms is by no means necessarily the best compromise to absence of sexual fulfillment in long-term love relationships, although it is a very common one. When not mutually agreed upon, infidelity always reflects betrayal and dishonesty and leaves great potential for pain.

Because of this last factor it is often tempting for analysts to take a moral stand with respect to injury to our patients' significant others and to their breaches in the analytically cherished qualities of openness and honesty. Each unique analyst draws implicit (or explicit) lines at points where one may impose values or moral standards, and these lines are likely to be at least somewhat affected by each unique patient. I believe that each analyst will impose moral judgments at some moments with some patients, although when doing so it is very important to present these as subjectively or countertransference based and not as a declaration that a patient's acts are perverse or pathological per se. When very extreme acts are committed, however, this rather idealistic stance becomes quite difficult to sustain. Of course there is much risk in taking moral positions, for they may imply that we do not accept a patient, warts and all, for who he or she is, and perhaps, that we ourselves, in our own personal lives, live by higher moral standards. As well, imposing a moral judgment suggests that we may view people as perfectable, and in so doing, we create aims for patients that are not reachable for them, and that we have not reached in our own lives. This ranks high among the lessons I learned from my unfortunate experience with Z. I was threatened personally by his effeminately tinged infidelities, and my imposition of a view of him as perverse was quite harmful to him.

I do not believe that I have any greater perspective than any of my colleagues about determining at what point harm to others calls for an imposition of moral prohibitions. For me, physical violence and harm to children are most likely to qualify. Although I know that some individuals I have discussed here have hurt their significant others by the former's betrayals and lies, I view such phenomena as part of living an imperfect life. Although it is absolutely central to any analytic process to help patients recognize that they are angry, hurtful, and destructive to others, I prefer to refrain from attempting to change this by moral approbation or disapprobation, and when it comes to matters sexual, by invoking the pseudoscientific term, perversion. Analytic ideals should not be confounded with analytic aims, and when analysts' aims are idealistic, we are likely to be in a state of denial about our own flaws. Our patients' lives, like our own, will always be imperfect, and through sexual behavior or in other ways, each of us will be hurtful to significant others. We may risk harming our patients by exhibiting disappointment in them in our efforts to be protective of their significant others.

Love, Lust, and Attachment: Discussion and Clinical Example

In his essay on this question of sex, love and infidelity, and moral judgment, Eagle (2003), extrapolating from psychoanalytic attachment research, concludes that attachment and sexuality are two different systems, and that these two systems are antagonistic to each other. This is essentially an affirmation of an observation made by Freud (1912) in the early days of psychoanalysis. Eagle posits that sexual desire brings people together long enough to afford the possibility of attachment. When relationships endure, it is because love develops from attachment, and indeed, adults very commonly love while experiencing minimal or no sexual desire for the person who is loved. These thoughts are compatible with the evolutionary thinking summarized by Fisher (2004), who explains that across species, familiarity breeds friendship and runs counter to sexual desire. She points out how infatuation can only last so long without such stimulation becoming dangerous to one's body and psyche both. Blechner (2003) notes that there are large individual differences, both between cultures and within them, about how passion and fidelity are played out. Speaking from an historical psychoanalytic perspective, he documents that the primary purpose of marriage throughout the ages has been pragmatic, the wish to create stability and family. Only in recent centuries has marriage been associated with romantic sexual love, and in some subcultures it still is not, where marriages are arranged. Although romantic love and marriage indeed constitute the modern Western ideal, Blechner observes that not all long-term relationships sustain the inclusion of sexual pleasure. He further observes that for some people, either sexual fantasy or sexual infidelity provides pleasure, while marriage-like relations provide stability, dependency, and loving attachments. Blechner notes a cultural preference that evokes my patient Y.'s personal views: in some societies, it is expected that men in particular have lovers, especially for men who have power. He also states that in homosexual subcultures, where legal marriage is not yet possible, there may be more experimentation with the parameters of erotic attachments and commitment.

Some of the current interest in this subject was inspired by Mitchell's (2003) posthumous book, *Can Love Last?* In attempting to answer why it is so difficult for sexual desire to endure in long-term relationships, he suggests (along with Fisher, Eagle, and others) that feelings of familiarity and dependence tend to be antierotic, while romance (read sexual desire) has always been normally fueled by novelty, mystery, pursuit, and the hope of conquest. He posits that even the most intensely passionate desire for relatively unknown partners constitutes but a very small emotional risk, since these relative strangers are not the objects of our dependency or of our attachment love. To feel this intense sexual desire and love and dependence toward the same person, however, is an emotional risk of immense proportion, and one that relatively few dare to take. For Mitchell, the degree of potential humiliation and loss in loving and desiring the same person over time leads to the normal compromise of dividing these affects into two categories. Much of what is called romance or "falling in love" refers to the erotic wish to conquer a new lover. This helps make new sex or "no strings" sexual infidelities extremely desirable, and when not acted upon, such desire often consumes much space in a fantasy life. For most people I know personally and clinically, optimally exciting sex is synonymous with relatively anonymous sex, and Mitchell's thesis makes sense to me as an explanation for this. Most long-term relationships are fueled by love other than romantic love (i.e., feelings of attachment, friendship, shared interests, and dependency).

Perhaps a more appropriate title for Mitchell's book would have been *Can Lust Last?* since it does appear easier to sustain long-term love than long-term lust. I believe that romantic fiction and American cinema have helped mislead us by playing to what most of us want, equating raw sexual attraction with true love. This helps make long-term love seem to be more of an exciting prospect, and less the quotidian, flawed, and laborious project, as Mitchell suggests, that most people find in long and stable relationships. Romance and attachment love are related to the extent that some loving relationships begin with sexual attraction. The concept of romance should refer to primarily erotic desire, and the latter is indeed often difficult to sustain in most long-term loving relationships. As my patient Y., suggests, one may be most fortunate to want to fuck the same person whom one loves. Mitchell himself offers no easy counsel with regard to the dilemma of how to keep lust alive in long-term love relationships. He says essentially that it takes a strong commitment to this project and consistent hard work.

U.

Married with two preadolescent children, U. tries to do this hard work, as he struggles to remain sexually faithful to his tense and overworked wife, whom he sees as aging physically more rapidly than he. She juggles the demands of motherhood and serious career and reportedly has little time to engage with U., much less have anything like the relaxed and playful sex they enjoyed before parenthood. Sex is further inhibited by the discomforts of early menopause, and U.'s wife accuses him of being unsympathetic to her total situation. U. alternates between angrily lamenting about the loving attention he used to receive and fantasizing about extramarital sex. He is charming, good-looking, and in the world. He has much opportunity for infidelity, but he holds the integrity of marital commitment in high regard. He believes that if he just screwed around a little, he would be much less angry toward his wife, feel far less deprived, and his marriage might improve. He looks to me to gauge how I would feel if he were to find extramarital sex, and wonders what I have done in my own marriage in this regard. I try not to influence him and am relieved at not consciously feeling strongly about either of his choices, although I do believe he may ultimately feel better about himself if he does not make the choices he associates with his mother's excessive narcissism.

U. recalls his parents' relationship—a father who maintained his caring and gentle ways with his wife, despite her demanding, narcissistic, and demeaning character traits. U.'s mother spoke openly about her crushes on celebrities and on powerful acquaintances, and he suspects that she probably had some affairs. He has great compassion for his humbled father and much anger toward his mother and is in considerable conflict about indulging himself in ways he associates with her. He wishes to be kind and giving like his father, yet fears the humiliation of what he also felt was his father's castrated passivity. He associates his "good boy" fidelity with being a fool and a cuckold like his father. U. still has faith that he can revive the sexual dimension of his life with the woman he still loves, but only rarely feels lust toward her. In the context of this struggle so far, he claims he feels better about himself than if he were to take the easier road that he associates with his mother's selfishness and hurtfulness.

Epilogue: Gender and the Question of Universals

Not all analysts who address this subject believe that familiarity and dependence dampen sexual desire. In a dissenting response to Mitchell, Goldner (2004) argues that the very familiarity that many experience as antierotic provides for others an erotogenic condition of safety. She suggests optimistically that many individuals in long and safe relationships allow themselves to disinhibit sexually, and this freedom and absence of anxiety can readily lead to better and better sex. Goldner refers to normal arguments and fights that occur in long-term relationships, and the getting together again after these mini break-ups (rupture and repair) as providing some of the erotic mystery and novelty that is otherwise absent. In the context of safety, this "make-up sex" (a term originating in the television comedy series *Seinfeld*), Goldner suggests, can be as arousing for some as novelty is for others.

Clearly, individuals are sexually aroused in different ways, although it is awfully tempting for me to suggest that Mitchell and Goldner may be representing, in an aggregate or normative way, their respective genders (Mitchell is male, Goldner is female). My own observation, from patients and personal life, suggests that even if married men and women are equally unfaithful, men's extramarital sex commonly entails a wider variety of sexual practices, which might give them more opportunities for infidelity.

If wives' unfaithfulness principally entails literal sexual encounters with other men and women, husbands' adultery goes beyond that. Perhaps as many women as men use pornography and engage in cybersex, although anecdotally this seems not to be the case. But men also partake of lap-dancing and, of course, patronize prostitutes, activities that are for women nonexistent in the first case and relatively rare in the second.

The argument for coupled men as generally more inclined toward infidelity than coupled women finds some support in the psychoanalytic literature. Stoller (e.g., 1975, 1979) has made the most meaningful contributions to this literature, emphasizing the inherently sadomasochistic nature of most heterosexual relatedness. He views men as essentially living with an inherent sense of weakness in relation to women, an inadequacy born of prolonged dependency on mothers or on maternal figures. He sees men as perennially trying to compensate for feeling like boys, longing for maternal nurture and humiliated by neediness toward and dependency on women. Compensation often takes the form of turning the tables on women, of efforts to transform weakness into strength. Anger, physical intimidation, and contempt for women's lower status work are among these compensatory expressions, as are sexual acts and sexual positions that emphasize the power and the dominance of the man. Hirsch (1997) observes that heterosexual men's common preoccupation with sex, particularly in the form of gazing at women in person and in photos and in talking with other heterosexual men about women, is an everyday way that many men attempt to convert feelings of weakness into strength. Stoller suggests that pursuit of prostitutes and other illicit sex is often in the service of trying to control both the prostitute and the significant love interest in the man's life. Childhood humiliation at the hands of powerful women is converted to unconscious strategies to control and to humiliate women—to sexualize them, to purchase them, and to betray them through infidelity. Hirsch (1999) offers the perception that many or perhaps most heterosexual men prefer the companionship of other men to that of women, turning fear of women into a male bonding characterized by sexualized preoccupation with dominating or otherwise humiliating women. Along similar lines Person (1999) emphasizes the role played by the male fear of engulfment by women as a major motivating force in men's effort at emotional distance from their lovers or spouses. Sexual infidelity has the advantage of creating emotional distance, gaining emotional control over dependent longings, and exacting revenge for childhood humiliations at the hands of powerful mothers. For all of these reasons it appears plausible that men are less sanguine about long-term love relationships than are their female counterparts and may be more inclined to use sex as a way of maintaining emotional equilibrium in relation to female partners. The very safety that Goldner suggests may make some people more free to enjoy sex makes all too many others feel trapped and stifled, leading potentially to a profound loss of erotic desire for a long-term lover.

Despite my sense that many men may have more readily understandable, historically internalized reasons for sexual infidelity than do women, I believe that we always lose much when we speak in universals. As well, it seems more difficult to identify generalized hypotheses that attempt to explain sexual infidelity, specifically in women. Our psychoanalytic literature does not make such convenient generalizations available, and this is probably for the better. Highly complex feelings and acts like love and sex and fidelity are best addressed in relation to human uniqueness and idiosyncrasy, not in reference to aggregates, although Freud (1912), Eagle (2003), Fisher (2004), and Blechner (2003) have offered some ideas about normative sexual behavior and the motivations involved. The more we think in diagnostic or in other universal splits and binaries, the more we are inclined to be disapproving with our patients and to impose our own personal moral judgments standards on them. Indeed, both men and women have difficulty integrating sexual vitality with long-term love and dependency, and various forms of infidelity are one compromise for what is most likely a majority of both genders. If we do not see sex and love as inherently synonymous—as intrinsically linked in the idealistic way dictated by both our psychoanalytic history and cultural fictions—how we view infidelity, whether as inevitably destructive or as sometimes a very imperfect compromise that suits the ordinary imperfections of life, depends on the flexible analysis of each unique situation. Needless to say, we must respect the aims of our patients. These aims quite often fall short of those dictated by some of our cherished psychoanalytic constructs, idealistic principels that we ourselves as analysts, in our own personal lives, fail to live up to at no less frequency than our patients.

Acknowledgment

A version of this chapter originally appeared in *Studies in Gender and Sexuality*, 8(4), 2007, 355–372. Reprinted with permission.

References

Blechner, M. (2003). Commentary: What happens when love lasts? An exploration of intimacy and erotic life. IARPP Online colloquium series, #2. www.iarpp.org accessed March 2003.

Dimen, M. (2002). Perversion is us? Eight notes. *Psychoanalytic Dialogues, 11*, 825–860.

Eagle, M. (2003, February). *Attachment and sexuality.* Paper presented to the Society of Medical Psychoanalysis, Columbia University, New York.

Fisher, H. (2004). *Why We Love.* New York: Holt.

Freud, S. (1912). On the universal tendency to debasement in the sphere of love. *Standard Edition, 11*, 179–190.

Glass, S., & Wright, T. (1992). Justification for extramarital relationships: The association between attitude, behaviors and gender. *Journal of Sex Research, 29*, 361–387.

Goldner, V. (2004). Attachment and eros: Opposed or synergistic? *Psychoanalytic Dialogues, 14*, 381–396.

Hirsch, I. (1997). On men's preference for men. *Gender and Psychoanalysis, 2*, 469–486.

Hirsch, I. (1999). Men's love for men: Contrasting classical American film with *The Crying Game. Journal of the American Academy of Psychoanalysis, 27*, 151–166.

Jones, E. (1955). *The Life and Works of Sigmund Freud,* Vol. 2. New York: Basic Books.

Mitchell, S. (2003). *Can Love Last?* New York: Norton.

Stoller, R. (1975). *Perversion: The Erotic Form of Hatred.* New York: Pantheon.

Stoller, R. (1979). *Sexual Excitement: Diagnosis of Erotic Life.* New York: Pantheon.

6

On Intimacy Between Men

Emmanuel Kaftal

The fantasy self-image of the hero is common to many men. When these men come to psychotherapy, they present a variety of symptoms that may be linked to this self-image. These include grandiosity, the need to control the therapist, empty depression, and a preoccupation with the imagery of death and battle. These patients tend to evoke in the therapist emotional responses that the patients subsequently deny. These characteristics are so pervasive among men that they may be endemic to manhood.

The heroic model of manhood is an attempt to strengthen and stabilize the gendered self-representation. Because fathers tend to be absent from the nurturing matrix, their sons have little early experience in an affective, preverbal relationship of mutual influence with another who is essentially like themselves yet outside their omnipotent control. Men, therefore, are raised with a pervasive experience of "otherness," their infantile experience and affectivity forever trapped in the world of women. Although the yearning of men for their fathers is recognized in psychoanalytic theory, the wish for the nurturing father has been underemphasized. The underemphasis causes the analyst to miss, or misunderstand, important transferential constellations.

Long before I became interested in the healing power of storytelling in psychotherapy, I was simply interested in stories. For a while, I was particularly interested in personal narratives and autobiographies, perhaps because they seemed to promise some clue about the future or, perhaps, a prescription that would immunize me against the danger of an unlived life. In 1968 André Malraux, who was then French minister of culture, published an autobiography of sorts in the United States, with the characteristic title *Anti-Memoirs*. I was almost finished with college and was faced with a number of very real, very adult decisions. Although I did not think about it in those terms, masculinity operated powerfully and silently in my deliberations, like a riddle that I did not know I was answering. At that time, Malraux was, for me, a masculine ideal. The quintessential artist-hero, he maintained a brash, imagistic, transcendent vision of art and lived a life of opposition that bridged the gap between the life of the imagination and the life of action. Malraux played a role in the political upheaval in Indochina and China, organized and led the air force of the republic of Spain in the civil war, fought in the French army, was captured by the fascists, escaped, joined the French resistance, and so forth. His books include *Man's Hope, Man's Fate, The Temptation of the West*, and *The Conquerors*. In one of them, a character asks, "What is a man? a collection of secrets?" The other responds, "A man is what he does."

In the *Anti-Memoirs* (1968) he elaborates somewhat on the primacy of action in the life of manhood:

> Almost all the writers I know love their childhood; I hate mine. I have never learned to re-create myself, if to do so means coming to terms with that lonely halfway house which we call life. I have sometimes managed to act, but the interest of action, except when it rises to the level of history, lies in what we do and not in what we say. (p. 1)

In conclusion, Malraux claims, as so many heroes do: "I do not find myself very interesting." But Malraux writes, and he writes only about himself. He tells us that he writes because he is "haunted." He is driven to remember and re-create "those moments when the mystery of life appears to each one of us as it appears to almost every woman when she looks into a child's face and to almost every man when he looks into the face of someone dead" (p. 2).

I remember being dimly disturbed on first reading that line, not because of its sexual stereotypy, which is so striking today but which was lost on me at the time, but, rather, because it resonated with something familiar. Almost 20 years after reading that book it is the only thing that I remember from it, and as I planned this chapter, it kept intruding itself into my thoughts. Whenever I try to understand the image or my own participation in it, I begin by imagining Malraux as its subject, staring into the face of another man, another soldier perhaps, more likely that of his suicide father, as if into a mirror, and having an experience that he feels is definitive of his "manness," something beyond his ken and therefore uncanny (Freud, 1919) perhaps, but something that binds him wordlessly to the other—something that is symbolized for him by death and, of course, something that distinguishes and separates him unequivocally from every woman.

Malraux evokes an image of relationship—illusive, paradoxical, and, to my ear, filled with longing. But it is at the same time a negation of relationship, or, to borrow from the title of Malraux's book, it is an image of anti-relationship, of the lonely encounter between the sentient and the infinite. It is an image of silence and the sequelae of destruction, yet it is seductive and pulls at me to experience the missing emotion in the scene. Malraux is as much a painter as he is a writer, and his work is more imagistic than narrative. He uses imagery to form an objective correlative (Eliot, 1919) of his emotional experience, and it creates, thereby, an emotional analogue in the reader.

This style is a tacit form of emotional communication, and to be successful it demands that one's emotional life be unlabeled and undescribed. This is a common style among men both in and out of treatment. It is among the pillars of fraternity, and ultimately it relies on identification for its existence (Freud, 1921). It is easy for me to sit in silence with one or more other men and pay attention to something. At those times, if I stop to think about it, I realize that our mutual attention creates a subtle but powerful emotional bond. Indeed, one young patient made this kind of relating his psychological litmus test of intimacy and said to me, "I know that I'm really close to somebody when I can go on a 3-hour car ride with them without saying anything." At these times emotion is both acknowledged and negated. Sharing the focus of attention carries the intersubjective function of sharing emotion (Stern, 1985, p. 129).

For example, whenever I asked another male patient how he felt about something, he would respond with a reference to a piece of music. He believed that if I could focus on an emotional stimulus that was meaningful to him, I could also discover his meaning. He also believed that the task of denotatively explaining his experience undermined the significance of our relationship. I was to understand without having to be told.

Indeed, a third patient, a male writer, became angry when I wondered at his need to communicate to me only through action, symbol, and symptom. "After all," he pleaded, "that's how my characters express themselves. They never tell each other, or me, how they feel, and I never need to ask." The expectation is for deep, almost sensate understanding as well as respectful distance. As another patient said even more clearly, "If people want to know me, they must experience me."

In Malraux's world the medium of communication is political upheaval, war, and death, and the image of death binds men together in very powerful ways and generates a reverence and awe that seem to cast a shadow over much of emotional expression—a shadow that reveals itself as both symbol and substance, a shadow that so definitively carries with it the intimations of a disruption of the continuity of personal experience (Bollas, 1987).

Why does this imagery play so prominent a role in the stories of so many men? The experience of being in battle creates an almost passionate attachment between men, and the fantasy of battle has such allure that men establish both games and business on that model. Furthermore, why the emotional silence, the reverential awe in the face of death?

It would, of course, be foolish to offer a single answer. We can be literal and say that, compared with women, men die earlier and, in the world of childhood, more often; that they are the warriors; and that they are born to be—or taught to be—both more aggressive and less emotional. Or might we profit from pursuing Freud's lead and understand this imagery as only symbolic of conflict? For Freud, death and manhood are inextricably bound together by the workings of the Oedipus complex. It is an issue of narcissism. Humans are simply incapable of conceiving of their own deaths. Images of death are derivative of guilt and its antecedent, castration, that bête noire of phallic grandeur.

A more comprehensive answer demands a consideration of the peculiar structure of manhood. Manhood is a unique developmental status as well as a social designation. It is not something that one becomes naturally; it is something that an adult male attains, something that he earns and that is given to him primarily by other men and only to a lesser degree by women. Indeed, the American poet Robert Bly (1990) argues that only men can initiate other males into manhood. Because it is given by others, manhood may therefore be lost or taken away. Manhood is also a subjective status, a way of seeing oneself. The development of the self-perception of manhood and its function may be traced to the structuralization left in the wake of the earliest object relations and through the countless fantasies that precede the ritual moment when a boy feels himself to be a man.

In these fantasies every boy lives a life with other men on the scale of Malraux's. In this life of the imagination he may be given his manhood, or he may steal it; he may serve it as a ward or a coquette; manhood may protect him, nurture him, or torment him. Yet an irreducible sense of continuity should form and be internalized very early in life between the boy and the man, an integrity that should not be dissolved by maturation. This often does not happen.

Many men have only tenuous and conflicted ties to the other males in their developmental lives, and they turn inward to find what is missing. Thus, fantasies of manhood come to be told in a grammar of the heroic. That is, men tend to conceive of their life stories as turning on a decisive, individual confrontation with the other during which they attain the symbolic wounds (Bettelheim, 1962) that transform them from boys into men or through which they reaffirm their manhood and save it. They emerge from these experiences with an uncompromising sense of individuality.

The rite of passage is a rebirth as a man into the world of men. The boy must leave behind the self-experience of childhood. To the degree that nurturance and emotionality have, because of lack of paternal involvement, been assimilated only to the schema of women with children, he is separated from his emotional self. Thus, for many men, manhood becomes defined by personal isolation that requires repetitive re-creation of the self in the world through personal agency. This constant re-creation is the heroic subtext to their lives. Like Malraux they must stare at the dead and re-create the heroic rite of initiation, while the personal self-re-creation remains forever beyond their grasp.

When such a man has a son and brings this structure of manhood to their relationship, the isolation and longing are again re-created, this time across the generations. The father is emotionally distant from the infant, in whom he can see only a dim, forbidden image of himself. Later, as the infant grows, the father is always experienced as distant and reachable only through the son's subsequent initiation into the world of men. What is missing between them is the experience that Benjamin (1988) aptly calls mutual recognition, the affirming, mutual emotional bond with another who is essentially like the self but who remains independent and outside of one's control.

Rank (1914/1971, 1941/1958) spent a good deal of time studying these phenomena in the form of wish and dread of "the double" in literature, myth, and fantasy. Rank (1914/1971) understood that for many men the need for recognition and identification often comes in conflict with the need to differentiate:

> This fear of a real double … brings us to man's eternal conflict with himself and others, the struggle between his need for likeness and his desire for difference. Torn between those two opposing tendencies within himself, he creates a spiritual double in his own image only to repudiate his natural double in the physical resemblance of his son. (pp. 99–100)

The failure of recognition between father and son creates in each of them a rupture in the sense of personal continuity. Men compensate for this rupture by the creation of spiritual doubles, false selves (Winnicott, 1960), fetishes, the secret identity of the super hero. They remain locked in an ongoing struggle with the other, who is ultimately concretized as the image of death.

When these men come to treatment, they therefore present a variety of symptoms: grandiosity and a need to control or even dominate the therapist; underlying depression; sometimes passivity, hypochondria, and, of course, preoccupation with death. They are often experienced as emotionally with-holding, but, like Malraux, they evoke a wide range of emotional reactions, which, when presented to them by the therapist, are denied, negated, and disavowed and which often precipitate a bout of passive rage, contempt, and withdrawal. This heroic "phallic-narcissistic" stance may be very intracta-ble for a very long period of time and tax the therapist's endurance.

Indeed, Freud (1937), near the end of his career, despaired at the task:

> At no other point in one's analytic work does one suffer more from the oppres-sive feeling that all one's efforts have been in vain, and from a suspicion that one has been "preaching to the winds," than when one is ... seeking to convince a man that a passive attitude to men does not always signify castration and that it is indispensable in many relations in life. The rebellious overcompensation of the male produces one of the strongest transference-resistances. (p. 252)

Freud's clinical despair was, I believe, inevitable. He always felt that he was an objective observer of internal conflict. Yet, he continually equated health with an individual mastery over emotion and infantile experience. This understanding of health is particularly dire for the treatment out-come of men who have detached themselves so decisively from the self-experience of childhood. These men live in a mythical world and believe that nurturance and receptivity are inherently feminine. Thus, women become symbolic beings, objects in a world of fantasy, while the analyst remains, like the father of childhood, always out of reach.

These patients require an experience with the other in imagination, an experience that is facilitated by the analyst's attempt to enter the narcis-sistic system by maintaining a basically neutral, empathic-introspective connection with the patient. Analytic interventions must be informed by the therapist's affective recognition to allow a prestage of intersubjectivity. Thus, transferential experience becomes a transitional area that functions for the patient as the "spiritual double in his own image" once did, and he can loosen the death grip in which he has held it.

In this period of treatment it is easy to feel narcissistically exploited in a futile endeavor. But it is in this transitional area that the patient can begin to experience his longings and fears toward other men, even if the thera-pist does not happen to be male. A sense of the analyst as a true external other develops in the growing context of affective interpenetration, a unique kind of intimacy, a sense of "sharing" one's inner and private self with another without undue anxiety and with relative confidence that one will remain in possession of one's own body and mind, despite profound experiences of commonality that may, for some people, include the sense of merger (Kohut, 1971, 1977). Thus, the experience of treatment offers the possibility of simultaneously experiencing the desire for sameness and the need for difference. This intimacy is transformational, helps turn conflict into paradox, and provides the context for analytic insight.

So, I am advocating an essentially reparative attitude in the treatment of these patients, an attitude that I am tempted to extend to male patients in general. What is repaired is the web of fantasy that is manhood, and with it the stance toward the world of others. Manhood is no longer defined by its distance from the nurturing matrix, nor does it set the subject in opposition to others.

Reparative treatments are often criticized for naively suggesting that it is possible to turn back the clock and give the patient something that he missed in life. I am not suggesting that the analyst behave like the father whom the patient needed or believes he needed. Nor am I saying that the analyst should provide a corrective emotional experience in the premeditated sense of that phrase. Rather, I am saying that the elaboration of narcissistic fantasy and affect within a human relationship heals a very basic failure of integration of identity. When the treatment is focused on the male's specific problem of continuity of being with the other, one may observe and participate in the patient's renewed attempts to integrate maleness, masculinity, and manhood into an in-depth experience of self and other that is structurally cohesive, stable over time, and of positive affective coloration (Stoller & Lachmann, 1980).

Questions of male relatedness and typically male structures of self-esteem have been a consistent subtext in psychoanalysis. I would like now to turn to a brief discussion of this subtext and its clinical implications and then add some thoughts of my own.

The Freudian Tradition: The Hero as Psychoanalytic Ideal

Freud's work, taken as a whole, is the longest, most consistent meditation that I know of on the experience of manhood. Again and again he returned to the same theme: conflict. The metaphors and images in which he concertized his vision of conflict were not unlike those of Malraux, consistently military or derived from heroic, biblical, or classical mythology. Kronos, Oedipus, Narcissus, Faust, and Moses were the figures who gripped his imagination. These are unique individuals and lonely sensibilities, unmatched in grandeur by anyone except, perhaps, their adversaries. They are the children of fate.

Freud's commitment to the brave, isolated human mind was always central to his thinking. It was among the major accomplishments of his self-analysis and his friendship with the "transference figure" Fliess. Isolation was so seminal to Freud's thinking that he regarded any group thought as primitive, emotional, and a residue of animal heritage. He argued:

> We must conclude that the psychology of groups is the oldest human psychology; what we have isolated as individual psychology, by neglecting all traces of the group, has only since come into prominence out of the old group psychology, by a gradual process which may still, perhaps, be described as incomplete. (1921, p. 123)

His vision is both tragic and heroic, for man is ultimately "a lonely wanderer in the universe" (M. Bergmann, personal communication) with only reason to provide him with some insight into his archaic, biological irrationality and rapacity.

Relations between men are predetermined by the inevitability of the oedipal crisis. The father and the son have something in common, their wish to possess the mother, and something more—the inheritance of the primal horde (Freud, 1912). In Freud's anthropological fantasy there is an original father who dominates all his sons:

> The members of the group were subject to [emotional] ties just as we see them today, but the father of the primal horde was free. His intellectual acts were strong and independent even in isolation, and his will needed no reinforcement from others. Consistency leads us to assume that his ego had few libidinal ties; he loved no one but himself, or other people only insofar as they served his needs. (1921, p. 123)

This father is killed, castrated, and eaten in an attempt to assimilate his power. Guilt supervenes; however, the father is internalized and becomes a god, and fear of him motivates the brothers to form a system of law both as an atonement (Loewald, 1980) and as an act of survival. The primal horde is transformed into the totemic group. The murder of the father and his deification are constantly relived in the totem meal. The brothers become the fathers of families and the fathers of sons.

This myth, according to Freud, is lived over and over again in the developmental life of males. The oral incorporation of the father is a primary ambivalent identification with him that appears very early in life, long before the consolidation of gender identity in the oedipal phase, and is a prerequisite of oedipal development. There is, in the subjective life of most men, a deep sense of longing for the father.

Freud (1921) did recognize a need for the father that was at variance with his general theoretical, oedipally oriented vision of masculinity:

> A little boy will exhibit a special interest in his father; he would like to grow like him and be like him, and take his place everywhere. We may say simply that he takes his father as his ideal. This behavior has nothing to do with a passive or feminine attitude towards the father (and towards males in general); it is on the contrary typically masculine. (p. 105)

It is this very idealization of the father that sets the stage for the Oedipus complex and makes it so poignant; it awaits only the development of object-love, which acts as a releaser. Likewise, it is this narcissistic attachment that allows the boy to project his own hostility on to the father and experience it in the vocabulary of his own infantile mind as castration anxiety. By renouncing the wish for the mother and identifying himself with his father, he makes a momentous step toward consolidation of his superego. By selecting the same ego ideal as do his fellows, a man makes an important compromise with his own narcissism and is rewarded for it with self-respect. It is not in the nature of Freud's view that a man could ever become the father of his earliest fantasies of awe, but he can come closest through submission to the group ideal and participation in the patriarchy, which is actually a covert brotherhood.

Chasseguet-Smirgel (1985) writes, however, from a somewhat different point of view:

> It is ... the case that the wish to be one's own ideal, as at the beginning of life, seems never to be given up entirely by most men. To differing degrees, it persists unchanged despite the vicissitudes it suffers at another level, in parallel with the development of the ego. The latter seemingly undergoes in this a splitting process analogous to that described by Freud in the case of the fetishist. (p. 77)

In Freud's world, a man is never able to resolve his ambivalence toward his father. The only real intimacy between them is the intimacy of opposition, where resolution comes to mean submission. Freud did not elaborate the possibility that the ongoing relationship to the father might mitigate the form and content of the Oedipus complex. But analytic experience suggests that the son needs a great deal from the father to help in the resolution of oedipal issues.

For example, when Jim, who was an aggressive litigator, came to treatment, he complained of a persistent sense of alienation in his marriage. He recovered a memory that he dated from approximately his seventh year. He had wanted to build a wooden boat and, after some difficulty, turned to his father for help. His father was accomplished at woodworking and had an extensive shop in the basement of the house. Jim had some thought as to working with his father on the project. The father "took over" and after a few hours presented his son a perfectly machined wooden gunboat. Jim took it and drove some nails into it to add more firepower. He knew that this action would ruin the boat, and he cringed somewhat at the disapproving look on his father's face when he saw it. "But," he said in therapy, "I had to put something of my own on it, and my father could never understand that."

Many elements of oedipal pathology are part of this memory, which summarizes Jim's relationship to and with his father. But the father is not simply the object of the son's aggression and envy. The father's subjective lack of appreciation of his son's need for a collaborative response turned the constellation traumatic and overtly rivalrous. Jim's endless, unrealizable, self-idealizing fantasies were attempts to repair this failure of self with other.

In the preface to the second edition of *The Interpretation of Dreams*, Freud (1900) wrote that the book was a product of his own self-analysis, "my reaction to my father's death—that is to say, to the most important event, the most poignant loss, of a man's life" (p. xxvi). That it is the most important event, that it moves a man forward in the cycle of generations, and that he must bear the guilt for the history of his ambitions are very clear in Freud's work. But the poignancy of the loss and the reasons for it are, to my mind, often cloudy. The attachments between men were always a struggle for Freud; he was always clear about the dynamics that kept men apart and always conflicted about those that held them together. The clinical power of Freudian theory remains its sensitivity to the subtle nuances of fantasy. But the philosophical commitment to isolation makes an understanding of the function of fantasy impossible. These factors combine to foster a clinical neglect of the patient's experience of the subjective depth of the other. Thus, although he saw so clearly that the boy needed and longed for the father, this very need was destined to remain forever frustrated—a potential source of panic.

Symbiosis and Gender Identity

The ego psychologists, elaborating on the work of Freud, made the under-standing of masculinity and manhood an essential part of their project, though with the exception of Blos (1985), there have been few attempts to create a coherent theory of male development from birth into and through adolescence to adulthood. They generally accepted Freud's vision of an isolated inner psyche pressed by drives to turn reluctantly toward the world of others. Individuality, self-control, and neutralization remain the ultimate achievements of maturity. They were more interested than was Freud, however, in the way in which experience with objects shapes and structures the mind. Their basic developmental design rests on the assumption of a primary diffusion of the infant in the maternal matrix and the infant's subsequent organization, separation, and individuation. Mahler was among the most influential thinkers in this tradition.

The first important organization for the infant, in Mahler's view, is the "symbiotic phase" of development. This phase of development is charac-terized by the formation of a stable dual unity between the child and the mother, not in terms of their prewired capacity but rather in terms of their internal psychic experience. During this phase, the "mutual cuing … cre-ates that indelibly imprinted configuration—that complex pattern—that becomes the leitmotif for the 'infant's becoming the child of his particular mother'" (Lichtenstein, cited in Mahler, 1967, p. 87). Mahler envisioned the mother as the active agent:

> It is the specific unconcious need of the mother that activates, out of the infant's infinite potentialities, those in particular that create for each mother "the child" who reflects her own unique and individual needs. This process takes place, of course, within the range of the child's innate endowments. (1967, p. 86)

During optimal symbiosis there is a consolidation of a large number of developmental processes that together form the weave of the ego (Mahler, 1961, 1966). The infant's mind is, for Mahler, the passive psychic clay in which the personality of the mother leaves indelible markings.

The enmeshment with the mother is a motivating and adaptive necessity that becomes noxious with further development. By the fifth or sixth month of life the child is differentiating, pushing at the mother and separating his body from hers, and seeking others, often the father. Mahler suggests that the reason for the "turning toward the father" by children of both sexes is that he is "uncontaminated" by the powerful symbiotic representations that characterize the experience of mother. The father beckons to the child from outside the symbiotic orbit and so cuts the umbilical cord to the mother at the psychological birth of the human infant (Blos, 1985). With the advent of the upright posture and locomotion comes the practicing subphase of separation-individuation, the "love affair with the world" and, not long thereafter, the awareness of the anatomical difference between the sexes and the rapprochement crisis. The role of the father in this process of elation, deflation, and modulation of narcissistic experience has been a center of analytic interest for more than 30 years (Greenacre, 1957/1971).

In this developmental phase we can most clearly see a prototype of male intimacy, of joyous parental participation in the physical, emotional, and interpersonal unfolding of the child; however, the internalizations that are theoretically available for the father and son remain circumscribed by tradition. Again, the father's lack of emotional involvement and his distance from the nurturing dyad are emphasized. The father promotes the separation of self and object representations and provides a modulating effect on the ebb and flow of the attachment to the mother, which remains center stage in the psychic life of the child.

The most important clinical application of this theory to the treatment of men is the Stoller-Greenson hypothesis (Greenson, 1966/1978, 1968/1978; Stoller, 1968, 1985). These analysts, while working at the Gender Identity Research Center of UCLA, became aware that the incidence of cross-gender behavior and fantasy among men was much higher than it was among women, contrary to the predictions of Freudian theory. They argued that the boy is faced with a much more difficult developmental task in terms of gender identity than is the girl. He must first identify with the mother during the symbiotic phase and then disidentify from her and identify with the father. Thus, the first core gender identity is female, and maleness is a difficult and perhaps never quite successful renunciation of that "protofemininity."

Much of male bonding, then, is the mutual underwriting of this never entirely accomplished renunciation. The brothers of the primal horde form societies not to atone for the murder of the father but rather to find strength in numbers against the engulfing, all-powerful mother. Again, as in the case of Freud, the theory offers abundant insight into the fantasy life of men. Many men harbor vast reservoirs of narcissistic rage and envy toward women.

The problem is that this theory implies that "protofemininity" is a structure that is innate, inevitable, and definitive of manhood. Although there is provocative evidence for the role of biology in the determination of the psychological experience of gender (Green, 1987; Stoller, 1968, 1985), the weight of evidence is that gender experience is socially determined (Money & Ehrhardt, 1972). Despite a preoedipal role for the father, these authors continue to regard masculinity as a measure of one's aggressive detachment. The capacity for intimate relatedness and attunement is "receptive" and is, therefore, characteristic of the feminine self. Intimacy between men continues as a defensive activity. We are no closer to an understanding of the transferential implications of poignant yearning for the father, which is so often found in the treatment of men, nor does this view of masculinity help us to understand the possibility of a structure of masculinity that has oedipal and preoedipal continuity.

Fast (1984) argues that concepts of male and female are not structured elaborations of an innate bisexuality disposition but, rather, that they differentiate out of a common matrix. Originally, gender categorization and identity are overinclusive for both males and females, and children identify from an indiscriminate array of attributes that carry none of their eventual social gender meaning. Thus, for the boy

> a broad range of identifications with [the mother], including her functions in nurturing and care giving may be included in his sense of himself as masculine. It may in fact be that "dis-identification" or "repudiation" signals failure in optimum development of masculinity, an organization too exclusively phallic, denying the actual procreative capacity and nurturing possibilities of a man. (pp. 72–73)

Gender differentiation occurs in the context of an unambivalent developmental pull toward masculinity on the part of both parents. Failures in differentiation stamp the structure of gender with a sense of the passivity and shame that was present in the child's original experience of his parents. The differentiation model does not rule out the influence of biology, but it allows us to imagine a wider relational matrix for the infant, who is no longer understood to be essentially passive. Furthermore, differentiation theory allows us to investigate relations with others as a primary, rather than a secondary, determinant of gender structure.

The Role of Intimacy: Harry Stack Sullivan

The interpersonal school has, more than any other, focused the attention of analysts on the central role of intimacy in psychoanalysis, primarily on the function of intimacy in the therapeutic situation (Newirth, 1982). I think it is without question that among the classic psychoanalytic theorists, no one was more aware of the crucial role of intimacy in human life than was Sullivan. Nor has there been another theorist who made the experience of similarity among people more central to a developmental scheme. Beginning with the "one genus postulate," that is, "that we are all more human than otherwise" and in each of the levels of development of a person in the interpersonal field, Sullivan (1953) was keenly aware of the facilitating function of the experience of sameness. Moreover, he emphasized the importance of the developmental leap whereby we experience that human sameness continues in depth—that is, into the mind and emotional life of the other.

Essentially, Sullivan understood this developmental leap to occur in preadolescence with the emergence of chumship. At this time of life, from 8 and a half to 10, one selects a friend, almost always of the same sex, and engages in a collaborative, reciprocal relationship that is intimate—a closeness "which permits validation of all components of personal worth" (p. 246). This relationship is the satisfaction of a need "for the most intimate type of exchange with respect to satisfactions and security" (p. 261).

Sullivan continuously stressed the uniqueness of this transformation of relatedness. "Nothing remotely like that has ever happened before," he wrote, referring to the value one places on one's chum, and he thought it to be the prototype of love; only the lust dynamism is left to be integrated in the following developmental phase, when one moves from isophilic to heterophilic others. The price for the lack of this crucial relationship is loneliness, which may endure for an entire life and which may motivate even more powerfully than does anxiety.

Of course, Sullivan understood that interpersonal intimacy had its roots in the mother–infant dyad. But he nevertheless maintained a sharp disjunction in the development of interpersonal relatedness in the preadolescent phase. The communication at this phase is largely verbal and takes place via both the sharing of "intimacies" and the participation in "common and more-or-less impersonal objective[s], such as the success of 'our team'" (p. 246).

It has been fateful for the development of much interpersonal practice that Sullivan located perhaps the most crucial transformation of self-experience at a stage of such highly developed cognitive operations. Although Sullivan's theory suggests that the first true experience of love involves a narcissistic object choice (in the sense that the prerequisite for the choice is sameness), the learning that emerges is the ability to value the other, and this ability remains the hallmark of intimate relatedness. In Sullivan's understanding, relationships between men go quite deep, but a distance remains and abstract communication allows for the new depth, which is crucially unlike anything that has preceded it.

Sullivan more than recognized the possibility of intimate male relationships based on a primary fraternity, and this alone would constitute a major contribution to an emerging psychology of men. It allows the male analyst to listen to the patient's transference without the vigilance that must come with the assumption of a basic ambivalence or underlying hostility between men. The very strength of Sullivan's contribution, however, is his insistence on a basic human similarity and identity; to the degree that gender subdivides that identity, it cuts across the grain of his primary theoretical interest. Although there are important exceptions, such as Miller (1976), gender theory has tended not to be a primary interpersonal theme.

What is clinically more important is that the creation of a watershed in the developmental line of intersubjective relatedness during preadolescence places an arbitrary premium on the forms of communication and relationship used by males at that time of life. Here we have again a relational idea that, for men at least, is consonant with traditionally delimited experience. To a large degree, preadolescent intimacy relies on a kind of mediation and depersonification. It is the intimacy of shared rules, values, and goals, the intimacy of "our team," and requires a clearly demarcated individuality. It is the intimacy of time of life noted for its preoccupation with clear gender role classification.

The conception of "chumship" as a model for intimacy can move an analytic treatment toward the use of confrontation as the primary mode of intervention and a relative neglect of an empathic interpretation of the fantasy. For example, Ehrenberg (1975) writes about working on the "intimate edge" in treatment and the need for the edge to be defined for there to be a true chance at intimacy. She points out that for intimacy to be real, each person must be aware of his or her own boundaries. "Intimacy cannot occur if either participant in a relationship is relating to a fantasy or a projection, or is relating … in the service of self-evasion to avoid the experience of personal anxieties" (p. 324).

In my experience, there is a paradox here. There is no doubt that mature forms of intimacy like mature empathy depend on a responsible mutuality between people. Yet, the development of genuine mutuality in treatment is often the product of long periods of projection, fantasy, and self-evasion. Although intimacy cannot occur if a person is relating to "projection," it cannot deepen if, to some degree, we cannot be transformed and used in accordance with the needs of the other.

Male patients often need to keep the boundaries of the self clearly defined. Such men may flourish in a treatment that emphasizes benign yet constant confrontation and that therefore sounds a tone of virile bonhomie, only to have much of their infantile longings left unacknowledged. These patients do, in fact, make progress by learning to understand the stated needs of the other. Their improved relationships are mutually honest and open and, as such, are intimate but lack something that is essential for a deep sense of intimacy.

Intimacy itself is a paradoxical experience, involving both an intensification of self-experience and a suspension of self-experience in favor of the other. Only a developmental approach that emphasizes the origins of gendered experience can, I believe, clarify the difficulties many grown men have in establishing the paradox of intimacy, both in treatment and in their lives with others.

Toward a Theory of Male Intimacy

This reading of the received psychoanalytic traditions suggests that very basic clinical relationships may be foreclosed for many men and that transferential expressions of longing for intimate male relatedness may go unrecognized or misunderstood. This result occurs despite the growth of interest in fathers and fathering and despite our generally greater understanding of the developmental significance of what were once collectively called "passive strivings."

Continued adherence to the theory of constitutional bisexuality and the belief that masculinity is equated with biological activity continue to confound our attempt to understand the early structuralization of gendered self-experience. Myers and Schore (1986), for example, in a review of "combined, hidden, and neglected transference paradigms" that emerge in the male-male analytic dyad, find "that research into the primacy paternal role of the affectionate, supportive, noncompetitive, and facilitating preoedipal father has been neglected in favor of the parental role of the aggressive, threatening, competitive oedipal father" (p. 247). They argue, however, that the reconstruction of these primitive internalizations is difficult because they are "early, ill-defined, composite imagos in which early maternal and paternal elements are not clearly distinguished or are condensed. ... [It is unclear] as well how preoedipal internalizations are integrated with the oedipal" (p. 246).

It seems to me that the difficulty here is conceptual rather than empirical. The patient's expression of wishes to be held, fed, and nurtured—to be understood and recognized—is, from this point of view, always directed toward the primitive representation of the mother. If the primary caretaker is male, it is assumed that his masculinity, at best, goes unnoticed and that he functions as a kind of *mater manqué*, whose behavior is guided by an internal female. It is further assumed that oedipal and preoedipal phenomena are entirely discontinuous (Mitchell, 1988, pp. 123–172), an assumption that can only further distort our image of development and confuse normal development with average, traditional, or acceptable development. This distortion allows for the most blatant stereotypes to enter the analytic relationship, creating a situation in which the male analyst can, as it were, hide behind the skirts of the internalized mother and fail to connect emotionally with his male patient.

Clinical experience suggests that the early role of the father does find clear, if ambivalent, expression in the transference, and a number of theoretical metaphors exist that acknowledge this fact. Grunberger (1979), for example, considers that the ultimate matrix of narcissism is what he calls the narcissistic triad of mother, father, and self. He understands this fantasy of a three-into-one unity as a basic image of the unconscious. Likewise, Abelin (1975) suggests that the prerepresentational parents function as a double mirror for the emerging child, and that this stage precedes the early triangulation that determines the child's gender identity. The male child's robust assumption of the virtual image of himself in that double mirror forms an essential precondition of the ability to be intimate as a man.

Research has demonstrated that children are attached to both parents from quite early on (Lamb, 1977a, 1977b), and Pruette's (1983) study of fathers as primary caretakers does not indicate any feminization of boys because the father plays an essentially nurturing role. Abelin (1975) presents a case of an infant who has a symbiotic relationship to both parents and who displays refueling behavior to both.

Indeed, the father is better understood psychologically as a second other:

> The father's availability may enhance not only the depth and range of affect in the early attachment patterns ... but also the ability of the environment to maintain stability. ... [He] will relate to his infant somewhat differently than mother and provide an additional and beneficial set of experiences through which the infant comes to know him ... self, others and a world of loving relationships. (Greenspan, 1982, p. 125)

Sexual stereotypy and its expression in personal psychopathology can seriously limit the utility of this "second other" in both the developmental life of the child and its re-creation in analytic treatment. This problem occurs, most commonly, because of the exclusion of males from the nurturing dyad in which the fabric of intersubjective relatedness is woven. Stern (1985) argues that intersubjective relatedness begins at approximately 9 months of age with "three mental states that do not require language. ... These are sharing joint attention, sharing intentions, and sharing affect states" (p. 128). The sharing of affect states with the caretaker establishes a bedrock of intimacy, which can be experienced in the analytic transference. The sharing of attention states and joint intentionality cannot duplicate the same experience of shared depth.

In optimal development the infant utilizes his or her inherent organizing capacities to maintain reciprocal communication and regulation with caretakers. Although this interaction first supports self-regulating functions and promotes the experience of self-cohesion, it is, from the first, an early structured representational system of being with others (Beebe & Lachmann, 1988). The medium of this communication is largely affective and establishes the affective core of the prerepresentational self (Emde, 1983). The affect attunement of the caretaking surround makes this interaffectivity possible, which is so fateful for the shape and coloration of the subjective world. As Stern (1985, p. 152) points out, interaffectivity plays an important role in the infant's coming to recognize that internal feeling states are forms of human experience that are shareable with other humans. The converse is also true: feeling states that are never attuned to will be experienced only alone, isolated from the context of shareable experience. What is at stake here is nothing less than the shape of and extent of the shareable universe.

Simultaneously, other schemata of "like me/not like me" are being established. They help organize the interpersonal world and contribute to the sense of self-cohesion; they channelize empathic responses. Intimate experience with others who are "like me" is crucial in establishing the continuity of the self with others throughout the life cycle. Among the central schemata is the core dimension of gender.

The core of gender identity is also forming during this time of life, and all children seek out others who are like themselves. Children between the ages of 10 and 18 months tend to prefer to look at pictures of the faces of same-sex rather than opposite-sex children (Lewis & Weintraub, 1974). Still more convincing is the paradigm in which two boys and two girls, each 1 year old, are placed in opposite corners of a room. The odds of crawling to an opposite-sex child are two to one, yet children crawl to the same-sex child more often (Lewis, 1975). By the end of the second year, the child has attained a gendered self-classification that is generally held to be unchangeable. Even in the deepest of regressions, gender is a deeply ingrained aspect of the child's perception of the world. The body-self is the most basic register of affective experience, and by the age of 2 it is profoundly gendered. Bower (1982) attached lights to the limbs and torsos of children and filmed them in the dark. When the films of the moving lights were shown to other children, they preferred to look at those of the same sex. Gender classification facilitates the experience of recognition within a differentiating context.

Affect attunement plays a crucial role in the development of relatedness. Failures in affect attunement tend to cause defenses against affective experience, which is perceived as heralding traumatic states (Stolorow, Brandschaft, & Atwood, 1987). Such empathic failures impact upon the child's self-experience in a number of ways. First, failures of affect attunement signal potential fragmentation. Gendered imagery and behavior may become a pathway for the satisfaction of basic self-regulatory needs as well as concretizing narcissistic rage, as is seen clearly in cases of perversion (Goldberg, 1975). Second, since the structures of masculinity and femininity differentiate out of a common matrix, normal experiences of gender delimitation are inevitably experienced as narcissistic loss (Fast, 1984), and an attuned response from a same-sexed other is required to maintain the cohesion of the body-self affect and minimize the experience of pathological envy. Among men this is primarily the envy of the woman's procreative and nurturing functions; remember, for example, that Malraux could never re-create himself and that he believed that women had peak experiences when they looked into the face of a child. The absence of men in the early affective life of males leaves them at risk for the development of narcissistically vulnerable integrations of the gendered mind-body self.

Chodorow (1978) argues that the clinical cases she reviews "describe boys … who … intuitively react to their mothers' feelings and wishes as if they were the objects of their mothers' fantasies rather than the subjects. Girls, then, seem to become the self of the mother's fantasy, whereas boys become the other" (p. 103). Females, it is argued, come to organize interpersonal experience on the basis of subject-subject relationship with the mother, while males experience a subject-object relationship. Each of these relational modes is part of the uniquely human dance of engagement and detachment. When either mode becomes the only possible one, however, the personality is enslaved.

In the case of men, the subject-object relationship tends to militate against new interaffective experience, leaves males with a pervasive sense of otherness, and consigns many of their nurturing capacities to the "not me" world of the feminine. In treatment such men invite the analyst to broach their tragic and splendid isolation. Much of what is traditionally called "homosexual panic" is more accurately described as the terror of the emotional vulnerability that comes with the breakdown of this resistance and first intimations of the self in the other (Ghent, 1990). Fantasies of oneness seem to be both an inevitable and sometimes a beneficial human experience (Silverman, Lachmann, & Milich, 1982), and if the chronic sense of otherness is pervasive, it sets the stage for complex narcissistic psychopathology in later life. In response to the sense of otherness, males turn inward and create heroic private worlds rich in untapped, angry meanings.

Acknowledgment

This chapter originally appeared in *Psychoanalytic Dialogues, 1,* 1991, 305–328. Reprinted with permission.

References

Abelin, E. (1975). Some further observations and comments on the earliest role of the father. *International Journal of Psycho-Analysis, 56,* 293–302.

Beebe, B., & Lachmann, F. (1988). The contribution of mother-infant mutual influence to the origins of self- and object representations. *Psychoanalytic Psychology, 5,* 305–337.

Benjamin, J. (1988). *The Bonds of Love.* New York: Pantheon.

Bettelheim, B. (1962). *Symbolic Wounds.* New York: Collier Books.

Blos, P. (1985). *Son and Father.* New York: Free Press.

Bly, R. (1990). *Iron John.* Reading, MA: Addison-Wesley.

Bollas, C. (1987). *The Shadow of the Object.* New York: Columbia University Press.

Bower, T. G. R. (1982). *Development in Infancy,* 2nd ed. San Francisco: W. H. Freeman.

Chasseguet-Smirgel, J. (1985). *The Ego Ideal.* New York: Norton.

Chodorow, N. (1978). *The Reproduction of Mothering.* Berkeley: University of California Press.

Ehrenberg, D. (1975). The quest for intimate relatedness. *Contemporary Psychoanalysis, 11*, 320–331.

Eliot, T. S. (1919). Hamlet. In F. Kermode (Ed.), *Selected Prose* (pp. 45–50). New York: Harcourt Brace Jovanovich.

Emde, R. (1983). The prerepresentational self and its affective core. *Psychoanalytic Studies of the Child, 38*, 165–192.

Fast, I. (1984). *Gender Identity*. Hillsdale, NJ: Analytic Press.

Freud, S. (1900). The interpretation of dreams. *Standard Edition, 4–5*.

Freud, S. (1912). Totem and taboo. *Standard Edition, 13*, 1–161.

Freud, S. (1919). The uncanny. *Standard Edition, 17*, 219–256.

Freud, S. (1921). Group psychology and the analysis of the ego. *Standard Edition, 18*, 69–144.

Freud, S. (1937). Analysis terminable and interminable. *Standard Edition, 23*, 209–244.

Ghent, E. (1990). Masochism, submission and surrender. *Contemporary Psychoanalysis, 26*, 108–136.

Goldberg, A. (1975). A fresh look at perverse behavior. *International Journal of Psycho-Analysis, 56*, 335–342.

Green, R. (1987). *The "Sissy Boy Syndrome" and the Development of Homosexuality*. New Haven, CT: Yale University Press.

Greenacre, P. (1971). The childhood of the artist. In *Emotional Growth*, Vol. 1. New York: International Universities Press. (Originally published in 1957)

Greenson, R. (1978). A transsexual boy and a hypothesis. In *Explorations in Psychoanalysis* (pp. 289–305). New York: International Universities Press. (Originally published in 1978)

Greenson, R. (1978). Disidentifying from mother: Its special importance for the boy. In *Explorations in Psychoanalysis* (pp. 305–312). New York: International Universities Press. (Originally published in 1978)

Greenspan, S. (1982). "The second other": The role of the father in early personality formation and the dyadic-phallic phase of development. In S. Cath, A. Gurwitt, & J. Ross (Eds.), *Father and Child* (pp. 123–138). Boston: Little, Brown.

Grunberger, B. (1979). *Narcissism*. New York: International Universities Press.

Kohut, H. (1971). *The Analysis of the Self*. New York: International Universities Press.

Kohut, H. (1977). *The Restoration of the Self*. New York: International Universities Press.

Lamb, M. E. (1977a). The development of mother-infant and father-infant attachment in the second year of life. *Developmental Psychology, 13*, 637–648.

Lamb, M. E. (1977b). Father-infant and mother-infant interaction in the first year of life. *Child Development, 48*, 167–181.

Lewis, M. (1975). Early sex differences in the human: Studies of socioemotional development. *Archives of Sexual Behavior, 4*, 329–335.

Lewis, M., & Weintraub, M. (1974). Sex of parent; sex of child. In R. Friedman, R. Richart, & R. Vande Wiele, eds. *Sex Differences in Behavior*. New York: Wiley.

Loewald, H. (1980). The waning of the oedipus complex. In *Papers on Psychoanalysis* (pp. 384–404). New Haven, CT: Yale University Press.

Mahler, M. (1961). On sadness and grief in infancy and childhood. In *Selected Papers* (Vol. 1, pp. 261–280). New York: Jason Aronson, 1979.

Mahler, M. (1966). Notes on the development of basic moods. In *Selected Papers* (Vol. 2, pp. 59–77). New York: Jason Aronson, 1979.

Mahler, M. (1967). On human symbiosis and the vicissitudes of individuation. In *Selected Papers* (Vol. 2, pp. 77–98). New York: Aronson, 1979.

Malraux, A. (1970). *Anti-Memoirs*. New York: Bantam.

Miller, J. B. (1976). *Toward a New Psychology of Women*. Boston: Beacon Press.

Mitchell, S. (1988). *Relational Concepts in Psychoanalysis*. Cambridge, MA: Harvard University Press.

Money, J., & Ehrhardt, A. A. (1972). *Man and Woman; Boy and Girl*. Baltimore: Johns Hopkins University Press.

Myers, D., & Schore, A. (1986). The male-male analytic dyad: Combined, hidden and neglected transference paradigms. In G. Foel, F. Lane, & R. Liebert (Eds.), *The Psychology of Men* (pp. 245–261). New York: Basic Books.

Newirth, J. (1982). Intimacy in interpersonal psychoanalysis. In M. Fisher & G. Steiner (Eds.), *Intimacy* (pp. 79–98). New York: Plenum.

Pruette, K. (1983). Infants of primary nurturing fathers. *Psychoanalytic Studies of the Child, 38*, 257–277.

Rank, O. (1971). *The Double*. Trans. and ed. H. Tucker. New York: New American Library. (Originally published in 1914)

Rank, O. (1958). The double as immortal self. In *Beyond Psychology* (pp. 62–101). New York: Dover. (Originally published in 1941)

Silverman, L., Lachmann, F., & Milich, R. (1982). *The Search for Oneness*. New York: International Universities Press.

Stern, D. (1985). *The Interpersonal World of the Infant*. New York: Basic Books.

Stolorow, R.D., Brandschaft, B., Atwood, G.E. (1987). *Psychoanalytic treatment: An intersubjective approach*. Hillsdale, NJ: Analytic Press.

Stoller, R. J. (1968). *Sex and Gender*, Vol. 1. New York: Science House.

Stoller, R. J. (1985). *Presentations of Gender*. New Haven, CT: Yale University Press.

Stoller, R. J., & Lachmann, F. (1980). *Psychoanalysis of Developmental Arrests*. New York: International Universities Press.

Sullivan, H. S. (1953). *The Interpersonal Theory of Psychiatry*. New York: Norton.

Winnicott, D. W. (1960). Ego distortion in terms of true and false self. In *Maturational Processes and the Facilitating Environment* (pp. 140–152). New York: International Universities Press.

7

An Eruption of Erotic Vitality Between a Male Analyst and a Male Patient

William F. Cornell

> We both came out of this piece of analytic work with our own deep sense of having been changed by the impact of an intimacy with an other that was novel and disturbing, then acceptable and enhancing to us both. ... In this core experience is a moving power, by and for the two participants, that I do not fully fathom.
>
> James McLaughlin (2005, p. 220)

This autobiographical chapter, written from my experience as a patient, tells the story of the eruption of buried and disavowed erotics between my male analyst and me, erotic desires that blurred the boundaries (if indeed there are such boundaries) between hetero- and homosexual love and nearly destroyed our analytic relationship.

The case of my personal analysis, which I describe below, was first written as a contribution (Cornell, 2009) to a book on enactment in psychotherapy, *The Past in the Present: Therapy Enactments and the Return of Trauma* (Mann & Cunningham, 2009). When I was approached to further develop this narrative for a book on "male heterosexualities," I was more than a little dismayed. What, I wondered, did my tale of coming out into a gay relationship have to contribute to the understanding of heterosexual masculinity? While I neither identified as particularly straight or gay, I had a definite sense of maleness. Then I began to relish the project as I realized that my relationship with Dr. D. and of Dr. D. with me collapsed the distinctions between hetero- and homoerotics, a collapse of what might be considered the stereotypic "masculine" autonomy into "masculine" receptivity and erotic vitality.

The Case Narrative

I found myself a patient in a psychoanalyst's office as much by default as by choice. My previous psychotherapy had been terminated by unexpected, unwanted changes in external circumstances that required an abrupt termination of what had been a very productive, long-term psychotherapy. Living in a small city, it was difficult to find a therapist with whom I did not have some degree of professional or personal familiarity. I knew that the most likely choice would be someone within the psychoanalytic community, in which my involvement at that time was minimal. At my request, I was referred to Dr. D. by my clinical consultant, a Jungian trained analytical psychologist. I knew only that Dr. D. was one of the senior psychoanalysts in the city, and that he had been classically trained.

The night before my session I had a dream of the first session, which took place in Dr. D.'s yet unseen office. The office of my dream was large, handsome, full of good and varied artwork, the ceiling strung with lines of illuminated plastic fishes, lights that in fact decorated the bedroom of my oldest son. The dream office was considerably more interesting than Dr. D.'s actual office, which was rather nondescript. The dream analyst looked startlingly like my maternal grandfather, Grandpa Frank, a man I deeply loved. In the dream, I was immediately drawn to Dr. D. and felt that engaged me very directly, asking me questions that threw me back on myself. There was one anomaly in the office, a large curtain that covered most of one wall. When I inquired about the curtain, Dr. D. seemed evasive. It continued to distract and disturb me. I finally left my chair and pulled back the curtain. There was a smaller office hidden behind the curtain; seated at the desk was my previous therapist and around him were several of my friends, all of whom had been listening intently to my session. I was stunned and enraged. My recollection of the dream ended there.

Bypassing the dream, I began my initial session by recounting my marital conflicts and the disruption of my previous therapy. When I told Dr. D. that I had had an anticipatory dream the previous night, he said that he doesn't usually take up a dream in an initial session before a decision is made to work together, but that he was inclined to make an exception. I told him the dream, and he asked for my associations. My first associations were to the termination of my previous therapy. The termination was the result of my therapist being sued by a patient who had once been a client of mine in psychotherapy. I had had no idea that this client, who had terminated in the midst of our considerable mutual conflict, had then gone on into therapy with my own therapist. I did not know if she had known that he was my therapist. Yet she had been seeing my therapist at the same time I was seeing him. In her lawsuit, she had named me on her list of previous therapists and planned to depose me. My therapist had tried to keep me out of the proceedings, but his lawyer persisted in her own way. It became clear that I would be required to write a report, be deposed, and very likely called to testify in his malpractice case. Our therapy seemed suddenly filled with conflicts of interest and too compromised to continue effectively.

With deep mutual regret, we terminated. I was very worried about my therapist's well-being and quite frightened of the impending legal proceedings, although they ultimately turned out in his favor. My therapy with this man had been marked by prolonged negative transferences, with projections on him of my anger and distrust toward my father, who I had experienced as a remote and unreliable figure in my life. I had resisted depending on this therapist for years, keeping a wary, often sarcastic, distance. He met my reluctance and resistance with patient skill. As my transference gradually changed, we had begun to establish a much closer and trusting relationship. The termination for me was decidedly unexpected, out of my control, premature. I was unable to acknowledge the loss of him or our work. Instead, I shifted to a familiar stance of worrying about him and went on my way.

Other associations to the dream were to my maternal grandfather, my father, and others whom I had loved and whom had died young. There was, in fact, more than a passing resemblance between Dr. D. and my grandfather, who had pure white hair when he died at age 52, as did Dr. D., who was in his early 70s when we began treatment. My grandfather's death from lung cancer when I was 7 left deep wounds in the structure of my extended family. My maternal grandparents had been my primary caretakers until I was 4, and the loss of their care with the onset of his advanced cancer was profound for me. In the face of her relatively young husband's death my grandmother fell into a depression that consumed her through much of the remainder of my childhood. My grandfather, although not long in my life, was the closest I had had to a loving, engaged father figure. As I began my work with Dr. D., I was filled with an unvoiced, anticipatory hope for the interest and engagement of an elder, male colleague.

My other association to the dream—to that of my previous therapist and friends in the hidden room—was of my struggle to make a decision to seek a divorce. All of my friends, and my previous therapist, were urging me to get a divorce. I was desperate to talk with someone who did not know me, my wife, or anyone else in my life, who could give me the psychological space to sort this out for myself. It felt essential that I understand both my motivations in the structure of the marriage as it had evolved and my reluctance to leave it before coming to a final decision. I desperately needed the primacy and the privacy of this new relationship to sort these things through.

For the first 3 years, Dr. D. and I met twice a week, face to face. Dr. D. warned me that he planned to retire at 80, so he was willing to undertake psychoanalytic psychotherapy with me but would be reluctant to enter into a formal psychoanalysis. As our work evolved, it turned out that I would be his final analytic patient. I was focused in the initial, face-to-face years on my marital conflicts and the severe pressures of being the sole financial provider for my family with one son in university, another soon to go, the third in a private school, and the possibility of divorce pending. Long an opponent of the intrusion of third-party payment structures into psychotherapy, I had always paid for my personal psychotherapy out of pocket. Refusing to use my insurance coverage, I could only afford Dr. D.'s fee for a single weekly session. Both of us thought that twice a week was necessary, and Dr. D. offered to see me twice for the fee of a single session. I felt deeply grateful (and ashamed). We analyzed my gratitude and its possible consequences. But my shame passed unacknowledged by me and seemingly unnoticed and unanalyzed by Dr. D.

In the early years I constantly sought Dr. D.'s approval for my parenting, professional activities, and writing. I gave him copies of articles I was writing, eager for his thoughts and approval. He did indeed give me the approval I sought. We began to form what we sometimes nervously joked was a "mutual admiration society," which we both enjoyed rather than examined. Neither of us seemed willing to jeopardize the immediate pleasure by analyzing it. Looking back now I can see that we might have begun to own the emerging affections between us, and that our gratifications might have deepened into real intimacy had we undertaken the analytic task. I deluded myself by equating this admiration operation between us with Bollas's (1989) concept of "the psychoanalyst's celebration of the analysand." Unconsciously I had yet again established a pattern of setting myself up (and thus to the side) as an object of idealization.

My idealization of Dr. D. was fostered by his being far more personal and forthcoming than I had ever expected of a psychoanalyst. When I inquired about his openness, he explained that the prolonged illness and death of his wife a few years before, during which he maintained rigorously "proper" silence, had left him feeling that his classical analytic technique had profoundly dehumanized both himself and his patients. He had recently read Maroda's (1991) *The Power of Countertransference* and decided that he needed to learn to practice differently, to bring more of himself into the analytic frame. I had also just read Maroda's book and was deeply affected by it.

Dr. D. went on to tell me that he had found himself reviewing, yet again, his own training analysis with considerable resentment. His own analyst had been a man he greatly admired, but he had found his analysis wanting. After completing his analysis, as he continued to read and attend conferences, Dr. D. kept a retrospective log of all the errors he thought his analyst had made in his care. Thirty years after the completion of his training analysis, a psychoanalytic conference was held in the city to which his former analyst had retired. His log of analytic errors in hand, Dr. D. decided the time had come to confront his analyst. Dr. D. found himself greeted with a hug and obvious affection by his now frail analyst. They spent a warm and personal afternoon together reminiscing. "All those errors I logged," Dr. D. told me, "boiled down to two things, more sins than errors really—that he had never been himself with me and had never shown his love." Dr. D. said he was determined to learn how to be himself as an analyst, and that he hoped our work would afford that opportunity. I greeted this opportunity warmly. Neither of us analyzed the many layers of unspoken meaning and desire contained in this arrangement.

We had fallen into what McLaughlin (2005), drawing upon Sandler (1976), refers to as a "transference actualization," in which "the patient views his analyst's behavior as having fulfilled his expectations" (p. 188). Dr. D. and I were ensconced in the "unobjectionable" (Stein, 1981) aspects of a positive transferential arrangement, which Stein suggests may seem innocuous but must come to be analyzed. McLaughlin saw such "unobjectionable" transference actualizations as a form of unconscious enactment involving both parties of the analytic dyad, thereby eluding either identification or analysis. Dr. D. and I were later to pay dearly for the comfort of that period.

Most powerful for me during this period of our work was Dr. D.'s comprehension of the centrality of loss in the foundation of my character. Both the paternal and maternal sides of my family suffered premature deaths of parents, creating intergenerational patterns of depressive and schizoid withdrawal. My mother, seriously ill with leukemia, died suddenly as a result of a medical error when I was 18. Dr. D. had also lost his mother to cancer at 18, creating an area of deep, mutual identification between us. Dr. D. knew within himself the impact of early parental loss, and he understood something in me that had not been recognized in any of my previous therapy. He said to me in the midst of my internal conflicts about leaving my marriage, "Your entire character is founded in the determination to avoid unnecessary loss—be those losses of your sons, your wife, or your own. You cannot discriminate, and you cannot think in the face of projected losses. Loss has always been unbearable to you, devastating to those around you." With that interpretation, I finally began to think. I was able to end my marriage and still care for my sons. I felt profoundly grateful to Dr. D.

Once I had separated from my wife, Dr. D. and I decided to move from face to face to couch sessions in the hope of shifting my attention from coping with daily life to more intrapsychic reflection and a more purely analytic process. With the shift to the couch, I found myself going silent, mute, for long periods during many sessions. At first, Dr. D. seemed reluctant to accept my periods of silence. I found myself in the familiar state of mind I fall into when I am alone, of solitary thought with little sense of the presence or usefulness of others. It was a difficult struggle to remember to talk in session, to feel that there was any point in talking. Dr. D. became a kind of ghost to me. I lost track of him. I would have a session with him in my mind as I drove to the appointment (an hour's drive), and then feel I had nothing more to say in the session, as though it had all already been said. In our face-to-face sessions, under the pressure of my needing to make a decision about my marriage, take care of my sons, and keep my life going, I was acutely aware of Dr. D.'s presence and concern. I was able to allow myself to rely upon him, unlike with my previous therapist. I accepted both his interpretations and his advice. On the couch, with my attention turned inward, I lost track of him. I could not feel his importance or his function. Dr. D. would sometimes encourage me to talk more, challenging my silence as a resistance, but any real understanding/ analysis of the power and peculiarities of my muteness remained out of reach for a long time. I can see now, in retrospect, how hurt, helpless, and angry Dr. D., having given me so much, must have felt in the face of my silence. In retrospect, I suspect that Dr. D. did not have enough distance and understanding of his own reactions to my silence to effectively engage and analyze it.

Unknowingly, I had set in motion with Dr. D. two long-standing, rather paradoxical modes of relating: one of a silent, cutoff distancing, and the other an idealized and idealizing engagement. Each kept my most vulnerable and lonely aspects out of view and reach. As I often felt deeply alone in my sessions (in the presence of my analyst), I also felt deeply alone in my life (in the midst of many friends). I was, however, determined to at least find a sexual partner, if not a new life partner. I knew that with the ending of the marriage that I would be exploring sexual relationships with both genders. As an adolescent it was clear to me that I was attracted to both women and men. I came out to my parents as possibly gay while in college. Both were supportive of either choice of sexual partner. I spent my college years experimenting with straight and gay relationships, although I found my relationships with women significantly more sexually satisfying. I lived with one woman for nearly a year and then lived my senior year with the woman who would become my wife. At the point of separation from my wife I became involved with a man who lived in another state, hoping for some distance and privacy from my professional and home life. He was a gay activist whom I had known and admired for quite some time. He had recently broken up with his longtime lover, heard that I had separated from my wife, and proposed that we become lovers. It was to be a sexual arrangement; he had no interest in my sons or my life in my home city. I relished the freedom. I fell into an intense and complicated relationship with this man.

As issues of my sexual choices and activities came up in the sessions, I began to experience what I considered to be countertransference reactions on Dr. D.'s part. When I told Dr. D. of my sexual interest in men as well as women, he was both taken aback and interested. I had little inclination to discuss issues of bisexuality, homosexuality, sexual preference, and so forth, as I had no particular conflict about it. I was very concerned that with whomever I became involved, male or female, I not repeat the symbiotic patterns I had created and was unable to break in my marriage. But throughout this process Dr. D. would repeatedly inquire about my homosexual feelings, the history of my sexual activities, and my understanding of my same-sex desires. These were, to me, his needs and questions, not mine. He had not inquired into my heterosexual relations in a similar way. I told him on several occasions that he seemed more interested in my homosexual life than I was. I told him that I had fantasies, frustrated and hostile, to add an additional, unpaid session each week to respond to his questions about homosexuality, so that it would not detract from my time on the couch and my own concerns.

Finally, I asked Dr. D. to talk about himself and what this was all about for him. Reluctantly, he told me of doing an analysis early in his career with a gay candidate in analytic training, with whom he made an agreement to hide the patient's homosexuality so that would not interfere with his accreditation as an analyst. He had had deep respect for this patient's professional skill and had long felt guilty and conflicted about colluding with hiding his patient's sexual orientation. He was now trying to come to a better understanding of same-sex relationships, acknowledging that he had real questions about the capacity of two men to love each other. Dr. D. told me he was on a national task advocating for gays and lesbians within the American Psychoanalytic Association and was a member of a small group of local analysts and psychotherapists discussing gay, lesbian, and gender issues. It seemed clear to me that in the background for Dr. D. were broader, more vague issues of intimacy and passionate attachments between men. I continued to feel my familiar detachment and distance from him. I was losing track of why I was seeing him. I no longer found him so helpful. Quite to the contrary, I felt a growing irritation with him, which I lived in silence. We did not talk about what was happening between us.

One evening, as I was cooking a birthday dinner for my youngest son, I received a panicked phone call from a client of mine, who (unbeknown to me) was a member of the gay and lesbian study group to which Dr. D. belonged. In the meeting the night before Dr. D. had discussed his work with a patient who she realized was me. She left the meeting as soon as she realized Dr. D. was talking about me, but by then she had heard details of my sexual history and that I had recently become involved with a man. A bit later that evening I received an awkward phone call from the clinical supervisor of the gay and lesbian counseling center, who after telling me of his delight at learning I was now involved with a guy, then told me that he had learned this in the previous night's meeting. "I've seen a lot of guys outed," he said, "but this is the first time I've seen it done by someone's psychoanalyst." I later learned that a supervisee of mine was also in that meeting and recognized that it was me Dr. D. had been talking about.

I was furious. I was confused. I called Dr. D.'s answering machine to tell him what had happened, telling him under no circumstances to contact me before our next session, that I needed time to think and I hoped he would have as miserable a weekend as I was anticipating for myself. I called my clinical consultant and went to see him at his home the next evening. He had known of my recent relationship with a male lover and was shocked at Dr. D.'s lack of judgment. He said I would probably have to terminate and suggested I consider bringing ethics charges against Dr. D. I saw no sense in either possibility. I was certain this was not an ethical lapse but something extraordinarily stupid, unconsciously stupid, an acting out. I did not particularly care that Dr. D. had "outed" me. Most people who knew me knew I identified myself as bisexual. The violation for me was that he spoke of the privacy of our work in a setting where I was almost certain to be recognized without elaborate efforts to disguise my identity. The curtain in my initial, anticipatory dream of Dr. D.'s office and my "first session" with him had indeed been ripped away.

In our first session after the mess, Dr. D. explained that the discussion in the gay and lesbian study group had devolved into one of these classically intellectualized psychoanalytic discussions of the defensive functions of homosexuality. He had become intensely frustrated with the tome of the meeting and told the group that if the discussions continued in this vein, he would be leaving the group. He was not going to tolerate the pathologizing of same-sex love relationships. "Suddenly," he told me, "I found myself telling the group that I was learning a great deal about homosexuality and love between men from one of my patients. I went on to talk about our work without ever thinking of the consequences." He went on to suggest that we might have to terminate, that this was an error from which we could not recover. This was not acceptable to me. I thought we needed to recover, to sustain our work. I needed to understand how this had happened. We each had things to learn about ourselves in the creation of this situation. I was suddenly revisiting familiar relationship issues with great intensity. I felt thrown back upon myself to take care of myself in a way so familiar from my earliest memories. How could I continue to rely on this man? If I worked to preserve this relationship, was I creating another horridly compromised relationship? I knew in my gut that I should not remove myself. Compromise and withdrawal were far too familiar defensive reactions. I needed to hold Dr. D. on the hook to account for himself. Dr. D. assured me that he was engaged in self-analysis to understand what had happened. I was not the least bit reassured by this. I insisted he get consultation.

Facing the Music

> Among the ways of being that I value in the analytic setting … is the effort on the part of the analyst and the patient to face the truth, to be honest with themselves in the face of disturbing emotional experience. … In the absence of the effort on the part of patient and analyst to "face the music," what occurs in the analysis has a shallow, desultory, as-if quality to it.
>
> Thomas Ogden (2005, p. 21)

The following weekend I was having dinner with an analytic colleague from Great Britain. With visible distress I told him what happened with

Dr. D. He began to laugh. He continued to laugh, occasionally muttering, "Oh, what a glorious fuckup. What a glorious fuckup." His reaction was rather unexpected, to say the least, but rather refreshing in an odd way. When he eventually settled down, he said quite simply, "We only fuckup this badly with patients we love. We do seem to save our biggest mistakes for the patients we love. It's the patients we love the most, want the most for, where we act without thinking. What you and he have to deal with is how much you love each other. You're very lucky to have each other. You know, Dr. D. must be utterly in love with you. This was a rather clumsy way of telling you he loves you. You must talk to each other about your love for each other."

I took this dinner conversation back to session, much to Dr. D.'s initial embarrassment. We began to unravel what this enactment meant for each of us and between us. With considerable hesitation, Dr. D. spoke more openly of his affection for me, his admiration of how I moved rather aggressively in my professional world, and his envy of my relations with other men, my male friends as well as sexual partners. He talked in more detail of his guilt for his collusion with his gay analytic candidate, the paradox of regret for his secrecy then and his inadvertent exposure of me now. He told me about an enlisted man he had grown close to while serving in the military. Dr. D., as a physician and an officer, was not supposed to interact personally with the enlisted men, but he was drawn to this one man in particular. Neither of them felt at ease with the hypermasculine military environment. Both shared many interests, and they became close. The friendship was shrouded in secrecy—a double transgression of an officer and an enlisted man and of male affection. I did not see the relationship Dr. D. described as homosexual in nature, but certainly deeply intimate and perhaps homoerotic. They did not maintain the friendship after their military service ended.

It became clear how much Dr. D. hungered for male companionship and intimacy. He said it was not to be found within his psychoanalytic community, which he characterized as intellectual, competitive, secretly disdainful—men going though the motions of camaraderie but no true caring for one another. I was reminded of his story about his own analyst, and we began to look at the implications of that experience for the two of us. He told me he hoped our relationship would continue after termination. Perhaps most importantly, he talked of the complex meanings and feelings of my being his final analytic patient at the end of his career. His emotional charge around my gay relationships began to take on very different meanings for me.

I, in turn, had to acknowledge and examine my feelings of not deserving his attention (let alone affection) as the crises in my life were now past. I was taking care of my sons, working hard, earning school and college tuition for my sons, back fully into my distant, manic coping style. I had become oblivious to Dr. D.'s care and concern for me. I did not give him the space or opportunity to give any voice to how he was feeling toward me. Neither did he make that space for himself. I realized that I had closed him out (as I had so many others) and could see how his complex feelings toward me and our relationship spilled out in a different context. As we now spoke more openly of our feelings for each other, I started to feel my reactions to his aging, my admiration for the way he was living his life, now approaching 80. My admiration had been held too often in silence, as his going on living vigorously was such a painful contrast to the resignation and ending of my young father's life. I wanted to know more about how he maintained his vitality and enthusiasm for life. I wanted to witness his growing older, how he coped with it. I wanted to be with him when he died. I was finally able to give voice to these desires. I felt my own envy of his happiness in his second marriage after the death of his first wife and the despair it engendered in me about ever finding love and companionship in a new relationship, be it with a man or a woman.

I was thrown aback on the dream I had the night before my first session with Dr. D. I could not quite believe that we had somehow ended up living out that dream, my therapy suddenly exposed to colleagues and friends. I had to face that ways in which I had communicated an invincibility, even in the face of the depth of the work I had been doing my therapy; had managed to convey a false sense of resilience and invulnerability that fostered both Dr. D.'s losing track of me as a patient and his feelings of being cut off by me, which I think contributed substantially to the spilling over of his feelings in an enactment.

Our enactment and potential rupture demanded that we consciously attend to the field of desire, love, and intimacy opening between us. Dr. D. and I began to grapple with the task defined for us by my dinner companion—the examination of our unacknowledged and feared affections and desires. In our grapplings were myriad desires evoking fathers and sons, mentors, heterosexual and homosexual longings. The wish for a man's affection and passionate involvement, for the love of and for a man, to bring each of us more fully to life, was more than either of us could bear, even in the deeply committed relationship that we did have. We each unconsciously disavowed our loving desires for the other. Dr. D.'s disavowed desire burst out in his enactment at the gay and lesbian study group.

I would imagine that many readers, as you have watched this case unfold, could see the danger points, read the signals, recognize opportunities for intervention and analysis, or wonder, "Why doesn't he (one of them at least) say something?!" The fact that neither Dr. D. nor I could see or say something underscores the nature and the power of enactments. It was the behavioral manifestation that brought us to the surface, to the possibility of conscious recognition and exploration.

Ten Years Later

> Arrested in their capacity to love, subjects who are under the empire of the dead mother can only aspire to autonomy. Sharing remains forbidden to them. Thus, solitude, which was a situation creating anxiety and to be avoided, changes sign. From the negative it becomes positive. Having previously been shunned, it is now sought after. The subject nestles into it.
>
> Andre Green (1983, p. 156)

Ten years have passed since the enactment I have described above. Dr. D. regained his analytic stance and we continued for another 4 years of productive work together. I was his last patient, our work marking the end of his career. As we approached termination, I wrote up this incident for us to use as a reflection on the many layers of meaning about loss and anticipated endings embedded in our relationship.

Eigen (1998) cautions us that the

> dread of environmental failure is the outer shell of a deeper dread of the failure of one's own [psychological] equipment. The environment tries to make up for what the individual can not do (and vice versa), but never with more than partial success. We rely on each other all life long for help with agonies [and I would add passions] we can not handle. (p. 97)

I was in my late 40s when this enactment with Dr. D. unfolded. I had been with and loved, within my limits, a woman for more than 25 years, but I had never truly relied upon her. I had wished for but never truly expected reliability. I had many friends, but there were limits to my engagement with them as well. Solitude remained my most faithful companion. I was by then having sex quite happily with a man, but I did not open myself fully or rely upon my sexual partners, none of whom had even lived in the same city as I. I had not yet learned to truly love a man or receive the love of a man. Dr. D. was approaching 80 and the end of his career; the love and companionship of a man and his for a man had eluded him as well.

Andre Green's brilliant essay "The Dead Mother" (1983) afforded me particular insight into the process between us. Green describes mothers who are unable to metabolize and transform the losses in their own lives, living then in a profound deadness while still alive. For me, in my growing up, such an account characterized not only my mother but also my extended family. Deadness and depressive withdrawal permeated my early object relations. Vitality seems impossible, even hostile to the "dead" parent. The infant/child cannot bring life to the parent's being; the child often identifies with the parent's lifelessness or imagines himself as the cause of it. What is most desired becomes the deepest threat. Gerson (2003) eloquently evokes the dilemma addressed in Green's essay:

> The baby's lips are made moist by the mother's milk even while the mother's tears dampen them both. It is a confused joining as the good and the bad are internalized simultaneously into a combined experience that occurs prior to splitting ... a whole object that is a product of the deadliness that was ingested together with life. ... In this scenario, where the source of life is mixed with its failure to sustain liveliness ... the closer one gets, the more alone one feels ... the more of life, the more of death. (p.14)

During this period of work with Dr. D., I began to recognize how profoundly I had turned away from others, forming a primary and solitary relationship with my own mind (Corrigan & Gordon, 1995; Winnicott, 1965). Dr. D. and I had lived our lives in the shadow of "dead" mothers (psychically dead and then tragically, actually dead), with fathers who were unable to bring vitality and passion into the lives of their sons or themselves. Neither of us had ever relied on our fathers and had spent our adolescent and adult lives turning primarily to women for love and stability. My previous, suddenly interrupted therapy with a man and my subsequent work with Dr. D. fostered both trust and hope in my relationships with men. My turning to a man as a sexual partner and love object (with some certainty that there would be others in the future) excited and threatened Dr. D.

The reparative work between us was not easy. Dr. D. needed to examine his breach of my privacy and the meanings of his outburst about male love, not to be punished or chastised for it. I needed to remain engaged with Dr. D. rather than withdraw into myself, in spite of the breach, and examine my part in what was unfolding, although at that point I could not have understood this as an enactment. Gradually we were each able to comprehend our own contributions to this enactment, face our parallel fears of loss and rejection, and in so doing begin to find the capacities for love that we each so dearly sought and could finally relish.

The Enlivening (and Deadening) Transference (and Countertransference)

> Yet we often fear all such intense affective experience because passion does not easily dissipate, it always takes us elsewhere, toward promises of eternal union and threats of inevitable separation. Like quicksilver in an exotic alchemy, desire begets desire, and for every vibrant act of creation it inspires, it also reminds us of darkening disillusionments.
>
> Samuel Gerson (2003)

Gerson (2003), speaking of the continual and inevitable meshings of eros and thanatos within interplays of the transference and countertransference, observes that "the more overt expression of this [erotic] force may be most prominently at play in transferences of those patients who feel, or most frequently suffer from, a hollowness at the heart of their vitality." This force was certainly at play in my transference to Dr. D. As can be seen in the enactment between Dr. D. and me, this force can be at play, albeit disavowed, in the countertransference as well. Gerson expands the concept of the erotic transference to that of the "enlivening" transference, suggesting "this idea and terminology because I think it contains the advantage of highlighting the aim of the transference rather than its content or even its object. In the enlivening transference the motive is the evocation of desire itself rather than the object."

Desiring, as Gerson so eloquently underscores, is not so simple. One's erotic hopes are inevitably intertwined with the possibility, the likelihood, and the memories of loss. This is especially true when one's first and foundational loved ones are shot through with unresolved and unspoken grief. For Dr. D. and me alike, our dead mothers (whom we were each relatively successful in reanimating) were partnered with dead fathers, who had little to offer their sons as either vitalizing objects or as role models. It was in my reading of Gerson's talk that I was able to more fully grasp the impasse that had constrained our analytic/erotic relationship. Gerson observes:

> People who have lived with and through their own or others' experience of deadliness must, in their desire to re-create and sustain life, manage a struggle

forever informed by the psychological grip of the deceased in a traumatized mind. … The process [of mourning] that in the end accepts that there is no reparative act through which the dead can be brought to life nor is there any destruction that can join us with the dead. Rather, vitality requires the incorporation of loss in ways that leaves the experience emotionally alive even as the dead themselves are put to rest.

The analytic literature is replete with models and studies of maternal object relations and patterns of mother–infant attachment. The paucity of theory or observation of fathers and their sons impoverishes our work, renders stale our abilities to understand and nourish hetero- and homo-erotic relations or to begin to comprehend the complexities of male masculinities. What Dr. D. and I most wished for and feared was the evocation of passionate attachment and desire of (and as) a man, love—more simply stated—and a coming more fully to life with each other. It was the experience of myself coming more fully alive, not some exterior intrusion or disruption, that was traumatic for me, and so too for Dr. D. We are often too much for ourselves. For years, until the dam burst, neither of us could tolerate the force of that desire within ourselves and thus could not overtly seek it in the other.

"Masculine" Desires

The residues of the dyadic, i.e., preoedipal, attachment of son to father, lie, to a large extent, buried under a forceful repression once adolescence has passed. The profundity of this infantile experience, when roused into emotional reanimation during analysis, remains usually inaccessible in its latent intensity by verbalization alone. It finds expression via affect-motor channels, such as uncontrollable weeping and sobbing, when the patient is tormented by overwhelming feelings of love and loss in relation to the dyadic father.

Peter Blos (1985, pp. 48–49)

As I reviewed my session notes in preparation for writing this chapter, I was shocked to see the frequency of father–son themes and motifs of revitalization in my first few years of work with Dr. D. During that time I dreamt of my previous therapist coming to a workshop I was leading. He was so ill that I did not recognize him. He had come to my workshop in the hope that I would help him fight his illness and not give up. While commenting on my obvious and continuing concern for the impact the lawsuit was having on my former therapist, Dr. D. interpreted this dream in the context of my not giving up or letting go of hope to revitalize my marriage. There was no interpretation or association (from either of us) to our therapeutic relationship or of my wishes for his role in revitalizing me or his wishes that I was revitalizing him. I had numerous dreams of bringing one or another of my sons to sessions. At one point, as I became quite severely depressed following my marital separation, I became deeply worried for my sons, who stayed with me. As I saw one becoming overly concerned (and feeling responsible) for my well-being, I actually took him to a session. I introduced him to Dr. D. as "the guy who is taking care of me so that you don't have to," and left him in the waiting room during my session. Dr. D. responded to all of this by admiring my determination to take care of my sons. If he ever recognized the transference implications of all of this, he did not say so or interpret my transference. The impact of loss on my psyche was subject to frequent and important interpretation. We spoke often of our mothers and the continuing conscious and unconscious influences of our maternal relations, but rarely did we speak of our fathers. Our developing relationship to each other *as men* seemed taken for granted, not worthy of comment or scrutiny.

Working and writing before the era of acknowledging the richness of countertransference and mutual enactment, Blos (1985), nearly alone in his writing of fathers and sons, stressed that when the transferences of the preoedipal relations (or lack thereof) emerged in treatment they would typically "require affecto-motor expressions before the symbolic process via verbal communication can serve the work of insight and reconstruction" (p. 49). The father–son transferences that Dr. D. and I played out for years were of an "affecto-motor" deadening. Only with Dr. D.'s "affecto-motor" outburst in the gay and lesbian study group did our passions intrude into our conscious relations. Blos stresses that "the little boy seeks by active and persistent solicitation the father's approval, recognition, and confirmation, thus establishing a libidinal bond of a profound and lasting kind" (p. 11), which he refers to as a "blessing" conferred by the father upon the son.

Within the paucity of discussions of the father in the psychoanalytic literature (Blos, 1985; Britton, 1989; Diamond, 1997, 1998; Herzog, 2001, 2005; Trowell & Etchegoyen, 2002), most attention is paid to his role and functions in the oedipal conflicts and resolutions. Barrows and Barrows (2002) examine the role of the father in the transgenerational impact of losses, observing that "the father's ability to support the child [in the face of loss] ... will be profoundly influenced by his own history, particularly how he has dealt with losses in his own life" (p. 163). Dr. D. and I worked deeply within the terrain of maternal loss, the psychic impacts of our "dead" mothers. What we could not recognize was the even more profound impact of our "dead" fathers, neither of whom had been able to metabolize the losses in their own childhoods or adult lives. The actual and psychic losses of our fathers were even more unbearable than those of our mothers. To turn to each other as men for sustenance and revitalization was unimaginable, unsanctioned. Unimaginable and unsanctioned as these desires were, while deadened, they did not die but finally erupted back into our lives through our enactment.

Lessons From Our Enactment

> Each has learned from infancy, long before the words were there for the saying, how to appeal, coerce, clarify, and dissimulate through the signals of body language, gestures, facial expression, and vocal qualities … whether we are analyst or patient, our deepest hopes for what we may find the world to be, as well as our worst fears of what it will be, reflect our transference expectancies as shaped by our developmental past.
>
> James McLaughlin (2005, p. 187)

With these poetic words, McLaughlin captures the delicate and often unconscious underbelly of analytic relationships that often erupt in transferential and counter-transferential enactments. No one has written more extensively or openly about transference, counter-transference, therapeutic impasse, and enactment than McLaughlin (McLaughlin, 1987, 1991, 1994, 2005; see also Chodorow, 2007; Cornell, 2005). I am indebted to his work and the insights it offered to the complex dynamics that enveloped Dr. D. and me.

Writing about enactments has necessitated analysts to be willing to write quite openly about themselves and their own intrapsychic conflicts, characterological blind spots, and unconscious vulnerabilities, demonstrating courage on the part of the authors and introducing a personal frankness and level of self-examination to psychoanalytic writing seldom seen since Freud and Ferenczi. While we still tend to hope for the awareness and insight afforded by countertransference rather than the unconscious blindness of counter-transferential enactments, we seem to be coming to terms with the frequency and inevitability of enactments and seeing the challenge and opportunity embedded in enactment.

The enactment between Dr. D. and me could have been seen as an especially egregious error, an acting out on the part of Dr. D. That was certainly my first reaction to it, as I felt myself to be a victim rather than an unwitting participant. In our willingness to "face the music" Dr. D. and I learned about ourselves and each other. In the rule-bound, litigious atmosphere of our current era, Dr. D.'s behavior could all too easily have been cast as a violation of my confidentiality (which it was), an irreversible ethical breach or even act of malpractice (which it was not). In my own work as a consultant and trainer, therapists often bring me cases of impasse, counter-transferential knots, failure, or enactment, often accompanied by shame or anxieties of ethical charges or a lawsuit. What so often unfolds in the exploration of these therapeutic dilemmas is some form of unconscious enactment between therapist and patient. When the enactment is unrecognized, I suspect it is all too often further acted out in the arenas of ethical charges, law suits, or premature terminations (Elkins, 1992; Kantrowitz, 1996).

Over the course of many painful, bluntly honest sessions, my work with Dr. D. again deepened, my self-understanding grew, my capacity to sustain a passionate attachment in the face of severe disappointment became solidified. This was an opportunity for me to see Dr. D. struggle with a serious error and come alive more strongly and richly on my behalf and his own. In so doing, he provided me with a startling contrast to repeatedly watching my parents (especially my father) disintegrate, withdraw, or become avoidant in the face of conflict, disappointment, and potential loss. With the challenge and understanding offered me by my dinner companion that one night, I did not retreat into myself this time. I did not retreat but came at Dr. D. again and again with the expectation that we understand what this meant for each of us. I had broken ranks with my past and with my standard defenses of providing reason and comfort to others by sustaining this confrontation and engagement with Dr. D.

The relationship with the man I was seeing at the time of the events I relate here did not last, but the impact and meaning of what happened between Dr. D. and me has lasted and has grown in significance. It fundamentally changed what I knew to be possible between men. Although sex had always been relatively easy for me, vulnerability and commitment (especially with men) were not. With Dr. D. that began to change, and the changes continue. While still in treatment with Dr. D. I met another man, also a father, who has become the partner of my life; we have gradually forged a relationship that in the years of my analysis I would not have thought possible.

The influence of this experience with Dr. D. has had perhaps even more profound influences on my thinking and my work as a psychotherapist than on me as a person (written as though those two are somehow separable). Enactments within the therapeutic relationship may carry the potential for rupture and disaster; they also carry the vibrant possibilities for mutual transformation. I have come to be acutely aware and respectful of the transferential vulnerabilities therapist and client alike bring to our therapeutic endeavors when we work at depth and at the edges of our own intimate capacities. I have come to see the unconscious hope and potential embedded in these experiences when therapist and patient both have the commitment to face themselves and each other.

Bollas (1999) has written of the three different psychic positions of the oedipal triangle, three differing forms of knowledge—the child, the mother, the father. He delineates the maternal and paternal orders of knowledge and analytic intervention (while delinking the functions from the behaviors of mothers and fathers). A complete analysis, Bollas argues, creates room for all three functions, not valorizing one form of knowing over another:

> It requires the capacity to operate according to the three elements of authoring and knowing: a celebration of the dreamer, the infant, the child, the producer of vivid ideas; a capacity to receive life and bear a not knowing about what is taking place even though a profound mulling over and playing is the medium of such reception [the maternal order]; and finally, a search for the truth that calls for judgment [the paternal order]. (p. 44)

The facing and resolving of the enactment between Dr. D. and me required a fundamental shift in our working relationship to that of the paternal order, truth and judgment.

Long influenced by the work of Winnicott, as well as mother–infant and attachment theorists (not to mention my unconscious identification with my mother, limited and problematic though it was), my working style had a deeply maternal orientation. Mothers seemed quite obviously more necessary and useful than fathers. Even as I struggled in my own supervision, my reading, and my own writing (Cornell & Bonds-White, 2001) with the limits of the maternal and attachment models, I did not have an experiential base upon which to anchor a different stance. As I wrestled with the implications of our enactment and finally accepted my need for the paternal and the vitalization it engendered, my clinical position was able to evolve. Having long idealized myself in life and in work as a penultimate provider of a "secure" base, I began to appreciate and articulate the need for a "vital" base in the therapeutic relationship (Cornell, 2001, 2003). I stopped avoiding or apologizing for my maleness. I have learned to appreciate what particular vitalities maleness can bring to male and female clients alike.

Conclusion

> I emphasize how masculinity is forged from the boy's earliest wishes to be both his mother and his father, and how these early identifications require adaptations and accommodations throughout the life span. I argue that a male's gendered ideals and the sense of his masculinity, as well as the ambiguities of his gender, are continually being reworked throughout his life.
>
> Michael Diamond (2006, pp.100–101)

Dr. D. and I decided that should the right circumstances arise I would publish articles based on the narrative that I originally wrote as part of our termination process. We wanted to draw from our experience to explore both the disruptive impact of disavowed desires in both therapist and patient as well as the intimate and healing potentials of the emergence of such passions. Written from the point of view of the patient rather than the therapist, this chapter is centered on the disavowal and unmanageability of "positive" rather than "negative" feelings, and is descriptive of the traumatic intrusiveness of one's internal experience and passionate desires rather than the environmental intrusions and violations that we most often describe and relate to as traumatic. I think my experience mirrors the hopes and fears of many men—"hetero"-sexual, "homo"-sexual, and those on the infinite continuum between those polarities—for the erotic vitality of relations among men.

Psychoanalysts and psychotherapists have finally begun to recognize that heterosexuality, "maleness," "masculinity," gender, and sexual object choices are not monolithic and cannot be grasped by binary categorizations (Chodorow, 1992; Diamond, 2006; Dimen & Goldner, 2005; Fogel, 2006; Harris, 2005; Person, 2006). Is it useful or relevant to declare the love and passion that Dr. D. and I were finally able to bring to life between us as heterosexual or homosexual? I think not. I am quite certain that most who know one or the other of us would describe us as "masculine." I say, "So what?" The masculinities that Dr. D. and I inhabited most of our lives and then brought to each other were impoverished, deadened—profoundly shaped and constrained by our histories with our own fathers and perhaps even more deeply by social and professional biases.

I write here the story of myself as a patient, but what I learned for myself as a therapist was profound. I learned anew and at a more fundamental level through my experience of this enactment of the power of unconscious, disavowed desires and of passionate, loving engagement. I acquired a deep and abiding respect for the fundamental humanity of all of us in this practice of psychoanalysis, psychotherapy, counseling, and human relations work. I internalized a deep and abiding regard for the unstoppable, and often disruptive, force of our unconscious passions. I learned a more realistic meaning of love and commitment and of passionate attachments between men. I still love solitude and still have access to my manic and idealizing defenses, but now other options for coping and closeness are more readily available. I remain forever seduced by my mind and the eloquent minds of others, but there is more compelling space in my experience of life and our work for the uncertain, for the mistaken, for human troubles, for needing and learning together, for honesty and self-scrutiny, for loving and being loved.

Acknowledgment

A version of this chapter originally appeared in Mann, D. and Cunningham, V., *The Past in the Present: Therapy Enactments and the Return of Trauma* (London: Routledge, 2009), pp. 82–101. Reprinted with permission.

References

Barrows, P., & Barrows, K. (2002). Fathers and the transgenerational impact of loss. In J. Trowell & A. Etchegoyen (Eds.), *The Importance of Fathers: A Psychoanalytic Re-evaluation* (pp. 161–171). New York: Routledge.

Blos, P. (1985). *Son and Father: Before and Beyond the Oedipus Complex.* New York: Free Press.

Bollas, C. (1989). *Forces of Destiny.* London: Free Association Books.

Bollas, C. (1999). *The Mystery of Things.* London: Routledge.

Britton, R. (1989). The missing link: Parental sexuality in the oedipus complex. In R. Britton, M. Feldman, & E. O'Shaughnessy (Eds.), *The Oedipus Complex Today* (pp. 83–102). London: Karnac.

Chodorow, N. (1992). Heterosexuality as a compromise formation: Reflections on the psychoanalytic theory of sexual development. *Psychoanalysis and Contemporary Thought, 15,* 267–304.

Chodorow, N. (2007). Book review essay: McLaughlin's *The Healer's Bent: Solitude and Dialogue in the Clinical Encounter*. *Psychoanalytic Quarterly, 76,* 617–630.

Cornell, W. F. (2001). There ain't no cure without sex: The provision of a "vital base." *Transactional Analysis Journal, 31,* 233–239.

Cornell, W. F. (2003). The impassioned body: Erotic vitality and disturbance in psychotherapy. *British Gestalt Journal, 12,* 92–104.

Cornell, W. F. (2005). Deep in the shed: An analyst's mind at work. Introduction to J. T. McLaughlin, *The Healer's Bent: Solitude and Dialogue in the Clinical Encounter,* W. F. Cornell (Ed.) (pp. 1–16). Hillsdale, NJ: Analytic Press.

Cornell, W. F. (2009). Loves and losses: Enactments in the disavowal of intimate desires. In D. Mann & V. Cunningham (Eds.), *The Past in the Present: Therapy Enactments and the Return of Trauma.* London: Routledge.

Cornell, W. F., & Bonds-White, F. (2001). Therapeutic relatedness in transactional analysis: The truth of love or the love of the truth. *Transactional Analysis Journal, 31,* 71–83.

Diamond, M. J. (1997). Boys to men: The maturing of masculine gender identity through paternal watchful protectiveness. *Gender and Psychoanalysis, 2,* 443–468.

Diamond, M. J. (1998). Fathers with sons: Psychoanalytic perspectives on "good enough" fathering through the life cycle. *Gender and Psychoanalysis, 3,* 243–299.

Diamond, M. J. (2006). Masculinity unraveled: The roots of male gender identity and the shifting of male ego ideals throughout life. *Journal of the American Psychoanalytic Association, 54*(4), 1099–1130.

Dimen, M., & Goldner, V. (2005). Gender and sexuality. In E. S. Person, A. M. Cooper, & G. O. Gabbard (Eds.), *APPI Textbook of Psychoanalysis* (pp. 96–113). Washington, DC: American Psychiatric Press.

Eigen, M. (1998). *The Psychoanalytic Mystic.* Binghamton, NY: ESF Publishers.

Elkins, S. N. (1992). *Resolving Impasses in Therapeutic Relationships.* New York: Guilford.

Fogel, G. I. (2006). Riddles of masculinity: Gender, bisexuality, and thirdness. *Journal of the American Psychoanalytic Association, 54,* 1139–1163.

Gerson, S. (2003, May 3). *The enlivening transference and the shadow of deadliness.* Paper delivered to the Boston Psychoanalytic Society and Institute.

Green, A. (1983/1986). The dead mother. In *On Private Madness.* Madison, CT: International Universities Press.

Harris, A. (2005). *Gender as Soft Assembly.* Hillsdale, NJ: Analytic Press.

Herzog, J. M. (2001). *Father Hunger.* Hillsdale, NJ: Analytic Press.

Herzog, J. M. (2005). Triadic reality and the capacity to love. *Psychoanalytic Quarterly, 74,* 1029–1052.

Kantrowitz, J. L. (1996). *The Patient's Impact on the Analyst.* Hillsdale, NJ: Analytic Press.

Mann, D., & Cunningham. V. (Eds.). (2009). *The Past in the Present: Therapy Enactments and the Return of Trauma*. London: Routledge.

Maroda, K. (1991). *The Power of Countertransference: Innovations in Analytic Technique*. Chichester, UK: Wiley.

McLaughlin, J. T. (1987). The play of transference: Some reflections on enactment in the psychoanalytic situation. *Journal of the American Psychoanalytic Association, 35*, 557–582.

McLaughlin, J. T. (1991). Clinical and theoretical aspects of enactment. *Journal of the American Psychoanalytic Association, 39*, 595–614.

McLaughlin, J. T. (1994, March 5). *Analytic impasse: The interplay of dyadic transferences*. Paper presented to the Karen Horney Psychoanalytic Institute and Center and the Association for the Advancement of Psychoanalysis.

McLaughlin, J. T. (2005). *The Healer's Bent: Solitude and Dialogue in the Clinical Encounter*. W. F. Cornell (Ed.). Hillsdale, NJ: Analytic Press.

Ogden, T. H. (2005). *The Art of Psychoanalysis*. London: Routledge.

Person, E. S. (2006). Masculinites, plural. *Journal of the American Psychoanalytic Association, 54*, 1165–1186.

Sandler, J. (1976). Actualization and object relationships. *Journal of the Philadelphia Association of Psychoanalysis, 3*, 59–70.

Stein, M. (1981). The unobjectionable part of the transference. *Journal of the American Psychoanalytic Association, 29*, 869–892.

Trowell, J., & Etchegoyen, A. (2002). *The Importance of Fathers: A Psychoanalytic Re-evaluation*. New York: Routledge.

8

David and Jonathan

Eyal Rozmarin

In June 2007 the *Journal of the American Psychoanalytic Association* (*JAPA*) hosted an online colloquium on the topic of masculinity. One of the dynamics that emerged during the colloquium was a disagreement between some participants who called for the engagement of postmodern perspectives on the concepts of gender and gender identity, and others who expressed doubt or reluctance toward the idea and asked, instead, that the discussion be carried out using what they called "plain talk." Plain talk was portrayed as the experience-near language of patients and analysts in the clinical situation; plain talk, as opposed to critique-oriented theoretical abstractions that in the view of these participants do not figure prominently in individuals' narratives or the psychoanalytic relationship. The calls for plain talk evoked strong reactions. Those who wished to examine the notion of masculinity through a critical lens argued that the resistance encountered was fear-based and defensive. In return, there were calls for civility, even censorship. There was no doubt, the argument had turned into a heated conflict. Adrienne Harris, one of the panelists, remarked at that point:

> I think that the intensity of the process reflects the degree to which masculinity has been in some degree off-limits for discussion or critique or elaboration. The study of gender has been for a century the study of femininity and this means that many ideas brew, grow, get elaborated and worked on, over time, by generations of women analysts who agreed and disagreed and worked carefully on these topics. A critical discourse on masculinity has been so silenced that it's perhaps not surprising that the topic breaks open and the eruptions into speech are not so well regulated. (Harris, personal communication*)

---

* According to the rules of *JAPA* online colloquiums, the content of individuals' postings can be quoted only by permission, as personal communication. For this reason the above description of the colloquium process does not employ more detailed, attributed references.

Eruptions into speech and about speech, it might be added; since in the end what had happened in this *JAPA* colloquium was that a discussion about masculinity turned into a discussion about discursive practices and modes of speech—a discussion about the very possibility and conditions for having a discussion. And once the genie was out of the bottle there was no way of putting it back in. It has been demonstrated once again how much the appearance of clarity and intelligibility depends, perhaps paradoxically, on the assertion of unquestioned premises.

A closer look at the colloquium material reveals, besides the aimed-for engagement with the notion of masculinity, two additional concepts that took a central if less deliberately intended part in the unfolding exchange. First, lurking on the margin of the discussion about gender was the question of sexuality, or more accurately sexual orientation. Inevitably so since, as has been widely argued by gender theorists across disciplines (Benjamin, 1995; Butler, 1997; Corbett, 2001a, 2001b; Harris, 2005; Dimen, 2003; Goldner, 2003), most conceptions of gender and gender difference have been traditionally and to a large extent still are anchored on the premise of cross-gender, that is heterosexuality. To the same extent, same-gender, that is homosexuality, has posed a theoretical and practical challenge to the discourse of gender difference and the very definition of gender. This challenge manifested both explicitly and implicitly in the back and forth that took place in the *JAPA* colloquium. In what was perhaps the most lucid of these manifestations, one of the participants gave his posting the title "Pomo-sense and homo-sense," alluding to the common association between postmodernism and queer theory, and their critique of, among other domains of regulatory discourse, notions of sexuality and gender. Pomo-sense and homo-sense indeed aim to critique what is perceived at a given time and place as common-sense the plain, uncritical, normative talk of the collective.

Further, as the discussion about gender and sexuality unfolded, the concept of family also emerged. In an echo of one of Freud's own considerations of the issue (Freud, 1935), this concept appeared in colloquium in the figure of a mother concerned about her homosexual son's ability to have family and children. Harris (personal communication) commented that such a view is in our place and time uninformed, if not anachronistic. Yet as anyone who has read a newspaper in the past decade or so could testify, homosexual unions still appear to many today as the most dangerous challenge to the very essence, that is to what mainstream social norm decrees to be the legitimate form, of the family. It seemed that some uncertainty, if not concern, regarding the institution of the family stirred between the lines of this psychoanalytic colloquium when the notion of masculinity crossed paths with the idea of sexuality within the same gender.

Masculinity, the possibility of discourse, and in the wings heterosexuality, homosexuality, and the family, all were exchanged and argued in a vibrant online discussion. And during that same period, in my office, two of my patients (recently married) told me about their weddings. David married his girlfriend Abigail in a religious ceremony, followed by a big celebration hosted by proud parents. Jonathan married his boyfriend Ronen in Montreal's city hall, in the company of close friends. At the party a few weeks later there were many others, including his family, but his new husband's parents who reject their son's sexual preference refused to participate. Two men starting a family, with some obvious differences, having to do with how, where, and by whom their union is accepted. A straight man fully embraced by family, religion, and social milieu, of which he now seems to be a new kind of privileged member. A gay man whose marriage is a strained puzzle with pieces spread across time and space, some impossible, some painfully missing.

This chapter was born of my effort to make sense of the views exchanged among psychoanalysts at the *JAPA* online colloquium, while having the intimate experience that is psychoanalysis with Jonathan and David. It was born, more specifically, of my strong feeling that if the call for "plain talk" was conservatism masquerading as straightforwardness, *straight* forward indeed, the purely political-forward antithesis also failed to do these two men justice. To say, as psychoanalysis traditionally has, that the truth lies primarily in the subject and his relations with others is to be uncritically ideological. It is to accept the complex set of norms that underlie subjective and intersubjective experience without question, a common, and to my mind, justified critique leveled at psychoanalysis. But to say, on the other hand, that subjectivity is solely an effect of social forces is both simplistic and unethical. Simplistic since, as Foucault (1980) for example argued, social discourse is at any given time disorderly, paradoxical, and far from total, a multiplicity that leaves open as much as it defines and limits. Unethical, since locating all meaning-making power in the social realm denies human experience and robs the subject of both agency and responsibility.

As I sat in my room with David and Jonathan, the puzzle again became evident: we are all founded in the deepest sense in what social discourse enables. Language and norm open up and foreclose; they provide the conditions according to which our experiences can be had and make sense, or must remain senseless and nameless. Yet in steps as large as the French Revolution or as small as falling in love, individuals come up against such conditions—clauses in the social contract that we must all continuously sign—and break them. And when conditions break, there is the potential for both "normal" and "abnormal," normative and other, to see through the boundaries that antagonize their experiences toward new possibilities. Case in point, here was between us, in what turned out to be anything but certain terms, one of the most poignant and contested features of the social contact these days, the institution of marriage.

But first things first; it is not David's or Jonathan's weddings, nor their subsequent marriages that I would like to begin with. It is rather the way in which they were conceived, or more accurately, what happened in the space between proposal and acceptance. A few months earlier, both of these men brought their stories to therapy, making me part of the plot, calling on me to take a position. Needless to say, masculinity, sexuality, and family were all there, being considered and negotiated. But as happened in the *JAPA* colloquium, no less debated between these men and myself was the possibility of discourse itself, the potentials and risks, desire and resistance to our having a conversation about their experience. And there were between the two men dramatic differences.

Jonathan is a 28-year-old Israeli who lives in New York. He met his future husband on a visit to Israel. Having just come out of a string of disappointing affairs, it was a time in his life where he enjoyed being single and experimenting with the plenty New York has to offer; he was not looking for a relationship. But when he met Ronen, it was special. Within a few months Ronen came to live with him. Not long after, Jonathan came into my office and said, "We are going to get married!" It turned out that on a mundane weekend evening, Ronen asked, "Do you think we should get married?" "Of course," Jonathan replied, and he took out his wireless smartphone. By the time he and I met the next evening, they had already set a date and figured out the entire procedure.

I felt happy for him and was quick to say so. But at the same time it all seemed to me too rushed, too matter-of-fact; and I found myself uneasy and worried. It was true that Jonathan seemed happier than ever. This relationship was clearly good for him. Yet I could not see why there was such a rush to make it formal, except perhaps to counteract deep anxieties left in him by parents whose love was never certain. We should discuss this, I thought; explore the anxieties that had to be so fiercely overridden by action. Action, moreover, that felt more like a plan for war than a pleasurable stage in the progression of a romantic union. Toward the end of the session I decided to speak: "It's a bit fast, don't you think?" I said. Jonathan replied: "No, I don't think so. We love each other, what is there to wait for?" To that, I did not have a good answer. The plan proceeded. But if he did not wish to discuss his marriage, Jonathan very much wanted to share it. And share it we did, all the way to their wedding party, to which I was invited, and happily attended.

David, my other patient, has just turned 35. He has also been unhappy in love, alone, or ambivalent about the women he had been dating. But when he met Abigail the affair quickly became serious. A few months in, while on a romantic getaway, Abigail brought up the topic of marriage. She did it very much like Ronen did, she asked David if he thought that they should, at some point, if all goes well, get married. But David's response was different: he froze, for a long moment he could not say a word or feel anything. When he finally came back to his senses, all he felt was intense anger and a deep sense of betrayal. "What do you think happened to you?" I asked, confused by what seemed like a paradoxical reaction. "We had such a beautiful love," he said, "a love that is only ours. And now she wants to bring all of society between us!" I was surprised by the violence of his feelings, but I could understand his sentiment. "I think I know what you mean," I said. "Marriage really is where love between two people becomes the affair of society." "Yes," David said, "we need to talk about it."

David and Abigail got into an earnest dialogue about the meaning of marriage. During that time he used our sessions in an effort to understand himself, to understand her, and to make sense of their sudden conflict. He loved Abigail and respected her wishes, but what she saw as promising he saw as dangerous. He needed to trust that their relationship could withstand what seemed to him an invitation to overpowering intrusion. He gained this trust when Abigail told him, out of love, not out of exasperation, that if he needed to remain unmarried in order to feel safe, she would not dream of insisting.

Two very different spaces between proposal and acceptance, and likewise, two different spaces opening up, or not, in therapy. For Jonathan, question and answer grip each other like two sailors on a small boat on the high seas, facing a storm they could only survive together. And in such an emergency, resistance to anything but me immediately joining, as if saying you're either with us or against us, and if you're with us, jump on board, without questions seemed prudent. No time or place for a conversation. For David the question itself summoned the prospect of a dreadful storm, of which a positive answer is the assured forecast. What he asks of his future spouse, and of me, is to assure him that the storm could be weathered. But for him to feel so, neither she nor I can jump on board too quickly. We must all first explore the contingencies, then take the right side in a battle where the individual and society are antagonistic. As if he is saying: if you're with us without questioning, you must be against us! We have to talk until we understand each other. Why this radical difference?

There are differences between these two men that usually come under the term "psychological." These are, of course, relevant. During the years of our work together, I have come to expect quick decisions from Jonathan, although it often turned out that he secretly went through a long process of deliberation beforehand. In some crucial aspects of his life, particularly where there was a potential for him to be in need but at odds with the support of others, Jonathan did not invite anyone, including his therapist, to participate in his deliberations. But as he went through them he gathered clues as to how the people who mattered might approach his dilemmas, so that when a decision was reached, the reaction could be anticipated. What he could not ascertain with the power of his intelligence he achieved with a decisiveness that put the other in a take-it-or-leave-it position. There were no gray areas; at the end of the day, if you did not agree with him he would have to do without you and you without him.

And so it was often the case that our work together centered on understanding his decisions and their motivations in retrospect, not always an easy position for me to inhabit. It began to make sense once I realized that in this dynamic of ours I had been facing the hopeful yet soberly anxious repetition of an ultimate challenge. The deed was done; any discussion about it could have been carried out either from a position of doubt or acceptance. And there was a thin line between the former and failing the challenge. I was continuously tested; this was how Jonathan knew he could trust me. In regard to his marriage, by the time he decided to marry Ronen he had already introduced him to me in many ways, including in person, and he knew that I liked him. He also knew based on our history together that given a stark choice to join or abandon him in such an important decision, I would most certainly join him. This was the core of our corrective contract.

David needed the opposite; he needed me to be patient and reflective, without taking a position. I have learned during our work together that the worst I could do with him was to pull aggressively toward any given direction, to suggest that I had an agenda. If I did, he would simply lose his train of thought, or otherwise dissociate. What I could do with him was to try and expand the range of possibilities for subjective experience, fill out the spaces between unnamed feelings and abstract, often foreign or hostile ideas about how things should be. When, as on the occasion of the marriage proposal, an unsettling event brought about a surge of strong emotions that felt to him strange and alien, my role was to stay calm and think things through with him, to give his experience words and syntax, to make it legitimate.

It would not be a psychoanalytic innovation to say that to an important extent, David and Jonathan were both struggling to be men other than their fathers, and in their struggle, looking to our relationship to establish alternative modes of being and relating as gendered individuals. But if there were significant differences between the two of them and what they asked of me, having to do with who their fathers were and how they gave or did not give what their sons needed, it seems to me that both of them needed, before anything else, to feel in me a certain kind of loyalty. For Jonathan, whose father was too self-absorbed to attend to his son in a reliable manner and had repeatedly evoked and betrayed his deepest yearnings, my loyalty was measured by the passion of my involvement and the consistency of my presence. Most of all it was measured by my accepting his desires and decisions, but doing so not from a position of indifference or self-interest, but from one of passionate caring. For David, who was raised to realize his father's ambitions, insulted and beaten whenever he did not make a good grade in school, my loyalty was measured by my willingness to accept him no matter how confused or uncertain. But for him there was a need for us to be at some distance from each other. There was a buffer zone beyond which I had to stay, that if I were to cross it my presence would materialize too vividly and would become threatening. Perhaps it would be to the point to give this buffer zone its old wartime name, we had to have between us a no man's land where my desire could not enter. There was, in fact, a no-man's-land between Jonathan and myself as well; only with him it was one prohibitive of joint deliberation.

Yet, with both David and Jonathan, what appeared between us as no man's land had to do with more than the triangulation between father, son and (male) therapist. It also had to do, I strongly believe, with the fact that all of our relationships, past, present, and potential, as when these two men came upon the prospect of marriage and brought it into their relationship with me, are formed, beyond the register of intersubjectivity, in the register of collective social discourse. It is a register in which Jonathan, a gay man, determined to marry another gay man, and in that gesture take a precarious position vis-à-vis the complex social discourse through which love relations are made intelligible and legitimate; a register in which David, a straight man, hesitated to marry a woman for fear of being crushed under the weight of the tradition inherent—for him—in that gesture. It is the register, in other words, in which the meaning of subjective life clearly appears, in direct relation, to social possibilities and restrictions. In this register, what Jonathan aspired for David feared; what propelled Jonathan from the outside as an alluring frontier, threatened David from the inside like the gravitation of an overdetermined center. Yet, all the same, in this register, David trusted the two of us to be able to think and talk about it, while Jonathan felt it could only work against him. Why is it?

We have in psychoanalysis an almost absolute faith in thought; we believe that thought is better than thoughtless action. Even as we, hopefully, abandon the premise that what the analyst thinks is true and what the patient refuses to think is a sign of pathology, we still believe—in contemporary terms—that thirdness, that is, collaborative thought, is better than enactment. But what these two stories perhaps demonstrate is that what appears to some of us as an ideal, the freedom of reflection from a third position, can appear to others as a nightmare of hostility and antagonism. If David had trust in our ability to think together about his reality, Jonathan had about this prospect a profound sense of danger. Rightfully, since in many ways, the discourse we could have used does not allow his love a positive social meaning. If we were to seriously talk, we could not have ignored the many forms of shame and abjection evoked regarding homosexual love in history and contemporary politics. We could not have reflected about his motives except for within a framework that makes them questionable in principle. We could have talked about his wishes from a position of informed defiance, to strive for resignification, as Judith Butler (1997) would have it. But Jonathan did not wish to take a personal journey through queer and postmodern theory. He wanted to take a subjective stand that still does not have good and stable discursive coordinates. In this regard, talking would have been an adversary. If he wanted to get there, resistance was necessary, he had to keep on rowing. David felt differently because, in his case, the two of us thinking together did not imply existential danger. It did not necessitate straying into discursive terrains that so thoroughly unsettle his subject-position, or the possibility of his union. For him, discourse held the promise of intelligibility and reason. He did not see collective thought—in general, or as it would have manifested in our relationship—as hostile to his project, even as he was paralyzed with dread of the collective pressure gathering around him.

To recall the *JAPA* colloquium described earlier, the immediate lesson regarding "plain talk" is obvious and by now far from revolutionary; the allusion or illusion of plain talk is the luxury of those whose position normative discourse renders sensible. For Jonathan and me there was no option for a straightforward discussion about his wish to marry; it could have been a complicated and painful one, full of doubt, or action. The smart and sensitive man that he is, Jonathan realized that much, without words, and chose the latter. But, and here Harris's words quoted above resonate with full force, David's situation was also far from simple. Perhaps for this heterosexual man the prospect and meaning of marriage was even more confusing. Paradoxically, it seems that Jonathan, right at the margins of legitimacy and outside most forms of mainstream discourse, had a greater sense of subjective freedom than David had, trapped as he was—and felt—in the contracting heart of normativity. Somehow, Jonathan was clearer, less afraid, on a frontier where, all the same, meanings lurked on the horizon, strange and threatening. It might be that if there are discursive possibilities hostile or foreclosed for homosexual men, if basic tenets of their existence among others remain uncertain, the same is true for heterosexual men, insidiously so, in other registers—the unconscious, haunting ghosts of normative, unquestionable gender.

Not long ago, while talking about some aspects of his responsibility as a new husband, David became suspicious about my line of interrogation. Uncharacteristically impatient, looking as if he was all of a sudden hurt, he abruptly stopped our conversation and asked, "Are you asking all these questions because you want to guide me toward a certain conclusion, or do you really not understand what bothers me?" Surprised, I replied, "What makes you ask that?" I could not see what it was about my questions that fazed him. "I know we are here to explore everything," he said, "but I am a man and you are a man and there are things that men understand about each other without asking." What had been addressed by my questions at that time was seemingly a rather straightforward dilemma: his willingness to entertain personal desires that in his mind did not sit well with his wish to be considered the new family's main provider. It seemed as if I should have realized without too many words that losing this position would be very difficult for him. Yet curiously, I felt I did. My questions were, in fact, directed for him to explore these feelings.

In retrospect, I think it was precisely this: the difficulty and the conflict it inspired should have been recognized but not explicitly articulated. There should have been between us a secret bond, part of which involved mutual recognition of male wounds too raw to be exposed and treated. The thought that it was possible we did not share this secret bond in the mere fact of our common gender made him nervous. It was as if he and I were supposed to be burdened the same way and like good soldiers march along together without paying the heaviness of our load too much attention. Was this predicament, the doomed-to-silence bearing of the world's weight on his shoulders, the one he feared when Abigail proposed marriage?

I think it was. Once he got married David felt inducted into a new realm of social regulation. If previously his love with Abigail was a private matter, now he was compelled by a new set of rules, which he felt he had no choice but to accept without questioning. This unavoidable destiny, the gravitation of what appeared to him as common matrimonial law, is precisely what he dreaded. But as unavoidable as this destiny seemed to him, he somehow knew all men were so fated. Aren't all men afraid to marry? Is it not because all of them learn, from loud cultural references and subtle man-to-man hints, that marriage is, among other things, a special kind of servitude that in the end must be proudly if reluctantly accepted? But if so, there is in this inevitable male bondage the consolation of an intimate togetherness. Chosen soldiers of society bearing the weight of family norms like brothers in arms, shoulder to shoulder. On some level, David expected to feel that much with me, he expected to recognize both of us inside a discourse that makes sense—common sense—of both of us as men similarly positioned in the social order, similarly conditioned, similarly interpellated. When he did not, he was shaken. All of a sudden his fears overlapped with those of Jonathan; our discourse became suspicious, he could not afford to be questioned.

It would be, of course, grossly mistaken to portray a simple picture of the relationships between gender, sexuality, family, and normative social discourse, in general or as they are engaged in the experience of any particular subject. But a raw sketch applied to an admittedly limited range can sometimes be useful. What I hope to have so far demonstrated is some of the contingencies I encountered with two of my male patients when we attempted to collaborate in making sense of their experiences approaching and entering the institution of marriage. As happened in the exchange between scholars that took place in the *JAPA* colloquium, addressing the notions of gender, sexuality, and family brought up questions about the very nature and possibility of discourse between us. My gay patient, about to marry another man, refused to talk about it. I suggested that his reluctance reflected a sense of reality where there is no discourse that is friendly enough to his project. My straight patient, about to marry a woman, wanted to talk. He, I suggested, felt that the discourse available to us as two individual members of the collective could make his experience sensible. But, as I think it was revealed, his feeling that we shared a common sense depended on a conviction—firm if, or because, unarticulated—that we had between us an implicit male agreement, a shared collective

unconscious of sorts where men take upon themselves a common burden in return for unquestioned comradery, for an assumption of essential sameness. When this assumption frayed, common discourse became
distrustful and togetherness gave way to confusion and vigilance. It was
almost as if by making David feel that we did not share an unspoken bond,
where, in his case, certain aspects of male gender role in the family were
understood without question, I betrayed him. If so, what was the nature
of this betrayal?

   The Bible tells us ambiguously and in great length the story of the love
between David and Jonathan. When Jonathan is slain by the Philistines,
David laments his death in a manner that engendered many interpretations of their love as the one "that does not dare to speak its name":
"I am distressed for thee, my brother Jonathan; very pleasant hast thou
been unto me; wonderful was thy love to me, passing the love of women."*
Considering this, and other instances where the biblical text describes
their relationship as one of great devotion and tenderness, the suggestion
that David and Jonathan's love was an erotic one is nothing if not reasonable. But perhaps there could be another interpretation. "Wonderful" also
means—and this is even more so in the Hebrew origin—full of wonder,
mysterious, defying comprehension. Could it be that what the biblical
David speaks to is the mystery of the bond between men that is not sexual
yet not exclusive of sexuality either, something less clearly spoken, less
comprehensible than the sexual love between men and women? This is
perhaps something akin to what Foucault (1976) tried to expose when he
distinguished between sexuality and sex and traced the notion of sexuality prior to its being subsumed by the rigid notion of sex in Western
civilization. Could it be, then, that what alarmed my patient David when
he sensed we did not share a gendered understanding was the fraying of
the unconscious underpinning of a rigid discourse where sex is clearly
defined and regulated, sex that is either heterosexual or homosexual, born
in an historical tradeoff; where sexuality full of mystery and wonder, what
we may call in psychoanalysis polymorphous sexuality, is given up for an
allusion of uncontested gender difference and sameness?

   This does not mean that homosexuality appeared on the horizon.
Precisely not, although at the very moment David looked at me, hurt and
suspicious, I had the sense that for the first time in years of therapy he
wondered if I was like him, heterosexual. What happened, I believe, was
an unsettling of the tight arrangement by which social normativity, as it is

---

* 2 Samuel 1:26.

expressed in the family, gender difference, and sexual desire are co-configured. This arrangement: man is man, woman is woman, man desires woman and is the undesiring comrade of other men, a final tightening of this arrangement where subjectivity is subsumed by social categories, is what David dreaded. Why would you want to do that to us, he asked Abigail, why would you want to make us society's prisoners? A few months later he came into my office struggling to be a model "inmate." He thought I was one too; after all, do I not represent with my degrees, my poise, and my reasoning both the possibilities and sacrifice of social reason? But what perhaps had struck him most when he failed to sense that I as well abided by the rules was that he might be alone in his predicament. Alone, because all of a sudden a foreboding feeling came to bear that we did not share a common, friendly discourse. A discourse he relied on until then to reconcile what felt to him a conflict between the subjective and the social. This discourse cracked when he no longer found me in it. For a moment the social contract did not make sense, it could not provide an answer for his conflict, it could not account for his experience. Alone, perhaps like Jonathan felt, from the outset, when he decided to get married.

References

Benjamin, J. (1995). *Like Subjects, Love Objects: Essays on Recognition and Sexual Difference.* New Haven, CT: Yale University Press.

Butler, J. (1997). *The Psychic Life of Power: Theories of Subjection.* Stanford, CA: Stanford University Press.

Corbett, K. (2001a). Faggot = loser. *Studies in Gender and Sexuality, 2,* 3–28.

Corbett, K. (2001b). More life: Centrality and marginality in human development. *Psychoanalytic Dialogues, 11,* 313–336.

Dimen, M. (2003). *Sexuality, Intimacy, Power.* Hillsdale, NJ: Analytic Press.

Foucault, M. (1976/1980). *The History of Sexuality,* Vol 1: *An Introduction.* Trans. Robert Hurley. New York: Vintage.

Foucault, M. (1980/1997). Subjectivity and truth. In: S. Lotringer (Ed.), *The Politics of Truth.* Los Angeles: Semiotext(e).

Freud, S. (1935). Letter to an American woman concerned about her son. In: *The Letters of Sigmund Freud.* E. Freud (Ed.), 1960. New York: Basic Books pp. 423–424.

Goldner, V. (2003). Ironic gender/authentic sex. *Studies in Gender and Sexuality, 4,* 113–139.

Harris, A. (2005). *Gender as Soft Assembly.* Hillsdale, NJ: Analytic Press.

9

Psychotherapy With Poor African American Men
Challenges Around the Construction of Masculinities

C. Jama Adams

The bias, indeed the purpose, of psychoanalysis and its related psychotherapies has historically been to explore the vicissitudes of subjectivity as they manifest intrapsychically in such characteristic structures as conflict, compromise, and enactment. Psychoanalysis pays relatively little attention to the social forces that promulgate and enforce models of normality, dominance, and otherness and that facilitate and inhibit the attempts of individuals to love, work, and pursue whatever other goals they cherish. It is therefore not always obvious how social factors such as racism, sexism, and classism influence our work as psychoanalytically oriented therapists, or how we might integrate a more capacious understanding of these forces into better ways of working (Javier, 1996; Suchet, 2004; Walls, 2006).

To the extent that whiteness, for example, both racial and metaphoric, is portrayed in a culture as normal, benign, thoughtful, and aspirational, African Americans by contrast become containers for the qualities that whiteness rejects and for its opposites: deviance, danger, mindlessness, and rapacity (Altman, 2006; Smedley & Smedley, 2005; Laubscher, 2005; Parham, White, & Ajamu, 2000).

In a subtler manifestation, multiple negatively constructed social markers are promiscuously attributed to the identity category "race," as it is commonly used today, that more properly reflects body type, language style, skin color, occupation, or place of residence, to name just a few alternatives. The use of a supposedly biological category gives undeserved scientific authority to a very fluid concept, and under its rubric it contains and justifies a bewildering array of unconsciously coerced dominant/subordinate identifications. This is part of the covert dynamic by which "race" is expansively used as a definition of identity imposed by a dominant group on a subordinate one, who then must struggle against this definition to own their own identities (Layton, 2006).

As long as such dynamics remain at large but unacknowledged in a society, they will also be present, unspoken and unquestioned, in that society's therapeutic ideology, and so will the subordinate status that this ideology imposes upon so-called people—and patients—"of color." When we do acknowledge the social reality of race, we are then challenged to develop effective psychotherapeutic ways of responding. On the one hand, there is always the risk of marginalizing race as a critical enframing force, both within the therapeutic dyad and in the world at large. On the other, there is the counter-risk of overprivileging race (at the expense of personal subjectivity) as the preeminent force limiting a client's achievement of a "good-enough" life. For African American clients especially (but not only), it is critical that psychotherapists be able to navigate between these risks.

Furthermore, the imposition (through institutionalized practices and media portrayals) of these racialized identity forms do not have a uniform impact on the psyches and lifestyles of the individual members of subordinated groups. People in a racialized society, whether dominant or subordinate, engage intrapsychically with these issues, and interpersonally realize them, differently; resistance, ambivalent adoption, and adaptation are just some of the possibilities. Similarly, individual struggles against racism may be adaptive and may be dysfunctional. What is clear is that neither psychotherapists nor their clients are immune to the influence of these social templates (Adams, 2007; Holmes, 2006).

That being so, psychotherapists must learn to recognize how personal and macrocultural factors intersect in their impingement on their clients' self-development and find constructive ways to deal with both in their work. They must also bear in mind that the impact of macro cultural factors such as racism and its economic correlates will be especially evident in clients from subordinated groups, since these factors explicitly restrict their access to the resources and networks that facilitate healthy self-development.

In this chapter I will explore some of the ways these considerations have played out in my work as an African American psychotherapist with poor African American male clients whose lives have been lived under the constraints imposed by a racist society. I will focus on how these constraints impact two of the important facilitators of healthy self-development: the need for a supportive surround and the capacity for reflection. These considerations do not apply only to therapy with low-income African

American men, of course. The effects of racialization may be most glaringly evident among this unrepresentative but highly visible group, but they are relevant to all subordinated people, and, through the distortions that racism wreaks on societies as a whole, by extension to everyone.

The Self and Its Surround

Relational theory is the therapeutic framework that best encompasses the connection between the intimate personal, which is the domain of psychoanalysis, and culture writ large, which is often marginalized by psychoanalytic perspectives. A central tenet of relational theory is that self-construction takes place within a matrix of relationships that facilitate the internalization of habits of thinking, feeling, and handling feelings. These habits in turn inform how people love and work. Ideally, the relationships we grow up in are diverse, affectively attuned, cognitively sophisticated, socially connected, and materially well resourced; they afford us protection against grievous psychological and physical insult and allow us to develop a well-defined sense of the self as competent and loved (Bowlby, 1980; DeVos, 1982). But relationships like these are as much a function of macrocultural factors as they are of personal ones, and for many low-income African American males especially (and for many other low-income individuals as well) reality is relational networks that are emotionally, cognitively, and materially underresourced. Poor African American children are less likely than others to grow up in secure physical and psychological environments in which they can safely explore and reflect, thereby laying the foundations of a solid self.

Lance

Lance is a 22-year-old African American man who is in an alternative-to-incarceration program following conviction for attempted robbery of a convenience store. Psychological and educational screenings reveal him to be verbally adept and exceptionally gifted artistically. He is also contemptuous of authority and wary of relating. He has potent and well-elaborated fantasies of starting his own line of casual clothing.

Lance was raised by his mother and his maternal grandmother, both of whom, according to Lance, have low incomes and chronic health problems. He had regular but unsatisfactory contact with his father, who,

Lance says, "was just a lot of talk, but never had any money." He dropped out of school in the tenth grade after a verbal altercation with an assistant principal. Most of his peers were also doing poorly. They spent their time smoking marijuana and engaging in casual sex and petty crime, and becoming increasingly isolated from adaptive support networks. They were at risk most of the time, either of being attacked by equally dysfunctional peers or of being arrested by the police for their criminal behavior. This left Lance with a quandary not uncommon among young men of his background. He needed protection, but his ostensible protectors were as dangerous to him as those he needed protection from; hence his wariness about relating and his distrust of authority. He had to be vigilant to ensure his continued physical safety and had little opportunity in his life on the streets to pay attention to his own internal experience.

Lance worked for a while after dropping out as a clothes transporter for a designer. He portrays this job as one of the best times of his life. "You know the guy was a faggot, but he treated me right. I learned a lot from him. Not just about clothes, but about life." But he was paid off the books and was let go when business got slow.

Bruce

Bruce is a 19-year-old African American college freshman. He attended private primary and secondary schools growing up, and he feels that his family is too controlling. The only extracurricular activities that Bruce's mother, a bank clerk, permitted him as a teenager were church-related ones; she believed that the world was "a wicked place," and that it was Bruce's parents' job to protect their son. Bruce's view, however, is that he was bullied at church by his peers, and that his father has never stood up for him.

His parents wanted him to go to a small Christian college, but Bruce objected and is now attending a junior college close to home. He is seriously considering enlisting in the marines. "I want to see the world and I want to see how good I am."

Analysis of Vignettes

These two vignettes encapsulate dilemmas that face many low-income African American men. Some, like Lance, grow up in relationships that are emotionally impoverished and perhaps indifferent. They develop a wary stance toward emotional intimacy in both peer and love relationships. Alongside this wariness can often be found an antagonistic stance toward authority figures, a consequence of the harsh disciplinary regimens to which many of these men are subjected from a relatively early age. Lance, like many poor African American men, reported frequent indifferent or hostile responses on the part of teachers and police officers to their complaints, opinions, and sometimes even just to their presence. Bruce's growing up illustrates the other end of the spectrum—suffocatingly protective relationships in which caring comes at the cost of autonomy. Men like Bruce may lack age-appropriate experience in the world and thus never develop reliable confidence in themselves. Wherever an individual may fall between the two extremes, this combination—of emotionally and materially impoverished intimate networks, and institutional networks that are either hostile or indifferent to their strivings—put many low-income African American males at risk for underperformance and for enactments that are injurious to themselves or to others. Yet despite the significant deficits in their environments and the paucity of constructive support available to them, an experienced clinician may still sense in many of these men—as in both Lance and Bruce—the potential for reflection and for adaptive growth. And indeed, when men like Lance and Bruce have access to the safety and support of a reliable psychotherapy relationship that can take into account both the social and economic realities of their lives *and* the particulars of their individual subjectivities, they often do prove haltingly capable of the kind of reflection that facilitates self-development. They can also learn to modify self-destructive ways of pursuing love and glory into adaptive and age-appropriate ones, without undue risk to physical and psychological safety.

Psychotherapy, Society, and the Self

The low-income African American men whom I see in psychotherapy come to me reluctantly. They are invariably in crisis, and they come only on the strong urgings of a female partner or close male friend. They tend to share a deep preoccupation with what it means to be a man—what is owed to them as men, what as men they owe to others, whether they are succeeding as men, and above all how to value themselves, be valued by others, and engage intimately with the people they love. These concerns about masculinity intersect deeply with both the racist macro forces in these men's lives and also with the subjective dynamics that they construct as individuals. This is therefore an excellent arena in which to observe how macro and micro forces play out in psychotherapeutic work.

Masculinities in the United States

The dominant model of masculinity in the United States is characterized by heterosexuality, unfettered autonomy, and whiteness (Connell, 2002). It emphasizes the use of cognition to acquire and maintain material goods and power. To the extent that emotionality is acknowledged, it is the stoic and often unreflective endurance of pain in an arduous and often vain pursuit of a questionable ideal, a variant of "moral masochism" (Savran, 1998). I say "questionable" because the dominant model obscures the emotional price that men pay in pursuing the goal of radical, unconstrained individuality. Furthermore, the representation of this model as universal obscures two points: that subordinated men are in most cases forbidden the achievement, and sometimes even the pursuit, of the dominant model; and that there are other, less costly models of masculinity available. And in fact some alternative models of masculinity *are* adaptive, perhaps more adaptive than the dominant one. They are more egalitarian, they allow for a wider range of emotional experience, and they value reflectiveness and intimate engagement. Other alternative models, however, are maladaptive to the degree that they privilege an archaic view of manhood notable for its brittle hypermasculinity and its devaluation of reflection and empathy, both of which encourage behaviors dangerous to the self and to others (Mosher & Tomkins, 1988).

It is hard for the many African American men who live in a racist society with little money, impoverished networks, and poor reflective skills to establish the foundations of healthy masculinity. Men these days are expected to be physically well, psychologically resilient, and possessed of the marketable skills needful to garner dignity, respect, and material resources through work. Certainly these are desirable qualities. They are not only psychologically gratifying, but they also enable their possessors to be appropriately autonomous themselves and supportive of their partners and families. Yet while these expectations seem completely unremarkable to many of us, many statistical studies attest to the fact that health, resilience, and skill are not so easily within reach for poor African American men. Positive outcome indicators such as health status (Williams, 2003), school graduation (Smith, 2004), and employment rates (U.S. Department of Labor, 2008) are all low among African American males relative to national norms, while negative indicators such as suicide (U.S. Department of Health and Human Services, 2007) and incarceration rates (Bureau of Justice Statistics, 2006) are relatively high. Lacking the health, the skills, and the resources of men from the dominant group, many poor African American men are condemned to lives of humiliating dependency on an unwilling and often punitive state apparatus, or on (equally impoverished) significant others. They are also more likely than more prosperous men to end up victimizing either themselves or other people in their desperate but maladaptive struggles to achieve at least some semblance of an otherwise attainable sense of manhood.

Their plight is exacerbated by the tradition, shameful but still robust in the social sciences, of attributing to men of African descent a lesser intelligence than that of dominant white males, not to mention a host of other failings both moral and social (Gordon, Gordon, & Nembhard, 1994; Kang, 2005; Laubscher, 2005; Parham et al., 2000; Rushton, 1988). This is a deadly combination. Limitation and exclusion at the macro level, subordinate status at the subcultural level, and a personal sense of the self as embattled and devalued leaves many low-income African American men with an unreliable sense of themselves as men and a narrow and often inadequate endowment of the psychological and material resources necessary to construct a healthier one.

Space does not permit a comprehensive review of how African American males, especially poor ones, struggle to construct and live healthy masculinities in the United States (Adams, 2007), so I will limit myself here to the quixotic aspect of this struggle that I alluded to above: the difficulties for both client and therapist of developing an understanding that encompasses both macro forces and individual subjectivities in a balanced and realistic way.

The social constructivist perspective has sensitized us to the fact that the development of the self—as manifest in an individual's capacity for good-enough agency, creativity, love, and service—is shaped and facilitated by a host of relationships embedded in adequately resourced support systems, systems that include not only family, but also the wider community and the macro institutions that encompass both (Hoffman, 1992; Strenger, 2003; Walls, 2006). Inadequate levels of support significantly constrain the quality and depth of self-development.

Yet social constructions are not absolute determinants of the self. Postmodernist thinking rightly warns against accepting them at face value as organic, essentialized, and normative, and the intersectionist view (Brah

& Phoenix, 2004) encourages us to think about construction of identity as the vector sum of multiple factors and perspectives. Any African American man exists within an African American space as well as within the larger American cultural space. His African American experience offers him solidarity around suffering and possible points of ethical resistance to the dominant hegemonies, and it offers him temptations to nihilism and despair. But he is also an individual, and he has an *individual* psychological and cultural location within these larger spaces. Psychoanalysis has made clear that any man's subjectivity is a critical factor in how he will enact, modify, and resist the dominant hegemonies in his life. True sensitivity to his condition, and to the interactions between these various factors, must take into account not only the macro forces in his society, but also his individual subjectivity, and *with it the possibility that whatever his behavior, he may not be enacting the predicted (which in the case of poor African American men often implies "maladaptive") script.*

For example, the security arrangements in the buildings of a housing project have a major impact on the safety of the poor African American man who lives in them; so do the social climate and the quality of teaching in the classes he attends. But not all buildings in a project are identical, nor are the teachers in a school. Two men living in the same project and attending the same school may differ greatly in how safe they feel physically while growing up and in the quality of the education they received. Safe spaces encourage and permit reflective focus on the self; a person who has to be endlessly vigilant over physical safety may not have the luxury of reflection. Yet the capacity for reflectiveness is a major variable in the way people learn to handle affect, relationship, and other stressful life experiences, and so our two men are likely to come to very different accommodations with their environments and to very different senses of themselves as men.

But socioeconomic systems, even "liberal" ones, are increasingly depersonalized and indifferent, if not hostile, toward individual subjectivities, particularly those of low-income individuals from subordinate groups. Such systems also rely increasingly on techniques of surveillance and control, in a time when adroit use of technology and ideology permit restrictive practices to be exercised in near invisibility (Hollander & Gutwill, 2006). So, for example, many low-income men who have a criminal record cannot vote, cannot live in public housing, and, when they manage to find legitimate work, have their salaries automatically garnished to pay off the huge backlog of child support obligations they could not meet while unemployed. Their visitation rights may not be enforced by the courts, yet if they get angry at this they risk being subjected to orders of protection. If they violate these orders, they may find themselves back in prison. Men in situations like these may be forced to choose work in the underground economy and form disdain for the rule of law as the preferred way to express their manhood. The more invisible coercion becomes, the more easily it can be disguised as seduction, or at least as fait accompli, and this is where psychotherapists must tread warily. Psychotherapy is deeply informed by the behavioral and ideological norms of the social contract of any given time. For poor people and for people of color, a therapist who is unthoughtfully aligned with cultural assumptions may discourage, wittingly or not, any challenging of extant institutional practices, even when these are manifestly restrictive or otherwise unfair. Ultimately this produces psychotherapies in which the enactment of autonomy, productivity, and intimacy issues are perceived as unconnected to the sociopolitical forces that gave rise to them.

People surrounded by walls can see the constraints that limit them, but invisible constraints may be perceptible only as a nagging sense of psychological incompleteness. This may encourage people to seek out psychotherapy, but any psychotherapy that denies the invisible constraints in the name of individual responsibility is not psychotherapy at all, but a seduction into a glamorous but illusory freedom.

There are pitfalls particular to therapies where clients of color are working with therapists of color. In this case, the therapeutic pair might enact a bias by which the client marginalizes his own contribution to his situation and focuses only on the cultural component, presenting himself as a victim of macro forces. Some clients may vehemently deny any cultural constraints and instead insist unrealistically on an indomitable autonomy to which the therapist may unconsciously also aspire; the inability to realize this goal is then blamed on personal failings. Yet other clients may try unthoughtfully to challenge the reality of socially imposed constraints, and, perhaps with the therapist's unconscious approbation, enact scenarios that are archaic, dramatic, and sometimes even fatal. That is, a client may act out in personal or therapeutic relationships caricatures of social norms, an idealized model of the unfettered male, for example, or an intensely pathos-ridden version of the bound and victimized subordinate (fe)male.

More common are less dramatic compromises: ambivalence toward authority, for example, or struggle against (and at times seemingly willing, if costly, submission to) the seductions of consumerism and the performance ethic. These reflect internalizations of aspects of the dominant society within racialized and genderized individuals, aspects that are widely admired and useful, and yet may also be destructive and despised. All are enacted in fluid and ever-changing combinations of struggle, desire, mimicry, victimhood, resignation, and adaptive modification (Layton, 2006).

Working with such complexity is challenging, and so it should be, given the infinite psychic permutations that are possible. Yet our ideologies of treatment often impose invisible preferences as to what should be privileged among these competing aspects of self and environment (Layton, 2006; Suchet, 2004), thus apparently simplifying the therapeutic task, but at a high cost.

When an African American male client speaks to me, his black male therapist, with pain about racist workplace practices, he makes a not unreasonable assumption of solidarity, that I will be able to hear him about the cruelties of "white" society. Yet that solidarity should not foreclose upon a possibly *more* painful discussion about how his understandable rage at these cruelties makes it difficult for him to take advantages of opportunities that are in fact available to him. On the other hand, if our solidarity around exclusion and loss of dignity is *not* acknowledged, I risk losing the therapeutic alliance to accusations that I am a "white nigger" who does not understand an African American man's struggles against the system. At the same time, too much focus on the depredations of the system is another seduction. It induces the client to relinquish his own agency while reinforcing his sense of himself as victim, swept along by a current of powerful impersonal forces and with no hope or capacity to change his circumstances. Freire (1970) reminds us that oppression can generate within an individual sites of resistance, places where toxic introjects can be cauterized and adaptive countermoves made. But this happens best in the context of support networks that promote self-reflection and agency at the same time that they acknowledge socially imposed restrictions.

Other issues in these psychotherapies arise out of the emotional paucity that too often accompanies social and economic subordination. For many persons of low-income background, resource insufficiency extends even to the emotional supplies that are the bedrock of a child's self-sense of fundamental entitlement and agency. The declining purchasing power of the working class (and increasingly of the middle class) means that primary caregivers work longer hours and are less available to their children both physically and emotionally. Over the past three decades, fewer children have had the advantage of reliably available attachment objects, and ever more children are in the care of overtaxed relatives (single working mothers, grandmothers, older siblings), an ever-changing cast of contracted providers (nannies, babysitters, foster mothers, teachers, after school staff, coaches), or, for many poor African American males, criminal justice staff and their therapeutic surrogates. Such inadequate objects and the insecure attachments they engender impoverish the quality of the individual's other relationships (Adams, 2007), a situation that gets worse as weak or flawed attachments increasingly become a multigenerational reality (Altman, 1995; Fraiberg, 1980).

So, for low-income African American men who are fortunate enough to have access to psychotherapy, the potential for enactment is daunting (Holmes, 2006). The usual testings around trust and containment, dependency and autonomy are exacerbated by the deep resource insufficiency of their childhoods. There are likely to be transference/counter-transference storms around issues of impotence, rescue, and the wish to be sufficiently compensated. Furthermore, many of these men have had no substantive positive relationship with other men, which leaves them adrift with their own intensely felt need for tenderness, and no acceptable model of how it might be fulfilled. At the same time as they attempt to build intimate relationships, these men must vigilantly police the homosocial/homosexual border lest they trespass against the John Wayne caricature of male relating that the culture imposes on men (Savran, 1998) who have no deeper experience of the male sensibility with which to modulate it.

They must also struggle with a profound distrust of hope, and this is a heavy burden on psychotherapy. A further impediment to the development of a good therapeutic relationship is the fact that poor African American men have ample opportunity to see how early death can come. Therefore, survivors quickly learn not to invest in long-term relationships with other men. Sooner rather than later, they are taught by street violence, the criminal justice system, and ungenerous managed and mandated care arrangements that the men with whom they have caring relationships will disappear.

Some Psychological Features of African American Masculinities

Despite these obstacles to self-development, poor African American men still strive for self-fulfillment, including the sense of glorious individual achievement that characterizes current views of masculinity. These strivings manifest themselves on a spectrum defined by two extremes.

Some men pursue what I call a *respectable* lifestyle (Adams, 2007), that is, one consistent with mainstream American values around behavior, relationships, and success. They wrestle with issues of discipline and intimacy and find socially acceptable ways of pursuing the minor glories that are attainable by them in a limiting society. Adherence to mainstream values is a difficult psychological juggling act, as these men must simultaneously maintain inspirational fantasies of being dominant and unfettered alongside the melancholy recognition that they are *not* dominant or unfettered, and likely never will be.

In the best case, the result is the construction of a masculinity that is reflective, that privileges tenderness over aggression, that is affectively informed, and that deploys a multifaceted sense of self that can enjoy a healthy assertiveness and narcissism without having to obliterate or demean other healthy ways of understanding gender, sexuality, class, and race. Many such men, however, achieve their respectable successes at the cost of deep inhibitions in self-confidence and self-assertion; this is one reason that some of them seek psychotherapy.

The other end of the spectrum is what I have called a *reputational* masculinity (Adams, 2007), in which the appearance of dominance trumps all other considerations. Men who identify with the reputational lifestyle may also use the dominant model of masculinity as a ways of defining themselves, in that they wish to attain such mainstream goals as respect, dignity, and a certain level of material comfort. Believing, however, that such goals cannot be achieved within the established ethical framework (which paradoxically treats many African American men in an unethical manner), they establish an alternative value framework—a regressive archaic, hypermasculine, and misogynistic style of dominance in which respect is earned by rule-breaking and enforced by violence (Mosher & Tomkins, 1988).

This uber-masculinity, this spectacular caricature of the mainstream model, with its characteristic physicality, its drastic discounting of the future, its disdain for reflection, and the homophobia and aggression that defend against tenderness, puts men at great risk of maiming of the self, and sometimes of early death. It also may result in incarceration or other monitoring by the criminal justice system, and it is often through judicial mandate that men of the reputational style find themselves engaged in a psychotherapeutic relationship

Following are two vignettes that convey the flavor of these two masculinities.

Jonathan

Jonathan is a 24-year-old African American. He was referred to me by a former professor, who is a colleague of mine. He is the first in his family to graduate from college. He works as administrative assistant to the divisional vice president of a large retailer. He enjoys the work and he likes his boss, but he feels he is in a dead-end job. Even after taking many internal training courses, he cannot get into the company-sponsored management training program. He feels that racism is at work; many internal candidates of color apply to this program, but very few get in. In his therapy with me he often speaks of the importance of "playing by the rules" and "not acting ghetto." Jonathan has difficulty asserting himself out of fear that he might be seen as "disrespectful." His father and an honorary uncle, both of whom he admires, have cautioned him to be patient. When I ask him whether it is possible to be both African American and assertive, he says, "Not if you don't want to get your butt fired." Jonathan knows that his workplace may not be supporting his aspirations. But he recognizes too that his problems with assertiveness also reflect his own doubts about himself. In therapy, he was able to work profitably on the way his limiting work situation and his private doubts interacted and to develop a less constrained repertoire for thinking about both. Eventually he registered in a college-based management program and was recruited by another company for a managerial position.

Wade

Wade is a 21-year-old African American, and was referred to me by an African American police officer who worked in community affairs and was a former student of mine. Wade never completed high school, and since his early teens he has sold drugs and engaged in other illegal activities to make money. He tells me that he is good with numbers and "knows how to plan stuff so that it works," and indeed he has often acted as the bookkeeper for the gangs he gets involved in and served as their tactician. Wade still lives with his mother and complains that he never has money. Asked why he does not get some formal training that would allow him to use his skills in a legitimate and well-paying job, he argues that such work would be boring and that he would have to put up with "crap" from his supervisor. Further probing reveals a hypersensitivity to issues of respect and a preference for dealing with such issues by fighting. Wade claims that he is respected by his peers, but one senses that their respect is closer to fear of his violent outbursts and of his willingness and ability to harm others.

Wade told me in the course of our work that he feared he would never be respected, and that he was angry about that. I suggested to him that his fears about putting himself in a subordinate position in a real job had to do with his anger if he were to be taken advantage of. Furthermore, his relationship-disrupting violence ensured that he would never be in a position where he had to take the risk of trying to trust others. This line of inquiry resulted at first in a rash of missed sessions and late arrivals, as well as disparaging comments about my office décor. However, in time Wade was able to hear enough of my comments about what he was enacting that he stopped missing sessions and once again came on time. He also noted and commented that I did not seem upset about him "dissing" me, a recognition that challenges his previous conviction that any disrespect must be ferociously punished lest status be lost.

Self Compromise

Obviously not all men take one course or another in pure form. Chodorow (1986) and others have noted that a given personality constellation reflects identifications established during ongoing processes of compromise between the self and the biological, psychological, and socioeconomic surround to which it is related. In healthy individuals, these identifications coalesce in ways that permit the developing self to avoid the damaging extremes of fragmentation or deadening homogenization (Mitchell, 2002). The following clinical vignette is illustrative of one such set of compromises, and also of how they may be engaged in psychotherapy.

Wilson

Wilson is a 28-year-old African American casual laborer. He is in a stable, long-term relationship with Wanda, a teacher, with whom he has a 5-year-old daughter. Although Wilson is a highly skilled construction worker, he lacks credentials and is not a member of the union. He is having increasing difficulty finding well-paying work, and this has become a source of friction with Wanda, who thinks he should go back to school so that he will be qualified to get "a real job."

Wilson came into therapy at the recommendation of a friend who had become depressed upon the death of his infant son. Wilson's friend had a union job that had paid for some therapy sessions, and he reassured Wilson that, in Wilson's words, he "wasn't crazy, but that talking to a brother [that is, an African American male therapist] might be helpful."

It was not easy at first for Wilson to accept the idea of therapy. He kept the conversation light, asking me to question him or to share casual information about myself. As he did start speaking about his own life, he mentioned his joy in his daughter and his anxiety that he "would not do right by her"; further probing revealed fears that he could not be a good provider. He expressed a complex anger about his work situation, comprised of contempt for the white supervisor whom Wilson felt did not appreciate his skills, contempt for himself for not confronting this supervisor out of fear of losing what little work he could get, and anger at Wanda for not understanding "what it was like to be an African American man in a white man's world." Unbeknown to Wanda, he was smoking marijuana heavily, despite having promised her he would not.

Wilson's initial relief that I understood the harshness of an unfair and racialized workplace quickly turned to anxiety as I began to focus on his pain and his rage and how hard it was for him to think of returning to school. At first he rejected my suggestion that his anger was costly, but then he related an incident in which he had become so angry at something his daughter was doing that he had had to move away from her so he would not act inappropriately. I commended him on his self-control, and this triggered the recollection of a similar situation from his own childhood, in which Wilson thought he had been unfairly punished by his father.

Wilson harbored strong and detailed fantasies of being an architect. He had been admitted to a top technical high school in his teens, but had dropped out in response to constant belittling by his father, a chronic alcoholic. "I knew I was good, but I could never please that man. Nothing I did was ever good enough for him. Nothing."

I commented that a lot of the men in his life had let him down, and that it seemed hard for him to take advice from a woman. Wilson smiled and observed that Wanda had said the same thing. But, he noted, it was because of two women, Wanda and his daughter, that he had stuck with the therapy. I said that I thought he was telling me to be careful in how I dealt with him, and he responded that he had to be careful dealing with me, because he had never had any close male friends. Why not? I asked.

He told me that a lot of his friends were not going anywhere with their lives, and the men who were doing well made him feel uncomfortable. I wondered aloud if the pain of being an underachiever who had had some bad breaks was easier to cope with than his anger and anxiety in relation to other men. Wilson responded by asking me about the specifics of my cultural background, which I interpreted to mean that because I was a black man who had not grow up in the United States I really did not quite understand the more nuanced racialized aspects of his situation as an African American man.

Three months after this session, Wilson reported that he had built a table for a friend. He had received many compliments on it, and a few orders for other work. Furthermore, his father had commented favorably upon his craftsmanship and told Wilson that his paternal grandfather (whom Wilson had never met) had been a renowned furniture maker. He suggested that Wilson think of doing such work as a business. With some trepidation, Wilson faced up to his discomfort about engaging with successful men and was able to cultivate a series of professional relationships and develop a furniture business that has generated for him job satisfaction, status, and a steady income stream. Wilson still struggles with bouts of anger and immobilization, but less than he used to. Much of the work we do now centers on understanding his supportive relationships and preventing his intermittent attempts to sabotage them.

Pursuit of Hypermasculinity

The life possibilities for low-income men of all persuasions, but especially for African American men in this society, are tightly and painfully constrained. The pain of constraint is heightened by the incessant exhortations these men hear that if they would only work hard and absorb pain, they too could construct and enact dominant masculinities. The hegemony of the contemporary model of masculinity masks the reality that truly dominant men are a very small elite, and that *most* men, not just African American men, are subordinate to them (Connell, 2002; Savran, 1998). Most men will never achieve the dubious status of being a privileged and unfettered dominant man; in the case of African American men, this mythical vision of masculinity is even less likely to be achieved.

The powerful tide of improbability and the intensity of the strivings against it in these men's attempts to achieve the dominant paradigm give rise to much psychological pain and much maladaptive behavior. This often presents as the costly, unreflective, and shallow hypermasculinity of reputation, which society highlights and punishes especially harshly in low-income African American males. The doomed pursuit of this flawed masculinity is painful enough in itself, and more painful because its seekers know that even the seeking may be punished. Reputational masculinity evokes intensely competitive and punitive reactions in other men. Dominant males and their institutional surrogates repress it whenever possible, but it poses a danger within the African American world as well. African American males act out its rites of dominance for one another's scrutiny and approval, but they are likely to receive murderous retaliation—driven by envy or homophobia—instead of the validation they seek.

This struggle between the seductions and the dangers of hypermasculinity is played out by poor African American and other subordinated men in contests around assertiveness. These may be psychological contests, but often they are enacted physically, in repeated and costly combat performances that ritualize and glorify otherwise inevitable pain. The vignette below illustrates the characteristic attitude of one aspiring man of reputation toward pain.

Duane

Duane, a 24-year-old African American, has had a series of incarcerations for petty crimes. I was asked by a (white female) friend of mine, a program director, to "talk to him as one black man to another." Duane was raised by his mother, whom he portrays as moody, neglectful, and isolated. He has had no substantial or consistent contact with his father or with the families of either of his parents.

Duane had little adult supervision from the age of 9 onward. "All my mom cared was that I go to school. She would whip my ass if the school called to complain that I was not in class or was messing up. Other than that she didn't care where I was or what I was doing." (As he got to know me better, he revealed that his mother had always had health problems, including what sounded like depression.) He portrayed himself as a boisterous but academically average student, and he roamed the street after school with equally underachieving, unsupervised, and emotionally immature peers.

Duane portrayed himself as embattled as he became increasingly involved in thefts, robberies, and assaults. "Cops, my mother, my so-called friends, everyone was out to get me." He stated with pride that he could outrun any cop, that the beatings his mother gave him did not really hurt, and that the fights with his peers only made him tougher.

Even the beatings he sustained while incarcerated did not daunt him. He could not only absorb the pain, he said, but even detach himself from it, critiquing the manner in which he handled himself during the beating itself. This too was a source of great pride. "You got to learn from the shit. It's all about your head. You can't make them get there. You just gotta take it and learn from it." He felt that the men who beat him respected him for the way he managed himself, and that made him feel good.

A stance like this is costly, however, and Duane can neither talk about nor reflect upon the price he pays. I can see that he is scarred from knife and bullet wounds, and that he is forever vigilant. I can see too that he struggles with feelings of loneliness and depression in the periods of extended sleep and lassitude that he describes. But he does not think about these things, and he is willing only up to a point to let me bring them to his attention. The limit to his tolerance of a therapeutic relationship is a career management group, where issues of self-management are discussed in the context of positioning the men for success in the work world.

Therapeutic Challenges

One challenge in working with these men is their resistance to reflecting on vulnerable aspects of the self; in the all-too-frequent worst-case scenarios, there is no history of a safe base in which subjectivity and reflectivity could be nurtured or uniqueness celebrated. For these men, to be reflective is to experience pain, to be confronted with the absence of redemptive options. They have little experience of sustained relationships in which painful reflective work leads to the acknowledged right to be loved, to be appropriately autonomous, and to be treated with dignity. In the absence of self-reflective skills of their own, and without an empathic surround, these men's psychic pain is all the more intense because it is never articulated. In the absence of support and understanding, pain leads to despair and to ever more dangerous enacted attempts to exorcise it.

Another challenge is the need for the therapist to discern and define progressive motivations, even when they appear in the context of what may be seriously self-destructive behavior. The appropriate pursuit of rights, for example, may be fraught with costly enactments for many men in whom the fantasy of entitlement is blocked by the reality of subordination. These men are often reared under conditions of very harsh discipline, which denies age-appropriate autonomy and has no room for "safe" or low-stakes failure. In their understandable struggle for growth, self-protection, and personal authority, they may formulate and resort to dysfunctional strategies, strategies that, while effective in the short run, work against the possibility of good long-term outcomes. These men may not necessarily or intentionally reject mainstream values; in fact they may well argue for a principled position in support of these values. But as Steinberg (cited in Spencer, 1999) has noted, they may do so in a narrow and frequently dysfunctional way that is often unacceptable to the mainstream society they are trying to emulate. So, for example, one young man supports the principle of providing for his young child by stealing; another supports the principle of protecting women by threatening to shoot a man who shoved his girlfriend. In other words, while the principle is congruent with mainstream values, its operationalization is not (Adams, 2007).

Not all poorly thought-through enactments are physical. Some are psychological maneuvers, distancing moves that decrease anxiety at the expense of intrapsychic and interpersonal growth. This was evident in Wilson, who had to some degree accepted the pain of being unfulfilled professionally. He had cultural rationalizations for his less-than-adequate functioning, and he resisted the idea of exercising individual responsibility, using peer and love relationships, for example, to help him assuage his pain and become more productive. Despite his yearning for intimate and nurturing relationships, for a long time he replicated a relational style that itself was a replication of his painful and unproductive relationship with his father. At times he appeared to harbor the perverse wish to be as unsuccessful and as unhappy as his father had been.

A related source of pain is the inability to cultivate and maintain relationships with successful men (and women). These men have often lacked the opportunity to get to know or become comfortable with successful people, and they tend to shun networks that might facilitate such access out of the projected expectation that more successful peers will demean them. To approach them generates fears of being belittled; to avoid them generates feelings of envy and of self-contempt. This too was apparent at first in Wilson. Therapy enabled him to grapple with his anxieties about dealing with more successful men, and he was eventually able to make the kind of relationships that could support his own aspirations. Nurturing relationships can help people break out of such cycles of pain and blame. But the paucity of nurturing relationships in the lives of many poor African American men, and the anxieties around intimacy that they trigger, makes it hard for them to escape.

Adaptive Moves

"Men of reputation" and "men of respect" share a continuum, and their issues may to a greater or lesser degree overlap. But they have different fundamental preoccupations; where assertiveness without regard to danger is a characteristic problem for the men of reputation, for the men of respect assertiveness may be greatly feared, lest it prove dangerous.

Winnicott (1971) has sensitized us to how a primary caregiver facilitates self-development in his or her child, and how the child's eventual sense of self and affective dynamics reflects the caregiver's own affect management style. What is not well understood is how some caregivers are able, even under stress, to manage themselves in ways that protect the child from his or her own distress, and give the child psychological and physical room for exploration despite the parents' anxieties. It is not uncommon to hear African American adults comment that not only did they not feel poor or endangered in the low-income households where they grew up, but that they are still at a loss as to how their parents managed to shield them from the worries they must have suffered about their insufficient resources or about their children's safety and well-being. Similarly, some caregivers have the crucial capacity to engender a sense of hope and possibility in their offspring, despite daunting socioeconomic challenges. Once internalized, this model of hope and commitment to adaptive struggle, despite adversity, serves as a potent buffer against racist and sexist attacks on the self. It provides the individual with the psychological tools he needs to recognize, reflect on, and adaptively manage potentially damaging assaults by other people and by institutions. At the same time it allows him to identify and take advantage of such safe and nurturing networks that (even if not in abundance) may be available in underresourced communities—churches, community centers, and organized sports activities, for example.

Lyndon

Lyndon is a 27-year-old African American man whom I interviewed for a project on identifying the characteristics of successful black males. He is a licensed social worker and counsels teenagers who are at risk for becoming entangled in criminal activities. Although he grew up in the North, his parents insisted that he spend summers with his extended family in a Southern rural community. He portrays his parents as being fanatical about education, with his mother focusing on school and "being civil," and his father on "the university of hard knocks." He is amused by his father's legacy to him: "Do not trust the white man—he will always hold you back. But learn as much as you can from him." Lyndon followed this advice. He attended predominantly white schools during his elementary and secondary education and historically black colleges for his undergraduate and graduate degrees. He admits to being angry at the racism he sees in society, but he feels that as an assertive professional, racism is not something he personally worries about. He has cultivated a culturally diverse set of friends but admits to being careful around his some of white friends who often "forget" that he is black and make racist comments. He must also be careful around some of his black professional friends, who either condemn their low-income peers for being lazy, or rage at an abstraction called "the system," even as they decline to become mentors to their less-fortunate peers.

Balancing Autonomy and Safety

But not all caregivers are able to protect and inspire their children at the same time. On the one hand, the inspirational siren-song of hypermasculine parents and peers lures many young men onto the rocks of violence and danger. On the other, the protective messages of other parents worked against their aspirations on their children's behalf, conveying to them a sense of the world as a dangerous place, where the best strategy was to drastically moderate expectations of high achievement. These parents kept their offspring safe, but taught them to fear assertiveness and spontaneity lest they be negatively conspicuous and therefore subject to attack or denigration. Such constraints are part parental projection and part social reality, but either way they limit a child's capacity for full-bodied self-expression and contribute to anger and depression.

Network resources may reflect the same uneasy balance between autonomy and safety as families do, as my earlier vignettes of Lance and Bruce illustrate. Secular community activities may be underfunded, poorly organized, and potentially dangerous, bringing together groups of antagonistic youths with a high potential for violence. And church activities may not be sensitive to the developmental needs of older adolescents and young adult men, overprivileging moral strictures and marginalizing activities that are exciting and competitive, and that garner peer respect.

These tensions between hope and dread, safety and risk, autonomy and compliance, offer interesting insight into the fantasy lives of African American men. For the ones who have achieved some degree of normative glory, fantasies are voluptuous and can assuage painful feelings of subordination; but they are just fantasies, and the men know it. They maintain a safe *what if* quality. A man who works as a truck driver, for example, fantasizes himself as a talented but unrecognized poet. He spins couplets and rhymes in his mind and fantasizes about reading his poems on the *Oprah Winfrey* show, as soon as he gets around to writing them down. And why doesn't he write them down and achieve fame and fortune? Because, he points out, he has to work long hours to support his family.

For other men, fantasies are glorious dreams. They masquerade as real possibilities and are seductive enough that they distract the dreamer from the steps that actual achievement demands. I am thinking of a 22-year-old warehouse clerk, who was convinced that if he just practiced he would become a top-ranked professional basketball player. He was not in fact a distinguished amateur player, nor did he even play in an organized amateur league. But his commitment to his fantasy diverted him from building skills that would have fitted him for better-paying, if more prosaic, work.

Finally, there are men for whom fantasy reflects identification with an archaic and punitive masculinity; these men act their fantasies out in ways that are dangerous both to themselves and to others. This vision of manliness is a potent and long-standing iconic image within American culture and seems to be especially attractive to disempowered males, whatever their race. The young man who nearly shot a peer who had shoved his girlfriend is illustrative of this brittle but often dangerous form of masculinity.

Fortunately, the men who enact reputational masculinities are in the minority, although they are disproportionately visible. There are many more men who work quietly to shape masculinities that express both pride in themselves and a desire to live and to love. These men tend to be embedded (or tend to find ways to embed themselves) in support networks that engage them as reflective and volitional agents, despite the considerable constraints they face. Such networks validate not only a healthy affective self, but also the intellectual skills and high expectations that are so heavily privileged by the mainstream culture. They also speak to a model of African Americanism that evinces self-pride and specialness, while constraining conspiracy making and victimization. They encourage boys and young men to think of themselves as agents capable of influencing the effects of other contingencies in their lives. In this context, the men can struggle fruitfully with the challenges of constructing adaptive and gratifying models of a reflective and loving masculinity. Psychotherapy is one of the resources that can help poor African American men achieve this fruitful struggle, but psychotherapy of members of subordinated groups must always take into careful and balanced account both the realities of a racist, sexist, and classist society and the way individual subjectivities grapple with these realities.

Conclusion

Our primary relationships are embedded in a larger web of socioeconomic relationships that both constrain and facilitate how we love and how we work, often in unacknowledged ways. The impact of any given macrocultural factors on self-development is especially evident when dealing with clients from subordinated groups, given the restrictions they face on access to the resources and networks that facilitate self-development. Psychodynamic perspectives tend to recognize the effects of macro factors mostly as they are reflected in intimate relationships and in such personal issues as narcissism, lack of reflection, and work performance. These are issues that do in fact plague many psychotherapy clients, and they certainly are significantly shaped by larger culture forces. But psychodynamic thinking does not always conceptualize well the impact of socioeconomic impingements on the development of the self (Fairfield, et al. 2002). On the other hand, social constructions are not absolute determinants of the self either.

Psychodynamic theories have taught us much about difference, loss, longing, conflict, reconstruction, and reparation. But we must use them in the context of the social realities in which they exist. And we can understand those realities only through their impact on the individual people who live within them.

References

Adams, C. J. (2007). Respect and reputation: The construction of masculinity in poor African-American men. *Journal of African-American Studies, 11*(3–4), 157–172.

Altman, N. (1995). *The Analyst in the Inner City: Race, Class and Culture through a Psychoanalytic Lens*. Hillsdale, NJ: Analytic Press.

Altman, N. (2006). Whiteness. *Psychoanalytic Quarterly, 75*, 45–72.

Bowlby, J. (1988). *A Secure Base*. New York: Basic Books.

Brah, A., & Phoenix, A. (2004). Ain't I a woman? Revisiting intersectionality. *Journal of International Women's Studies, 5*(3), 75–86.

Bureau of Justice Statistics. (2006). *Prison statistics*. Retrieved April 24, 2008, from http://www.ojp.gov/bjs/prisons.htm

Chodorow, N. (1986). Toward a relational individualism: The mediation of self through psychoanalysis. In T. Heller, M. Sosna, & D. Wellbery (Eds.), *Autonomy, Individuality, and the Self in Western Thought* (pp. 197–207). Stanford, CA: Stanford University Press.

Connell, R.W. (2002). The history of masculinity. In R. Adams & D. Savran (Eds.), *The Masculinity Reader* (pp. 245–261). Malden, MA: Blackwell.

DeVos, G. (1982). Adaptive strategies in US minorities. In E. E. Jones & S. J. Korchin (Eds.), *Minority Mental Health* (pp. 74–117). New York: Praeger.

Fairfield, S., Layton, L., & Stack, C. (2002). *Bringing the Plague: Toward a Postmodern Psychoanalysis*. New York: Other Press

Fraiberg, S. (1980). *Clinical Studies in Infant Mental Health*. New York: Basic Books.

Freire, P. (1970) *Pedagogy of the Oppressed*. New York: The Seabury Press, Continuum International Publishing.

Gordon, E. T., Gordon, E.W., & Nembhard, J. (1994). Social science literature concerning African-American men. *Journal of Negro Education, 63*(4), 508–531.

Hoffman, I. Z. (1992). Discussion: Toward a social-constructionist view of the psychoanalytic solution. *Psychoanalytic Dialogues, 3*, 74–105.

Hollander, N., & Gutwill, S. (2006). Despair and hope in a culture of denial. In L. Layton, N. Caro Hollander, & S. Gutwill (Eds.), *Psychoanalysis, Class and Politics: Encounters in the Clinical Setting* (pp. 80–91). New York: Routledge.

Holmes, D. (2006). The wrecking effects of race and social class on self and success. *Psychoanalytic Quarterly, 75*(1), 215–235.

Javier, R. (1996). Psychodynamic treatment with the urban poor. In R. Perez-Foster, M. Moskowitz, & R. Javier (Eds.), *Reaching Across Boundaries of Culture and Class: Widening the Scope of Psychotherapy* (pp. 93–113). Northvale, NJ: Jason Aronson.

Kang, J. (2005). Trojan horses of race. *Harvard Law Review, 118*(5), 1490–2005.

Laubscher, L. (2005). Toward a (de)constructive psychology of African-American men. *Journal of Black Psychology, 31*(2), 111–129.

Layton, L. (2006). Racial identities, racial enactments and normative unconscious processes. *Psychoanalytic Quarterly, 75*(1), 237–269.

Mitchell, S. (2002). The treatment of choice: A response to Susan Fairfield. In S. Fairfield, L. Layton, & C. Stack, (Eds.), *Bringing the Plague: Toward a Postmodern Psychoanalysis* (pp. 69–102). New York: Other Press.

Mosher, D., & Tomkins, S. (1988). Scripting the macho man: Hypermasculine socialization and enculturation. *Journal of Sex Research, 25*(1), 60–84.

Parham, T., White J., & Ajamu, A. (2000). *The Psychology of Blacks,* 3rd ed. Englewood Cliffs, NJ: Prentice Hall.

Rushton, J. (1988). Race differences in behavior: A review and evolutionary analysis. *Personality and Individual Differences, 9*(6), 1009–1024.

Savran, D. (1998). *Taking It Like a Man: White Masculinity, Masochism, and Contemporary American Culture.* Princeton, NJ: Princeton University Press.

Smedley, A., & Smedley, B. (2005). Race as biology is fiction, racism as a social problem is real: Anthropological and historical perspectives on the social construction of race. *American Psychologist, 60*(1), 16–26.

Smith, R. A. (2004). *Saving Black Boys. The American Prospect.* Retrieved January, 2008 from http://www.prospect.org/print/V15/2/smith-ro.html

Spencer, M. B. (1999). Social and cultural influences on school adjustment: The application of an identity focused cultural ecological perspective. *Educational Psychologist, 34*(1), 43–57.

Strenger, C. (2002). The self as perpetual experiment: Psychodynamic comments on some aspects of contemporary urban culture. *Psychoanalytic Psychology, 20*(3), 425–440.

Suchet, M. (2004). A relational encounter with race. *Psychoanalytic Dialogues, 14*(4), 423–438.

U.S. Department of Health and Human Services, Centers for Disease Control and Prevention, National Center for Health Statistics. (2007). *Death rates for suicide, by sex, race, Hispanic origin, and age: United States, selected years 1950-2004.* Retrieved April 14, 2008, from http://www.cdc.gov/nchs/products/pubs/pubd/hus/injury.htm

U.S. Department of Labor, Bureau of Labor Statistics. (2008). *Labor force statistics from the current population survey, economics news releases: Current, employment situation.* Retrieved April 15, 2008, from http://www.bls.gov/news.release/pdf/empsit.pdf

Walls, G. (2006). The normative unconscious and the political contexts of change in psychotherapy. In L. Layton, N. Caro Hollander, & S. Gutwill (Eds.), *Psychoanalysis, Class and Politic* (pp. 118–128). New York: Routledge.

Williams, D. R. (2003). The health of men: Structured inequalities and opportunities. *American Journal of Public Health, 93*(5), 704.

Winnicott, D. W. (1971). *Playing and Reality.* London, Tavistock.

10

"Fathers" and "Daughters"

Adrienne Harris

Introduction

In trying to position this work on fathers and daughters into the context of Reis and Grossmark's creative and bold reconsideration of masculinities, fathering, and heterosexual masculinities in particular, I find I have some new terms to set into quotation marks, to interrogate, and to consider. These terms, once signifying stable, essential, definable experiences and traits are now considerably less clear-cut and reliable. Yet, I would argue, and this book clearly makes this argument, these terms can still be useful and important work in or understanding of human subjectivity and intersubjectivity. Gender and parenting terms within psychoanalysis occupy what Janine Puget has termed "radioactive" space. Masculinity, fathering, and heterosexuality are category terms and they come to constitute psychic, interpersonal, and intersubjective experiences that draw in and magnetize profound forces of culture, ideology, and personal meaning. We cannot step fully outside these categories and yet, mercifully, they are always under revision and reconstruction.

A gender category, or a sexual category, or a category denoting family position can be seen as a citadel, a prison, an opportunity, or a changing landscape. Masculinity across many cultural settings denotes power and certain dominance. Yet cultural privilege also entails cultural and psychosocial requirement. In their work on masculinity, Reis (Chapter 3), Grossmark (Chapter 4), Diamond (Chapter 2), Corbett (1999, 2001a, 2001b), and others have begun to examine and so, inevitably, to alter the brittleness and narrowness of these categories. In this essay I look at the links between two of these fundamental experiences, father and daughter, examining how these experiences are both culturally mediated and co-constructed.

A number of theorists have noted one particular problem of masculinity: its severing from tenderness. The rigor of early separation and the demand for autonomy imposed on boys from very early ages is notable. We can now finally see that the press for separation is an unnecessary but potent aspect of the traumatization of boys. Need is phallicized through the installation of masculinity, required in the performance of demand and proscribed in the manifestation of need. We can see through these new lenses on gender and sexuality the terrible costs of the prohibition on passivity and tenderness. Perhaps in the light of this new work on masculinity, we might see that in parenting, men (and women) have a new way to ventilate and create new vectors of masculinity.

To think through a historical lens we might say that psychoanalysis had an intrapsychic baby, a relational mom and behavioral dad. Dad, man, heterosexual: these are the unmarked categories. This new look at masculinity is making theory not merely drawing on it. Theorizing here is an act of resignification, in Butler's (1997) terms. How to reconceive masculinity and parenting as phenomenologically not naturally linked? And what can we now speculate about the textures of the relationships between parent and child, where gender, generation, and sexuality are in complex and emergent tensions?

To be more explicit, I work with a particular developmental model here: complexity theory, chaos theory, and nonlinear dynamic systems theory, to give this perspective its multiple names. Any process (psychic or social) or any system (interpersonal or familial) arises in a constructed, unpredictable but self-organizing pattern. Being a father would emerge in a particular historical and cultural moment, formed in relation and in active process with others in the family and cultural system. One of the glories of chaos theory is the understanding that highly significant forms and differences emerge from subtle shifts and changes as systems form and evolve. Systems and individuals form in context. No fathers without daughters, no daughters without fathers, provided we let these terms float and move.

There is something pleasing and perplexing about writing an essay on fathers and daughters at this period of our psychoanalytic and cultural history. This is a time in which gender categories are being creatively and rigorously challenged (Butler, 1990, 1993, 1997a, 1997b; Corbett, 1993, 1999, 2001a, 2001b; Dimen, 2003; Goldner, 1991, 2003; Harris, 2005; Layton, 1998, 2002). Are there still fathers and daughters? Or just "fathers" and "daughters," designations pinned by quotation marks so we see how very unstable and unsettled such meanings and categories must be.

This is an era in psychoanalytic thinking when maternal, phallic, or paternal functions jump the usual boundaries. Jessica Benjamin

(1988, 1991), in developing a critique of the simplified binary in which mother was the site of fusion and attachment and father the site of separation and difference, proposed that we see how maternal reflective functioning always had the potential to include a mother's recognition of difference in her child. Fogel (Chapter 12) is expanding our ideas of masculinity by the inclusion of "receptivity," usually a mark of femininity, as an aspect of postoedipal maturity in men. We can now ask whether the dyad of father and daughter is of any clinical or theoretical use or significance. Are relational and/or gender categories atavistic? Yes and no. Gender phenomena are present but can be fluid. The idea of the phallic woman is contested and deconstructed. Terms like penis envy engage us intrapsychically and interpersonally, pointing to the mother and/or the father (Harris, 2004; Torok, 1970; Zeavin, 2004).

One of the interesting problematics in considering Benjamin's (1991) ideal of father–daughter identificatory love is to think about how the loves and the identifications are and are not gendered for any particular father–daughter duo. Would you need to be claimed by a father or as a potential father to become one, at any of many distinct levels of representation? Is this identificatory love, so useful in the dismantling of fixed and lethal polarities and complementarities, free from gender, or is this love a way to negotiate gender? How free is any father or daughter to gender morph within these loving ties?

Our clinical work and our thinking have flourished when we cut ourselves loose from the icebergs and monoliths of essential constructs like gender. We can use many postmodern energies to deconstruct identity positions of many kinds: racialized, genderized, sexualized. Softly assembled, deconstructed, self assigned, socially assigned, fortress or freedom, gender is more useful as function than as structure. The protean experiences of gender (disappearing, supersaturated, hybridic, material, history laden, and/or mutative) suit our clinical needs, the complexity of the mix-ups of patient and analyst, parent and child. We need to keep gender but we need to keep it moving.

On the other hand, material circumstances, unique meanings, and archaic primary process residue adhere to category names like "father" and "daughter" and to histories and relationships. So we must continue to ask the question about any individual subject: How is gender constructed, assembled, maintained? Is gender relevant? Who is the father? What is a father? What is a daughter? Attributes of gender can shift and mutate in surprising ways. Imaginary fathers and daughters, material fathers and daughters: these pairs are also creatures of history, class, and subculture.

An inventory of fathers of daughters in my current practice reveals an exciting bad boy, an ego ideal, a lost hero, a dangerous and controlling sadist, a man too caught in the toils of his own father to be free to parent a daughter, a father who emanates a warm maternal presence, a good father in babyhood turned sinister and frightening in his daughter's adolescence. And all the daughters of these men, in strikingly different ways, take up these fathers as points of identification, sites of desire and zones of trauma.

Because, within psychoanalysis, we consider many facets of psychic life within the asymmetries of development, we tend to consider influence as a top-down matter. The child, here a daughter, forms in relation to an experience of a parent, here a father. Yet in thinking of childbirth in relation to femininity, we have no difficulty imagining that the child's birth is transformative for the mother. In fact, since the 1960s and now more than ever, with the burgeoning attachment literature and the relational turn, we have an understanding of the child partner in the parent–child dyad as the "competent infant." The child is coparticipant in the construction of the relational matrix from the beginning. Could one extend the same possibility to fathers, that is, that men are transformed by the experience of fathering and that this may have some unique characteristics when the child is a daughter?

Writing about Freud's case of homosexuality in a woman (Harris, 1991), I drew on two contemporary patients, patients whose gender identity and sexualities were complex and unpredictable. The fathers in these cases I now reflect offered very different prospects. BJ, a self-proclaimed "butch" was strongly identified with her father, a beloved but doomed figure. Crippled by failing health and by responsibilities to an ailing wife, BJ's father sank. But his kindness, the memories of his maternality/paternality remained for BJ a strong and important force. A caretaker for the women in her life, she also remained deeply bonded in fantasy to an adolescent boyfriend, both a sexual object and a point of identification.

Hannah, the other woman I wrote about in that essay, had a father more clearly dangerous and seductive than warm and helpful. His manipulation and odd obsessions with Hannah left her with lifetime distaste for too much immersion and intimacy with another. I say odd obsession because Hannah's father seemed equally involved with Hannah's sexuality and that of her real or imagined (her father's imagined) boyfriends. To what end was this father the voyeur of his daughter's developing power and vital sexuality? Creepiness settled over their relationship with long-term consequences and much alienation. Yet Hannah's memories of the father of her early years had strength and love and loyalty. Perhaps this is one of the losses worth noting. The father who drifts or veers away when a daughter grows and changes can leave a lethal effect on her aggression, her ambition, and her feel for power.

So perhaps the question need not be so baldly and confrontationally why write about fathers and daughters but rather how to write about fathers and daughters. For any subject for whom those terms have heft and significance, what might we say? For the moment, I am going to position myself simultaneously as a modernist and postmodernist and so hold to the materiality and historical contingency of the experiences of fathering and being a daughter. This means that I am thinking of these designations as placeholders not as essentials. How is meaning and power pulled into or emanated out of the particular circumstances of being a daughter or a father, given that "daughters" may be boys or girls, and father's housed in many distinct sites?

I find that when I start to think about my own history and my own father, the gender terms both hold and shift almost at once. I discover, in working on this essay, that I enter these categories more immediately and fluidly either as daughter and/or son than as father or mother. Some categories are more impenetrable than others for me and I see how my defenses set limits on the flow and play of identifications.

"A Good Little Soldier"

This description of me as a small child was offered retrospectively by my mother when we were discussing my early experience of fragile health, and the regimen of inoculations, medicines, and quite draconian dietary restrictions that I fell under. My father, the actual good soldier, was in Europe in the Second World War, and as the years went by, my mother sank under the weight of loneliness and uncertainty. This absence at home and away left my nanny and I to soldier on, battling the gloomy household and darkening depression emanating from my mother and waiting for the liberation we fervently hoped would arrive with my father.

Nanny and I evoked and watched for the soldier father in many ways. We read Babar attentive to the august king's battles with the terrible rhinos. We scrutinized my father's handsome and serious uniformed picture, kept in my room. We had a ritualized walk where trees were named in his honor. But how had my stoic, tough reaction to illness gotten identified with him? What amalgam of Nanny's character, her and my mother's imagination, and my own organization of responses to pain, had cashed out to "soldiering"?

When my father actually appeared, Nanny and I orchestrated neighborhood parades in his honor and I followed him as quickly as possible into the world of baseball and sports. So even starting with a simple story of my father and me as daughter, I have to notice that one powerful fantasy that swept me up is that he needed/wanted a son. I found this an easy and desirable reach. And of course, this shift to tomboy kept the pain-fighter identity I had been crafting quite intact. A tomboy persona is also very suitable for a little girl who needed to get away from her mother.

This story makes me want to begin to look at fathers and daughters by exploring how frequently a father is approached through the realm of the imaginary. (Wartime absence being only one kind of example of the distal nature of the father and child relationship.) My point is that any parent will be held in someone's imagination as an object of desire, of fear, of repudiation, or of idealized hopes. A father, one's father, will inevitably be someone else's deeply held object.

Father Through the Lens of the Imaginary

We might say that my imaginary father was held by two libidinal streams. First, there were fantasies from my Nanny who held my father for me, knowing that memory and fidelity were important. But why did this woman keep such fidelity for a man she had never met? This imaginary soldier father carries the residue of her own story, the lost love of the First World War and the emptiness of a Scottish village life in the 1920s that had her searching for meaning and sustenance through emigration to Canada.

The stream from my mother was sometimes underground and harder to follow. The mother's desire, consciously and unconsciously, is transmitted to the daughter. For my mother, the good soldier seemed more and more shadowy and unreal. Now in adulthood, I can empathize with two people separated for close to 5 years and unable to build the bridges back

At home my mother continued a devoted and daughterly tie to her father. She gave me a French name to please him. He arrived to view me when I was about a day or two old and pronounced, "This is a very intelligent baby. She has a very high forehead." In that moment, I am claimed by a "father," just not mine, exactly. I am interpellated in that instant as the carrier of my mother's desires in relation to her father as well as my grandfather's vision of his own capacities now mirrored in another. This is a multigenerational interlocking father–daughter story. Faimberg (2004) notes how often the oedipal triangles are actually multigenerational. One is bound into many imaginary father–daughter scenes, all read through the fantasies and longings of the parental figures. Becoming gendered as some object of desire is both a creative bid for freedom and a defense. In particular I think the material circumstances of my early childhood had all the sadness and uncertainty of wartime, and therefore the imaginary world seemed luscious and freeing to me and those taking care of me.

A rich part of my gendered character is already worked out through nostalgia, looking backward as much as forward.

At my father's funeral I had his grandchildren read sections of a letter written near the end of the war to my mother. I said it was to give them a picture of a man before aging and before Alzheimer's. The letter speaks with great emotion and almost lyrical attention to the landscape and site of a crucial battle in Italy. In the spirit of soldierly writing styles, danger is downplayed and the letter ends with an open expression of hope: "Our time will come." That is the man I had been waiting for, carrying the unconscious and semiconscious desires of my mother, my nanny, and myself. Of course, the man who came home had changed, was never that man again. There is in my longing a "telescoping of generations," the phrase Faimberg (2004) uses to describe the unconscious transmission of the psychic projects of one generation into the next. Nanny's history and my mother's history with their fathers has collapsed into, filled out, and animated mine. A softly assembled father, defined by waiting but also by vitality and play. The longing for this father, I can see in retrospect, was in everyone. For me what was most central was that he would appear and heal my mother. My father, like many returning veterans, was simply too traumatized or perhaps too distant from the relational matrix that had become imaginary in his mind as well.

My patient Patricia holds and offers an imaginary father to her daughter in a different way. Back from maternity leave after the birth of a second daughter, she is describing the routines of exhausted new parenting and the help she and her husband are providing to their firstborn, now 3. This situation is very charged and preoccupying for Patricia. She was a lonely and not well-contained firstborn daughter, and the conflictual and agonizing relationship with her younger sister, as both children struggled for very inadequate parental/maternal resources, continues to be devastating and painful.

Patricia describes a nightly scene where her 3-year-old wakes and comes into the parents' room. The dad sighs, groans, gets groggily out of bed and as Patricia describes it, night after night, his little daughter's hand fits into his and they walk back to her room and he settles her down. Patricia, always alert for the old objects, focuses on the sighs, the groans, and the exhaustion. But we talked about that hand, that absolutely reliable presence that the 3-year-old counts on and always finds. There is a new object, a paternal presence that keeps the links between mother and child, helps contain and hold uncertainty and change. Of course it is a weary hand, but it is a deeply loving hand. Patricia can notice that this scene feels different from her own screen memory of a cold night, an anxious wait at the parental bedroom door and finally her anxious entry only to find the spot between the parents' already taken by her sister.

I am describing this through the lens of Patricia's gaze, her imagination. What I believe is being established by mother, father, and daughter is a complex multidirectional holding in mind and body. The father's care of the daughter is held in the mother's mind, the daughter is held by her father. She holds his hand in mind in the nighttime. The analyst has a role in this holding as well as I work with Patricia to expand what she can imagine for herself and her daughters from a father and mother.

This is both a Winnicottian (1971) and a Laplanchian (1989, 1997) way to encounter the father, through the desires and imaginative transmissions (conscious and unconscious) of maternal figures, what Laplanche (1989) somewhat provocatively termed the maternal seduction. The desires the child absorbs (inevitably excessive and enigmatic) include desires for the child and desires for others. So the father arrives as another's object of desire, only ever incompletely absorbable by that child. The excitement for the father as other and different is constructed on part on desires already alive in the unconscious life of the child.

Again, I notice the unidirectional focus on the adult as the site of spectacle and the imaginative focus for the child. This is understandable perhaps considering that psychoanalysis is a theory of development, a theory of the instantiation of subjectivity, to use modern terminology. But in the light of thinking of co-construction and of adult development, might we think of what the daughter, as an imaginary figure, contributes to her father's sense of self and capacity. Might we think that for an adult man, the presence of a child, particularly a female child who may carry the markers of vulnerability, offers the potential to expand genderedness or to minimize it in an identification that stresses sameness not difference, but certainly to alter its more rigid contours. The capacity for empathy that is inherent in parenting may expand the repertoire for men, lightening the particular burden of autonomy and separation. This is of course an ideal of the encounter of father with daughter. We can equally imagine that terrors and anxieties in regard to connection and care may produce alienated or hostile parenting. But in the call to reimagine gender categories interacting with parenting, we need to notice and counteract the unidirectionality of influence and effect as well as the brittleness of the categories many men, most men, are enjoined to work and live within.

Activity and passivity, as animated forms of living and relating, are no longer valenced and polarized between the genders. Linked but not soldered to gender, those modes of being offered a site for more fluid co-construction. Patricia's husband is actually doing an act that is normally assigned to maternality. That is, he provides a quiet, receptive containment, a reliability that we usually think of as a cornerstone of early attachment and early maternal space. So we might need to think of an environmental father alongside an environmental mother. I also wonder about the reparative meaning to this father, who has his own history of loss, of being so capable of giving reliable parental care.

Daughters and the Paternal Body in Early Childhood

It is a centerpiece of classical and contemporary psychoanalytic theory that sensual intensity and fusion is a function of mother and daughter with the father as the more utilitarian and functional agent of separation. As I have just argued, the distal nature of the father in the experience of infant or toddler girl is one aspect of early family relational configurations. It is also a family dynamic that has changed historically.

The image of the distant, unavailable father is also a myth, a caricature; in many ways a caricature indebted not only to actual family dynamics but also to the intensity within psychoanalysis of dividing active and passive and therefore opposing regression and agency. Reviewing the literature reveals a contradiction that is quite longstanding between the concepts of the father as the guardian of rapprochement, of representation or the law or the word. Chasseguet-Smirgel (1970, 1985), for example, saw in the regressive pull of the mother, dangers that were on a large historical as well as modest familial scale. The mother must be beaten back, for the sake of reason, democracy, sanity, and generational difference. Abelin (1971) is a pivotal exemplar of this perspective, in which the father's appearance in the child's toddlerhood broke a dangerous fusion and paved a way for a child to move out of this morass.

Looked at with a more modern eye, this approach now sounds faintly (or more than faintly) hysterical. But we have yet to fully extricate ourselves from this theoretical quagmire, though many writers within the classical canon speak to the role of the father as a deeply textured and material figure in the preoedipal period (Balsam, 1989; Chiland, 1982; Chused, 1986). This tendency has evolved within the relational tradition as well (Benjamin, 1988, 1991).

One of the interesting questions regarding early bodily life is how and when to think of these bodies (parents and children as consciously and unconsciously gendered). In thinking of the dynamic interactions of father and daughter, for example, gender is likely to be more elaborated for the adult and only gradually so for the child. The paternal body of a daughter's early experience may be sensual, erotic, libidinizable and libidinizing (as the mother's can be), containing, or disturbing. The father of toddlerhood, in Benjamin's (1991) groundbreaking insight, can offer a girl (as well as a boy) an identificatory link. But how gender works in this process may be highly variable. The fluidity can be in parent or child. Or gender may not be the salient formation. A father may, consciously or unconsciously, extend his own gender identifications into his identificatory link to his daughter. He may see her as "masculine" like him. A father may find his femininity in his daughter or project it into her. In some father–daughter dyads, gender may not be one of the salient charged characteristics of their bond. A father and daughter may bond and coidentify as minds, characters, body types, looks, alliances, or affective styles. Gender's place in this mix will be highly variable and part of a unique dyadic co-construction.

My father's actual presence was the occasion of a quite dramatic gender shift for me. I seemed to have felt or known that my father would do better with a son than a daughter. I became instantly tomboy and I continued to live in the exciting fantasy world of soldiers and then the exciting world of sports. Nanny sewed my father's badges on my sweater. My father repudiated uniforms and returned to a life that could include perfectly tailored suits and perfectly chilled martinis, to disastrous effect. He also returned to baseball and since this was a pastime (as spectator and player) scorned by my mother, baseball was available to me as a way to be with him. Like many latency boys I spent hours absorbed in sports arcana and history. I found a way back to his boyhood.

Only recently have I begun to wonder about the impact on me of these encounters with boys' motility and aggression in early baseball games my father organized for neighborhood children, games I absolutely refused to be sidelined from. Perhaps the spirited encounters with the paternal body, observed in the play of fathers and young children, is a powerful permission for bodily vitality for a daughter. Early encounters with the paternal body may have the potential for vitalization and intensity different in tempo and style from the encounters with the maternal body.

To reverse this perspective, might we also consider how the experience of an active, identifying daughter may impact on the father and the construction of his body ego? Could it promote a more complex, bigendered experience in a male parent to find activity modeled by an active daughter? Narcissistic use of children by parents can be a grotesque and destructive process. The biographies of many athletes are stained with the tales of a father living through and colonizing his son. But might we, in the spirit of ventilating and rehabilitating the relation of father and daughter, think of the possibilities for growth in the parent through the encounter with a daughter's activity or prowess? We might add this idea to Benjamin's (1991) notion of identificatory love, where a child is claimed as "like me," a process that must be transformative for all, as identification is. Thinking relationally, we must recognize that any act of intersubjective encounter, any act of identification, transforms both parties. How easy it is now to see the frozen fathers of our theorizing. Masculinity and masculine parenting has been endowed with endless power and capacity, except the capacity to be moved and altered.

Fathers and Daughters in Psychoanalytic History

Psychoanalysis and its multiplying narratives are indebted to a man who analyzed his own daughter: Sigmund Freud and Anna. The founding father–daughter couples in early psychoanalytic texts—the *Studies on Hysteria* (S. Freud, 1895/1955a), the case histories (S. Freud, 1915/1957, 1920/1955c), and the half-buried evidence of Freud's analysis of Anna (A. Freud, 1923; S. Freud, 1919/1955b; Young-Bruehl, 1988, 1989)—are a daunting and rather terrifying group. Sabina Spielrein, Jung's patient, later his lover and still later a member of Freud's group in Vienna, had a violent, sexualizing father. A footnote in *Studies on Hysteria* (S. Freud, 1895/1955a) reveals that the molester in the case of Katharina was actually her father. Dora's father and Freud were caught up in a collusion in regard to framing her treatment, a collusion rather strikingly repeated in the case of homosexuality in a woman (S. Freud, 1919/1955b). Daughters are property. If damaged, they can be repaired to order. As property, they can be damaged at will by their owner.

Yet we might see another side to this experience of fathers and daughters within the Freudian canon, a picture mostly dominated by Freud's relationship to his youngest daughter, Anna. There are many signs and mementos of Freud's relationship with his oldest daughter, Sophie. One must imagine Freud observing Sophie and her child, and then noting and making creative use of the fort/da game with the cotton reel, a game through which a child constructs a psychic space for loss and absence. Freud is a father in mourning for a lost daughter in the paper in which the fort/da game is described. Beyond the pleasure principle, one might say, is written in the context of many deaths and traumas, but it is especially haunted by Sophie.

A key text for gender as performative is Joan Riviere's (1929) essay "Womanliness as a Masquerade," a text from which mothers and homoerotic desires have been erased. Instead we have a consideration of women's ambition and potency and phallic striving in which the discourse is entirely between a father and a daughter. In Riviere's essay, the striving woman speaks as a daughter to console and reassure her father (or his substitutes). Please don't be cross or upset or worry. None of my aggression or castrating power plays have real teeth. Girlyness coats the bitter pill of the daughter's potency and challenge. Riviere's essay is both enactment and theoretical progress (see biographical essay by Athol Hughes, 1991). At the end, after she has developed some incendiary ideas that take another 50 years to detonate, Riviere takes it all back and reassures Papa Freud, Jones (her analyst), and Abraham (who by this time is dead) that she is really just drawing on their ideas.

An interesting counterpoint to this is the published writing by the symbolist poet HD about her analysis with Freud in the mid-1930s. In a volume of letters to and from HD, Freud, and HD's lover Bryher, a clinical picture of a bisexual woman emerges (Friedman, 2002). The treatment, undertaken in the most fraught political and social circumstances (Vienna 1933–1934) aided HD in recovering from a debilitating writing block and did not attach or compromise her bisexual identifications or desires. What is intriguing in this context is that Freud interpreted and worked within a maternal transference, that is, the big father (and when one reads about HD's transference-readiness to be in analysis with Freud, one appreciates the bigness of the father) worked as mother.

Did HD have an impact on Freud? Certainly he was proud to have a famous poet for a patient and the accounts of the analytic work are full of the animated discussions of archeology and antiquities. But it is worth noting that during this time of analysis with HD, Freud was working on *Moses and Monotheism*, a book caught up in the meanings of that classical world for religion and for psychic life and identity. At the very least, one might see that the materials of use in that essay were under active discussion in his analytic work with HD.

Yet despite the rather lurid historical picture of the patriarch in the early psychoanalytic clinical picture, fatherhood makes its way into midcentury psychoanalytic theory as the site of safety, reason, lawfulness, and growth. In other words, despite an often quite different clinical picture, fathers and the paternal function carry idealizations of the power of reason, of law, and of language to cut the symbiotic regressive tie to the mother. The father in psychoanalytic theory is the wholesome alternative to madness, refusal of difference, the collapse of subjectivity. This idea persists in some intriguing ways. Benjamin's (1991) ideas of father's identificatory love is a kind of compromise between a feminist theory of gender-neutral parenting and a psychoanalytic model that counterpoises active and passive, reason and madness, regression and activity. The father, still possessing his particular potency as a site of bidirectional identification opens a pathway for a daughter in which he endows her with power, though this is not necessarily sexualized.

There is a viewpoint within the analytic canon that father–daughter incest is quite dramatically underrepresented, underplayed, and underinterpreted (Adams, 2000). But most strikingly viewed retrospectively, there is a subtle tension between theory and clinical practice and experience. This tension moves in a number of directions. There is increasing speculation and clinical evidence that the daughter's "shift" to a heterosexual object, her father, is not a shift, not a renunciation, but an addition, an expansion (Halberstadt-Freud, 1989, 1993). This shift is both initiated and confusingly obfuscated by Freud's own speculations. From Deutsch (1944–1945) and Mack-Brunswick (1940) onward, there is less rupture and repudiation and more movement and complexity to female object choice and father–daughter dynamics.

A second tension arises in the role of the father in preoedipal as well as oedipal life. This elaboration, aided by cultural and social changes, and also by changes in observation and analysis, point to the power of early paternal nurture and the overlay of preoedipal and oedipal life. Chused's (1986) extensively detailed clinical case gives a subtle view of the layering of oedipal and preoedipal feelings (longings and guilts) in the case of a young woman whose primary early nurturing figure was her father. A number of unique aspects of this case and Chused's analysis are worth noting. In some cases, including the case she reports, the father's nurturing and primary care came as a response to maternal illness. So the positive aspects of paternal early care are overlaid and interwoven with maternal absence and the meanings of this early care enter later oedipal guilt in complex triangulations that ensue when one parent is ill or compromised. In Chused's case, the good early father was lost to the daughter in later developmental crises of the family and took considerable analytic work to reconstruct in the transference and in the young woman's psychic experience and memory. But Chused's clinical story illuminates the power of early paternal care, the potency of the father's early attachment and bodily care of his daughter, and the evolution of these dynamics in the daughter's adult character. Pruett's (1983, 1992) accounts of early fathers (of sons and daughters) are more of an observational study with some clinical overlay. One interesting finding is the quality of early paternal play, a quality often remarked on in the baby watcher literature. Father's play with young children has a vitality and often boisterous quality, even with girls, a phenomenon noted by Parens (1990) as well. Chused also explores this idea in examining how to think about the concept of the phallus in the context of early dynamics. Does early father–daughter contact make not only for some identificatory links but also some quality of bodily being—a certain vitality and playful aggressivity—that may have an impact on a daughter's development? Chused's analysand retained a strong feeling about the potency of masculinity in various forms as an identification with her father, or perhaps also with his longings for masculinity.

Chused speculates on particular vicissitudes of oedipal life for girls who in turning away from a dangerous or disappointing oedipal father must erase and eclipse the preoedipal father as well. The patient's long-standing and extensive masochism in relational life, and simultaneously her idealization and dependency on men was shaped by the draconian repression and disavowal of early paternal love and connectedness. Chused and others (e.g., Munder Ross, 1990) are pointing to the dangers— in theory, development, and practice—of not considering the father as a primary object.

A third tension arises in considering the function of the paternal object: a site for autonomy or an organization of desire and object choice. In contemporary work on oedipal resolutions and postoedipality (Cooper, 2003; Davies 2003a, 2003b), there is a complex requirement of any parental object, but certainly the father, for exquisite titration of interest, excitement, and identification. These ideas have some echoing in an earlier work (Leonard, 1966) in which the negative effects of paternal seduction, paternal neglect, paternal possessiveness, or absence are all detailed.

Daughter–Father Oedipality: Heterosexuality Queried

Despite the centrality of oedipal structures and conflicts in the psychoanalytic canon, the elaboration and evolution of thinking psychoanalytically about girls and women has been quickly dominated by the preoedipal dimensions, the power of the maternal body, although it is also true that the homoerotic aspects of that tie have been more clearly elaborated in the cultural theorist world (most prominently Butler, 1993, and Irigaray, 1985) than in the psychoanalytic world. Much of the creative use of Laplanche's (1997) idea of enigmatic maternal seduction has not considered the question of gender, the parent's or the child's. The enigmatic seduction of the paternal body and the differing meanings (conscious or unconscious) attributed to a baby girl or baby boy's body are powerful avenues to consider clinically and theoretically.

An important exception to that tradition in psychoanalysis is Diane Elise (1997, 1998, 2002), who has made theoretical and clinical use of the potent link to the mother's body for the girl and its deep implications for her embodied pleasures. I have argued elsewhere (Harris, 2005) that the contemporary psychoanalytic work on the potency of female pleasure and maternal erotics has its ancestry in some early psychoanalytic figures (Lampl de Groot, 1933, in particular). To a marked degree, the Dora case begins to mark out a terrain for femininity and female sexuality that is multiply configured, bisexual, multilayered, and homoerotic.

What is intriguing and puzzling then is to really understand how it is that the daughter's desire gets refocused on the father. In a certain way, in the account of oedipal development, there is much that remains unmarked, unremarkable, and unanalyzable about heterosexuality. In a keynote address in 2004, Adam Phillips argued for the tenacity of the first objects, the strange dance of new but not too new, new really masking the oldness of the object. He marveled, he said, that women, after the struggle to link to one object had any strength at all to find a second one. The rather patronizing concern for female neurasthenia and exhaustion had many of us in the audience checking our day calendars to be sure this was 2004 not 1904, but the point is certainly interesting. Marie-Christine Hamon (2000) asked the question in a cheekier way. *Why Do Women Love Men and Not Their Mothers* is the title of her book in which she charts the long gap between Freud's struggles in regard to femininity and maternality, and a theoretical grasp on the meaning of early attachment and primary object love.

One of the most interesting tropes in American film from the silent era (perhaps with roots in 19th century melodrama and fiction) is the emblematic situation in which a widower father has the responsibility of raising a young daughter, usually at the outset a prepubescent child. Shirley Temple films mined this arrangement continuously. Curiously, when Graham Greene, undertaking some film criticism, questioned the moral probity of this arrangement, he was wildly attacked.

The films *Paper Moon*, *I'll Fly Away*, and *Because of Winn-Dixie* of the late 20th century continue this enduring fantasy. Does the father pine for a wife, a daughter, or a lover? How does the daughter relate to her father's grief and her own? The missing mother is on occasion replaced with a dog (Winn-Dixie) but mostly stays as a haunting absence. In a sense, all these films play with the safety and danger of fathers and daughters but without the safety net of the active maternal presence. The mother has been beaten back, killed off, eclipsed. This is often her fate and the fate of her desires in psychoanalytic accounts of heterosexuality.

So unexpectedly in examining fathers and daughters, I find myself querying heterosexuality. Not to acknowledge the pun here would be disingenuous, but in a certain way I am and am not "queerying" heterosexuality. The enterprise of queer theory had a particular task to resignify a pathologized form of loving and being. The enterprise was both epistemological and curative. In looking through the lens of father–daughter dyads, I want not to assume heterosexuality as unremarkable and obvious but at the same time to be interested in how (and perhaps why) men are exciting. In a way, this inquiry might be one that includes daughters/girls whose desires are for men and gay men whose objects are also men.

Is there any theoretical advantage in shifting the groupings from the same-sex/opposite sex polarity to a (perhaps) concrete focus on the problem of detaching or expanding desires from the maternal world to a world of men? How does masculinity get sexualized for anybody? Or to ask the question another way, are father–daughter erotics only derivative of maternal longings?

We might look to the question of "Otherness" in considering the power of the father as erotic object for a daughter. Otherness has been the term in Lacanian and some Freudian theory, carrying the desire of the other. But even the syntax is somewhat enigmatic here. Do we mean the mother's desire for the father? Who is being desired in the play of contact between parent and child? Is the mother's desire for the father an element in her sensuality with her child? Is that desire read in some way by the child so that the object of the mother's desire comes to enter as an element in the constituted subjectivity of that child? Is desire like free radicals or is desire a structure always outfitted with certain receptors (the old object Phillips, 2005, fears we can never leave or really effectively transform). Is the feral aspect of desire constituted out of these earlier transmissions?

Another possibility is to consider the paternal object as exciting *sui generis*, as exciting in its enigmatic otherness, its unassimilableness? Is the desire for a masculine or paternal object a connection to phallic power and to its mix of lawfulness and lawlessness? Annie Reich (1953) wrote about a certain kind of women whose object choice was really a narcissistic identification with a powerful phallic object, in which the woman immersed herself in a kind of erotic and identificatory fusion with the powerful man. In this way, the woman achieved a vicarious hit of pleasure in her proximity to power, even if also the woman inhabited this spot in a masochistic way. Might this be a remnant of the tie to a powerful paternal object in which the woman suspends her own agency, finding meaning and subjectivity only as an object of interest for a powerful man? Reich's case material made such women sound masochistic and cannibalistic, empty and voracious.

Or alternatively, is the old object never renounced, always found somewhere in the new object? Interestingly, does a daughter sometimes link herself to and identify the child in the father. Certainly Goldner (1991), writing on spousal violence, found that the women's "love" for the batterer is not for beatings but for a lost child. This could be a narcissistic identification, a telescoping of generations, the search for a lost parent–child part object as well as an accurate read into the psyche of the man–child.

There may be several generations of parent–child object relations collapsed into a particular father–daughter dyad, the psychic project of an earlier generation lived out unconsciously in a father–daughter duet.

Thinking personally, the tomboy persona I adopted in middle childhood might be a kind of compromise formation, retaining the soldiery father figure, linked to the androgynous vital nanny and sequestered from the fragility and depression in my mother.

I think of my transformation into femininity in theatrical terms. Literally, I began to be an actress, performing gender *avant le letter*. Retrospectively, I can see that my performances had a certain potent identification with the kind of women I could see that my father liked. So in entering the world of the theater, I was testing the possibility of being an oedipal winner, always a dubious project. Acting professionally and performing gender got quite entangled. The stage became a powerful but conflicted site for competition with women, exhibitionism, and the uneasy power for a woman in being an object.

But my father's objects were more complex. He did volunteer work for a group devoted to the care of delinquent boys, a group I therefore came to envy and then to desire myself. Now the bad boy as an object of desire is not an unfamiliar category. A twin, a brother, a forbidden love, a fellow criminal. Daphne Merkin writing in the *New York Times* (2005) about the alarming fact of women marrying and courting jailed serial killers could not quite decide how to imagine this phenomenon. A correspondent to the newspaper in which this essay appeared had a thought. A woman wants a bad guy who will be good just to her. Perhaps. But perhaps in the feral character, in an untamed other, a certain charge can arise. Then the father's distal nature, his coming and going, his power, his flight from control, may free him up as an object of desire.

Father–Daughter Oedipality: The Paternal Body and Heterosexuality Multiplied

It is much easier to gender the heterosexual oedipal scene from the father's side. The boy's immersion in and emergence from the maternal enigmatic seduction can leave the traces of an endlessly replicable desire for that maternal body. Lacanian's *petit objet a* comes powerfully and evocatively into place in psychic and unconscious life of the growing man.

Turning to the girl's story, we step right into the theoretical muddles begun by Freud and his colleagues (S. Freud, 1930/1961a, 1931/1961b; Horney, 1967; Jones, 1927, 1933, 1935; Kestenberg, 1968). Benjamin (1991) casts her account of the power of the father's identificatory love in a toddler, preoedipal world. But the implications for oedipal life are surely also present. What Faimberg (2004) has called an oedipal constellation includes the narcissistic as well as more usually oedipal conflicts over sexuality and identity. A number of writers are interested in the vitality and maturity in bisexual bidirectional identifications in postoedipal life (e.g., Bassin, 1996; Benjamin, 1991; Chodorow, 1992; Cooper, 2003; Davies, 2003a, 2003b; Fogel, chapter 12). What this would potentiate for fathers and daughters is a complex and multiply configured experience of admiration, competition, excitement, and containment. Tip in the narcissistic direction and the identificatory process can eclipse difference and sexuality. It is a formidable task from the father's side of the equation. Delight in the emerging sexuality and maturity of the daughter, rueful but steady renunciation of her moves to freedom and otherness in herself and in her loves. Davies (2003b) puts it quite frankly. The child must be an oedipal winner and a loser; the father as well. This is deeply examined and clinically worked by Cooper (2003).

In thinking about the oedipal father, we can recast the importance of the paternal body at a new level. Frequently, paternal anxiety about sexuality can lead to a turning away from a daughter, an eclipse of sexuality and of the developmentally earlier experiences of body connection with a daughter. In thinking both of the father as an object of imagination and desire and the father as an embodied subject, the daughter may find a vital link both as his object and in identification, desiring whom he might desire. This two-way street for desires, identifications, and oedipal engagements lies at the heart of the relational project.

To turn to other aspects of a daughter's subjectivity, to get out of a doer–done to world, a polarized complementarity, the father has the task of imagining his daughter as like him or as he like her. We have to extend and elaborate Benjamin's (1991) idea of identificatory love to inquire if such links from a father contains a feminine identification as well as an extension to her of all the father imagines for himself or a son. This relational matrix is what I would call softly assembled, fractal, manifold, often contradictory and endlessly dynamically transforming. In the idea of soft assembly (Harris, 2005) I propose a view of gender as co-constructed, as relationally elaborated and emergent from many transactions of meaning. A daughter's gender identity, as she experiences it and as her father imagines it (to cite only one relational configuration) could include a range of body states, self experiences, affective styles, ways of looking and acting, which all come into a complex web of meanings for father and daughter.

We can marvel at this ideal of a father's holding and recognizing a daughter because we more usually live in clinical situations in which the barrenness or dangerousness of the father's conception of and relating to his daughter is told with its devastating consequences. Not to be libidinized at all, Davies (2003a) has cogently argued, leaves a daughter often immobilized and without optimism in regard to her impact on lovers. Anxiety about a daughter's sexuality can default to terrifying repression, depression, and retreat and abandonment, or an often sexualized violence.

Dangerous Fathers

Despite our theorizing of the protective function of the paternal imago and its role in preserving the child from the dangers of fusion with the mother, actual fathers are quite dramatically, statistically speaking, a source of danger inside the family.

Lauren has spent several decades actively trying to manage the very fraught identifications of and projective identifications from her quite disturbed but often charismatic father. Lauren's father, a man with a lethal and perverse imagination, considered all family as property. He conjured up a terrifying world in which he was a secret mobster/cop/hero/villain and employed a psychic violence and recklessness in relation to his daughter that continues to this day to have its effect. Lauren's struggle to remain visible and palpable to herself, to remain unerased, plays in every sphere of her life.

She has understood how much she had to camouflage of her beauty, intelligence, ambition, and maternality in order to avoid his very devastating attacks, psychic and physical. Early in this excavation she would, in moments of conflict with her partner or indeed with anyone, become highly dissociative, almost depersonalized and passive, as though stunned with beating and beratement. She has learned to observe and understand these states of fragmentation and to be amazed and often concerned that too many of these situations are triggered by conflict with her partner, a woman, who, although officially determined to protect Lauren, also traumatizes her. The dangerous father has in a certain way been excavated into her partner. But in another way, Lauren is quite identified with the competent business man, workman father, although that identification was often felt to be too threatening to most of Lauren's family, but particularly her presentation of a highly skilled professional identity produced mocking and chaos in the father who had destroyed children (male) from an earlier marriage and was violently homophobically critical of Lauren and her brother.

When she had a child, she was able to make a bridge to her mother and to have some reparative experiences in a genealogy of mother/daughter/granddaughter. The father was simply too disturbed to be brought into this possibility. A very few visits with her young daughter and the father's ribald and highly perverse comments had Lauren dissociated again and the visits were soon abandoned.

Lauren's current task is to tolerate the flowering of both maternal and paternal identifications and to sort through the complex meaning of being a woman with some physicality. Conventional feminine manifestations, deeply important to both her parents, are not what Lauren searches for. Many of the conventional trappings of gender were contaminated by Lauren's parents' perverse use of such conventions. But she is interested in her own impulse toward disguise and camouflage, the danger of a father's sight. This father, now some years dead, can still dominate Lauren's internal world, even as she plays out some powerful forms of identification with him.

Looked at one way, Lauren and her brother switched gender positions, the brother staying very mother-identified and mother-dependent as a way to protect her from the violence of the marital circumstances she could not seem to escape. Lauren's gender enigmaticness, her androgyny, and her occupation of space between genders were perhaps her deep theory of safety in her family. One would have been doomed and under assault as son or daughter.

Is it only chance, or only related to other developments in her life, that Lauren is reclaiming sexuality? To parent and as it happened to do so in close geographic proximity to her parents, her sexual life became for a time eclipsed. Recently she purchased the first year of the TV series *The L Word* on DVD and the effect was profound. Her partner too frequently reproduces some thing of Lauren's father's rageful affect. Yet Lauren's evolution into a sexual being is her hope for something reparative for herself and her partner, a place where the father might not penetrate (I use that word deliberately).

Karen's relation to a dangerous father is somewhat different. Her father's quite odd obsessions with bodies (his, his wife's, and Karen's) have been taken up as quite severe and exacting internal regulatory and persecutory experiences. In early childhood I think this father was exciting and somewhat glamorous, though highly anxious and obsessional. He seemed an important and securing figure in relation to a more depressive and angry mother. This shifted after a very catastrophic divorce when Karen was 6 and Karen entered a strangely liminal state of go-between for the father's child-support check and the mother's collapse and despairing need for help and resources. Their conflict became a deep internal aspect of Karen's inner mental/bodily world, leaving her shaken and uncertain about worth, value, meaning, and love but very certain that money was a dangerous luxury and a frightening specter everywhere she turned. She became precociously independent, highly anxious, and immobilized under situations of anger or conflict. She could see over time how mad and perverse her father's obsessions were, that his fears about his own body and his preoccupations with hers were clearly toxic and mad. She came to feel more protected as her mother gained ground, maturity, and competence, but she needed an enormous degree of support and care from older women figures (including her therapist) for a significant period.

With Karen and Lauren, one sees the various price tags on rebellion and refusal and on obedience. One daughter responds to paternal violence with conformity and a very stereotypic femininity (certainly a kind of armor). Lauren's armor was a negation of gender and a hidden life as a good son. Karen has hidden out in a deeply carved conventional femininity, an almost hysterically charged and shallow performance of daughterliness.

Lost and Melancholy Fathers

Hope and sadness can also dominate a daughter's relation to her father. For some father–daughter pairs, negotiating a daughter's adolescence and burgeoning sexuality can be fraught with conflict. Charlotte retained a powerful feeling of bedrock, an undissolvable tie to her father though contact had actually stopped several decades earlier. Much examination of this in analysis revealed the power of her hopes and alongside a kind of uncanny disbelief that her father (the one held in mind) could vanish. We began to see together how he had perhaps vanished many, many years earlier. But talk and analytic work and reflection could never quite dispel the magical charm with which this father (of her very early memory) was endowed. The good dad who surely must return seemed to be a deep part of procedural memory. Hannah, who finally could not process the strange disturbing intrusiveness of her father in her adolescence, also held an experience of an earlier devoted and caring father, a father of early infancy who was actually more capable of love and attunement than her angry, unhappy mother. These are melancholy apparitions, never fully metabolizable as lost or gone.

At my father's funeral, a man who had been a contemporary of my younger sister stood up to say how much my father had helped him in his adolescence, how important and steadying a force he had been for this man when he was growing up. He was talking about style and an easy glamour that my father had in abundance. He was talking about emotional warmth. I now understand how much my father masked his anxiety with humor and genuine warmth. In his 20s, ready for the birth of his daughter, this man went to talk to my father. "How do you father a daughter?" he asked. "Well," my father said, "basically you just drive them around places, roll down the window, and hand out cash. That's really it." There was certainly a ring of truth to this. The anecdote conjures an image that took me up and down the emotional landscape. Passive, yes. Benevolent, yes. More dutiful than imaginatively engaged, certainly. But whether it was as trivial as shopping or as fraught as a large formal party, my father was happy to launch us and make sure we were supplied. It was liberation from the more anxious and often angry intrusion of our mother. Yet, of course, the soldier, the involved competent, the engaged warrior is gone. That confidence leeched away over the years.

Conclusion

Fathers and daughters are softly assembled. There are systems within systems, multiple narrative scenarios, and many ways gender, sexuality, identity positions dependent and independent of these phenomena coevolve. Perhaps, in all such configurations we see the long hand of history, even as Faimberg (2004) has described, the telescoping of generations in which object ties from other generations work their way into the gender arrangements of men and women, parents and children. "Fathering" and "daughtering" can cross gender, can multiply and eclipse. I could not just write of one father and daughter. My own situation is one story of many. One of the surprising lessons for me in writing this chapter is that I have understood that while I always felt gender fluid in childhood, the parental and fatherly aspects of my adult character have never felt gendered as father. So in thinking of "fathers" and "daughters," it will be important to pay attention to a lot of clinical individuality and specificity. For some, gender is a significant factor in character, for others gender may not be salient or may be variably salient.

In tracing this history of psychoanalytic theorizing of father–daughter relatedness, I unexpectedly discovered that of all the potential dyads of parent–child (i.e., mother–son, mother–daughter, father–son, father–daughter) it is the dyad of father–daughter that has changed most dramatically over the century of psychoanalytic history and writing. I am also mindful that I may be tracing a line of inquiry that is altering and perhaps disappearing. As functions like containment, authorizing sexuality, paving a way to separation and autonomy, cultivating dependency and regression get dislocated from gender, becoming more gender agnostic, many other features of character and subjectivity may carry these psychic and intersubjective functions. Generational differences rather than more strictly gender differences may be more prominent. If gender saturation is variable, historically contingent, and mutative, fathers and daughters will have highly idiosyncratic forms in some but not all relational configurations. Even as particularly material phenomena, maternal or paternal bodies may evolve within histories and contexts of great variability. People may come to conduct the psychic projects of identification, evolving desires, and objects of love and need, and orchestrating many intersubjective agendas is ways that may or may not involve gender.

In revising this chapter for this book on heterosexual masculinities, I am mindful of the need to see how a father and daughter are involved inevitably in a co-construction, asymmetrical to be sure but interdependent. This idea, central to Reis and Grossmark's revision of masculinity and fathering, requires a lot of rethinking about development and about gender meaning.

I have a number of concluding thoughts and speculations. In looking at case material involving some pattern of father–daughter pairing, I am struck by how hard it is to see the impact of the child upon the parent. I am thinking particularly of daughters where they bear some powerful form of intergenerational transmission of trauma. A woman, now in middle age, can see in the tiny nooks and crannies of her daily life how much deep terror and anxiety transmitted from her father's boyhood shapes her every move. Looking back on this deeply loved though flawed parent, she feels that she could not make an impact, could have no reparative or healing effect. This does not mean she did not have an effect, only that it is opaque to her. Another woman, also now middle aged, was able to do considerable reparation with her father at the end of his life and a big component of that reparation was the father's relationship with the woman's daughter. One might think about the possibility of cross-generational work in co-construction, that a compromised father may function remarkably well as a grandfather.

A second thought is that my examples and much of the theorizing of masculinity keeps us within a mostly white, middle- or upper-middle class Western world. If one laces race, culture, ethnicity, and class into these matrices, more complex effects no doubt pertain. An added factor is history. Our patients' experiences inevitably cross historical periods and currently do so in a period of rapid cultural change. Masculinity, perhaps as potently as femininity a generation ago, is under construction. It is actually impossible to know whether the frozen rigidity of many experiences of fathers is an artifact of theory or a fact of history.

I am also aware that a number of my examples of father–daughter that explore the transmission of masculinities or femininities within a heterosexual context could easily be reconfigured for their homoerotic potential. These terms appear but not with fixed meanings, at least not always. There are material conditions; men identify as heterosexual or homosexual, feminine or masculine, and these experiences have weight and gravitas and meaning. But I am reminded of a fascinating case reported by Quinodoz (1998, 2002) who treated a 40-year-old male-to-female transsexual. Masculinity and father identification had been powerfully evacuated by the analysand. The treatment, an analysis that deepened the patient's feminine identification, did so through a deep reconnection to lost masculinity, a grieving over a broken tie to the father, and through mourning a bigendered identity within a heterosexually lived marriage as a woman to a man. The conclusion I would draw from this case is that when deep ties to gendered experience can be held in mind, many forms of life can be lived with vitality and imagination. Desire was organized in a heterosexual scene with a man, alongside many currents and multiplicities of self and object. It is a case in which gender matters and it does not, or where it matters but matter is in motion.

Acknowledgment

This chapter is an expansion of "Fathers' and 'Daughters," *Psychoanalytic Inquiry*, 28(1), 2008, pp. 39–59. Reprinted with permission.

References

Abelin, E. (1971). The role of the father in the separation-individuation process. In J. B. McDevitt & C. F. Settlage (Eds.), *Separation-Individuation* (pp. 229–252). New York: International University Press.

Adams, P. L. (2000). Childism as vestiges of infanticide. *Journal of the American Academy of Psychoanalysis, 28*, 541–556.

Balsam, R. (1989). The paternal possiblity. In S. H. Cath, A. Gurwitt, & L. Gunsberg (Eds.), *Fathers and Their Families* (p. 584). Hillsdale, NJ: Analytic Press.

Bassin, D. (1996). Beyond the he and the she: Toward the reconciliation of masculinity and femininity in the post-oedipal female mind. *Journal of the American Psychoanalytic Association, 44*(Suppl.), 157–190.

Benjamin, J. (1988). *The Bonds of Love. Psychoanalysis, Feminism and the Problem of Domination*. New York: Pantheon Books.

Benjamin, J. (1991). Father and daughter: Identification with difference—A contribution to gender heterodoxy. *Psychoanalytic Dialogues, 1*, 277–299.

Butler, J. (1990). *Gender Trouble: Feminism and the Subversion of Identity*. New York: Routledge.

Butler, J. (1993). *Bodies That Matter: On the Discursive Limits of Sex*. New York: Routledge.

Butler, J. (1997a). *Excitable Speech*. New York: Routledge.

Butler, J. (1997b). *The Psychic Life of Power: Theories of Subjection*. Stanford, CA: Stanford University Press.

Chasseguet-Smirgel, J. (1970). Feminine guilt and the Oedipus complex. In J. Chasseguet-Smirgel, *Female Sexuality* (pp. 94–134). London: Maresfield Library. (Original French edition, 1964)

Chasseguet-Smirgel, J. (1985). *Creativity and Perversion*. London: Free Association Books.

Chiland, C. (1982). A new look at fathers. *Psychoanalytic Study of the Child, 37*, 367–379.

Chodorow, N. (1992). Heterosexuality as a compromise formation. Reflections on the psycho-analytic theory of sexual development. *Psychoanalysis and Contemporary Thought, 15*, 267–304.

Chused, J. F. (1986). Consequences of paternal nurturing. *Psychoanalytic Study of the Child, 41,* 419–438.

Cooper, S. (2003). You say oedipal, I say postoedipal: A consideration of desire and hostility in the analytic relationship. *Psychoanalytic Dialogues, 13*(1), 41–63.

Corbett, K. (1993). The mystery of homosexuality. *Psychoanalytic Psychology, 10*, 345–357.

Corbett, K. (1999). Homosexual boyhood: Notes on girlyboys. In M. Rottnek (Ed.), *Sissies and Tomboys: Gender Nonconformity and Homosexual Childhood* (pp. 107–139). New York: New York University Press.

Corbett, K. (2001a). Faggot = loser. *Studies in Gender and Sexuality, 2*, 3–28.

Corbett, K. (2001b). More life: Centrality and marginality in human development. *Psychoanalytic Dialogues, 11*, 313–335.

Davies, J. (2003a), Falling in love with love: Oedipal and postoedipal manifestations of idealization, mourning, and erotic masochism. *Psychoanalytic Dialogues, 13*, 1–27.

Davies, J. (2003b). Reflections on Oedipus, post-oedipus and termination. *Psychoanalytic Dialogues, 13*(1), 65–75.

Deutsch, H. (1944–1945). *The Psychology of Women* (Vols. 1 and 2). New York: Grune & Stratton.

Dimen, M. (2003). *Sexuality, Intimacy, Power*. Hillsdale, NJ: The Analytic Press.

Elise, D. (1997). Primary femininity, bisexuality and the female ego ideal: A re-examination of female developmental theory. *Psychoanalytic Quarterly, 66*, 489–517.

Elise, D. (1998). The absence of the paternal penis. *Journal of the American Psychoanalytic Association, 46*, 413–442.

Elise, D. (2002). The primary maternal oedipal situation and female homoerotic desire. *Psychoanalytic Inquiry, 22*(2), 209–228.

Faimberg, H. (2004). *The Telescoping of Generations*. London: Karnac.

Freud, A. (1923). The relation of beating phantasies to a day-dream. *International Journal of Psycho-Analysis, 4*, 89–102.

Freud, S. (1955a). Studies on hysteria. In J. Strachey (Ed.), *The Standard Edition of the Complete Psychological Works of Sigmund Freud* (Vol. 1, pp. 1–305). London: Hogarth Press. (Original work published 1895)

Freud, S. (1955b). A child is being beaten. In J. Strachey (Ed.), *The Standard Edition of the Complete Psychological Works of Sigmund Freud* (Vol. 17, pp. 179–204). London. Hogarth Press. (Original work published 1919)

Freud, S. (1955c). The psychogenesis of a case of homosexuality in a woman. In J. Strachey (Ed.), *The Standard Edition of the Complete Psychological Works of Sigmund Freud* (Vol. 18, pp. 147–172). London: Hogarth Press. (Original work published 1920)

Freud, S. (1957). A case of paranoia running counter to the psychoanalytic theory of the disease. In J. Strachey (Ed.), *The Standard Edition of the Complete Psychological Works of Sigmund Freud* (Vol. 14, pp. 261–272). London: Hogarth Press. (Original work published 1915)

Freud, S. (1961a). Civilization and its discontents. In J. Strachey (Ed.), *The Standard Edition of the Complete Psychological Works of Sigmund Freud* (Vol. 21, pp. 59–145). London: Hogarth Press. (Original work published 1930)

Freud, S. (1961b). Female sexuality. In J. Strachey (Ed.), *The Standard Edition of the Complete Psychological Works of Sigmund Freud* (Vol. 21, pp. 223–243). London: Hogarth Press. (Original work published 1931)

Friedman, S. (2002), *Analyzing Freud. Letters of HD, Bryher and Their Circle.* New York: New Directions.

Goldner, V. (1991). Toward a critical relational theory of gender. *Psychoanalytic Dialogues, 1,* 249–272.

Goldner, V. (2003). Ironic gender/authentic sex. *Studies in Gender and Sexuality, 4,* 113–139.

Halberstadt-Freud, H. C. (1989). Electra in bondage: On symbiosis and the symbiotic illusion between mother and daughter and the consequences for the Oedipus Complex. *Free Associations, 17,* 58–89.

Halberstadt-Freud, H. C. (1993). Do women change their object? In H. Groen-Prakken & A. Ladan (Eds.), *The Dutch Annual of Psychoanalysis* (Vol. 1, pp. 169–190). Amsterdam/Lisse: Swets and Zeitlinger.

Hamon, M.-C. (1992). *Pourquoi les femmes aiment-elles les hommes?* Paris: Seuil.

Harris, A. (1991). Gender as contradiction. *Psychoanalytic Dialogues, 1,* 107–244.

Harris, A. (2004). Hatred at close range. In D. Moss (Ed.), *Hatred in the First Person Plural* (pp. 249–278). New York: Other Press..

Harris, A. (2005). *Gender as Soft Assembly.* Hillsdale, NJ: The Analytic Press

Horney, K. (1967). On the genesis of the castration complex in women. *International Journal of Psychoanalysis, 5,* 50–66.

Hughes, A. (1991). Joan Riviere: Her life and work. In A. Hughes (Ed.), *Joan Riviere: Collected Papers: 1920–1958* (pp. 1–55). London: Karnac.

Irigaray, L. (1985). *The Speculum of the Other Woman.* Ithaca, NY: Cornell University Press.

Jones, E. (1927). The early development of female sexuality. *International Journal of Psycho-Analysis, 8,* 459–472.

Jones, E. (1933). The phallic phase. *International Journal of Psycho-Analysis, 14,* 1–33.

Jones, E. (1935). Early female sexuality. *International Journal of Psycho-Analysis, 16,* 263–273.

Kestenberg, J. (1968). Outside and inside, male and female. *Journal of the American Psychoanalytic Association, 16,* 457–520.

Lampl de Groot, J. (1933). Problems of femininity. *Psychoanalytic Quarterly, 2,* 489–518.

Laplanche, J. (1989). *New Foundations for Psychoanalysis.* London: Blackwell.

Laplanche, J. (1997). The theory of seduction and the problem of the other. *International Journal of Psycho-Analysis, 78,* 653–666.

Layton, L. (1998). *Who's That Girl? Who's That Boy? Clinical Practice Meets Postmodernism*. Northvale, NJ: Aronson.

Layton, L. (2002). Gendered subjects, gendered agents: Toward an integration of postmodern theory and relational analytic practice. In M. Dimen & V. Goldner (Eds.), *Gender in Psychoanalytic Space: Between Clinic and Culture* (pp. 285–311). New York: Other Press.

Leonard, M. R. (1966). Fathers and daughters—The significance of "fathering" in the psychosexual development of the girl. *International Journal of Psycho-Analysis, 47*, 325 –334.

Mack-Brunswick, R. (1940). The preoedipal phase of the libido development. *Psychoanalytic Quarterly, 9*, 293–319.

Merkin, D. (2005, August 28). Passion and the prisoner. *New York Times*.

Munder Ross, J. (1990). The eye of the beholder: On the developmental dialogue between fathers and daughters. In R. A. Nemiroff & C. A. Colarusso (Eds.), *New Dimensions in Adult Development* (pp. 47–72). New York: Basic Books.

Parens, H. (1990). On the girl's psychosexual development: Reconsiderations suggested from direct observation. *Journal of the American Psychoanalytic Association, 38*, 743–772.

Phillips, A. (2004, April 10–14). *Freud as Modernist*. Keynote paper presented at Division 39, American Psychological Association, New York.

Pruett, K. D. (1983). Infants of primary nurturing fathers. *Psychoanalytic Study of the Child, 38*, 257–277

Pruett, K. D. (1992). Latency development in children of primary nurturing fathers—Eight-year follow-up. *Psychoanalytic Study of the Child, 47*, 85–101.

Quinodoz, D. (1998). A fe/male transsexual patient in psychoanalysis. *International Journal of Psycho-Analysis, 79*, 95–111.

Quinodoz, D. (2002). Termination of a fe/male transsexual patient's analysis: An example of general validity. *International Journal of Psycho-Analysis, 83*, 783–798.

Reich, A. (1953). Narcissistic object choice in women. *Journal of the American Psychoanalytic Association, 1*, 22–44

Riviere, J. (1929). Womanliness as a masquerade. *International Journal of Psycho-Analysis, 9*, 303–313.

Silverman, M. A. (2002). Homosexuality in two women treated from the age of nine years. *Psychoanalytic Inquiry, 22*, 259–277.

Torok, M. (1970). The significance of penis envy in women. In J. Chasseguet-Smirgel (Ed.), *Female Sexuality* (pp. 135–170). London: Maresfield Library. (Original French edition, 1964)

Winnicott, D. W. (1971). *Playing and Reality*. London: Tavistock Publications.

Young-Bruehl, E. (1988). *Anna Freud*. London: Macmillan.

Young-Bruehl, E. (1989). Looking for Anna Freud's mother. *Psychoanalytic Study of the Child, 44*, 391–408.

Zeavin, L. (2004). As useless as tits on a bull? Psychoanalytic reflections on misogyny. In D. Moss (Ed.), *Hating in the First Person Plural* (pp. 227–258). New York: Other Press. 10

11

Finding a Father
Repetition, Difference, and Fantasy in *Finding Nemo*

Louis Rothschild

Over a decade ago a shift occurred within a majority of the public men's bathrooms in the United States. At issue was the appearance of changing tables. In response to the appearance of these tables, Calvin Trillin (1995) wondered within the pages of the *New Yorker* if the presence of a cooing baby being changed by a soft, sensitive father would alter the traditional edginess found in men's rooms. Trillin's observation of traditional edginess and his curiosity regarding contemporary softness depict significant features of the social representation and compromise formation that characterize a general psychology of masculinities.

Edginess may be understood as an enactment of the belief that masculinity requires a clandestine if not adamant renunciation of traits marked feminine, coupled with a lived inability to banish feminine identification from psychic life. A task-oriented steadiness that attempts to bypass the conflict of compromise by devaluing experiences marked feminine has been referred to as pathological arrhythmicity (Kupers, 1993). Within psychoanalysis, such wishful pathology has long been observed and illustrated from Little Hans' fear of being bitten to the tragedy of Sophocles' Oedipus. In these studies and stories, we see experiential dread over the thought that masculine security may be an oxymoron. Put somewhat differently, due to the partiality of defense, an active doubting is a part of masculinity—what Judith Butler (1992) has playfully called penis size envy. Such doubting appears to often lead to a homosocial enactment of desperation for approval (cf. Connell, 1990; Rothschild, 2003).

Engaged fathering heightens a pragmatic need for a psychological security that can comfortably acknowledge uncertainty and flexibility (cf. Diamond, 1998; Ducat, 2004; Herzog, 2001). This need may be attributed

to a normative trend in which dual income families require that men perform work previously categorized as women's work that is now referred to
as second shift work (Marsiglio & Peck, 2004). Such a trend might afford
enhanced sex role flexibility (cf. Diamond, 1998). However, diapering in
the men's room or any second shift labor for that matter could equally
be understood as a ritualized womb envy (cf. Munroe & Munroe, 1994)
that reactively thwarts such flexibility via compartmentalization and disavowal. A Kleinian formulation of womb envy (Ducat, 2004) posits that
men disavow a feminine identity and transfer their envy of devalued and
relegated traits to women's subjective desire. In this transfer, men's womb
envy becomes woman's envy of masculine social roles (cf. Layton, 2004a,
2004b). Such defensive disavowal would serve to inoculate the explicit
identification with a feminine softness experienced by an edgy (read anxious) man. Taken as a generalized social representation that is experienced
in particular compromise formations, mothering in the men's room war-
rants a critical evaluation of whether a contemporary heterosexual father
is different from a traditional father in terms of degree or kind. By addressing father–son matrixes as depicted in the popular film *Finding Nemo*
(Stanton, 2003), I aim to show that this tale of a father's and son's quest
for relatedness may be understood as a move beyond and something of a
perpetuation of the edgy distancing that has been considered a primary
ingredient of father hunger (Herzog, 2001).

This popular film affords an opportunity to assess contemporary nego-
tiations between an ideal and what is real. As with any artistic creation,
this film is approached below as a mechanized artifact that simultaneously perpetuates hegemony, while creating a space in which a new experience might occur (Fischer, 1963). Framing this evaluation is what might
now be considered a substantial outcropping of work on fathering within
psychoanalysis. Diamond (1998) notes that when a good enough father is
available, a reassurance may be found that allows a boy a space in which
identification with mother, and therefore softness, need not be disavowed.
Similarly, Ducat (2004) states that apron strings may adhere to both mother
and father in a manner that values mothering and fathering by mothers
and fathers. Yet, Diamond (1998) has also noted that despite social changes
such as enhanced sex role flexibility found in contemporary culture, that
father's are typically portrayed in an idealized fashion, not as real people,
and that our view of development continues to be matricentric.

In regard to contemporary portrayals of fathering, *Finding Nemo* is
refreshing in that it conveys a narrative of masculine development as
a lifelong process in which *softness* and uncertainty are as primary as

assertive *hardness*, but the film's cathartic end suggests that true complete-ness and certainty are possible, while simultaneously devaluing women in a manner that is consistent with the womb envy of hegemonic masculin-ity described above. Additionally, the film's narrative illustrates structural and psychological changes within a subset of contemporary nuclear fami-lies now headed by people born into the cohort referred to as generation X, those born between 1960 and 1980, and such changes have implications for hegemonic masculinity.

A Personal Frame

In regard to the post–baby boomer cohort referred to as generation X, Carlo Strenger (2005) has noted that fathering is fraught with uncertainty as one's frame from which to act is altered in a social world in which mar-ketability and therefore a tantalizing transience are viewed as inherently more valuable than the continuity of cultural tradition. Similarly, Milan Kundera (2007) has noted that one sign of modernism is that comfort with the status quo is comfort with continual change. Kundera and Strenger are describing a zeitgeist in which uncertainty is certain. Utilizing Lacan, Strenger describes fatherlessness as the disruption of the familial trans-mission of cultural values due to a privileging of the horizontal values of the cohort. To the extent that a father feels outside of the world inhabited by offspring, the ability to perform what Campbell (1949/1973) has referred to as atonement with the father, which may be considered a second birth of initiation into the order of the world, is truncated.

It is my contention that the film *Finding Nemo* may be understood as a portrait of fathering in a poststructural world, as the central plot rotates around a doubting father whose ability to maintain relational continuity with his son is in jeopardy. In this regard, the film is viewed as depict-ing changes and challenges in contemporary life in a fashion similar to Freud's understanding that the differences between the stories of Hamlet and Oedipus revealed changes in those respective civilizations (Freud, 1900). For my purpose here, *Finding Nemo* is to *Pinocchio* (Collodi, 1892/2001) what Hamlet is to Oedipus. Simply, although each father pos-sess a strong drive for a relatedness and continuity with their respective son, Pinocchio's father Geppetto possess a certainty of the larger world and subsequently a sense of self that Nemo's father does not, and this loss of an intergenerational holding environment has significant implications in regard to autonomy and generativity (cf. Blatt, 2008).

An interpretation that connects art to the psychology of the author was not far from the mind of Andrew Stanton, who wrote and directed the film. Stanton, a member of generation X, was 37 years old when *Finding Nemo* was released in 2003. He was candid regarding the manner in which feelings of protectiveness in response to uncertainty regarding his own sons, then 10 and 7, underscored an anxious daydream of abandonment and loss experienced while visiting a crowded aquarium (Corliss, 2003). Although Stanton does not speak to his particular uncertainty as culturally mediated, the writer's commentary and film's primary focus on uncertainty co-occur with the demands of contemporary social role flexibility and fractured generational continuity. My own experience in fathering supports the idea that in addition to unique individual history, shared cultural representations significantly shape mental life in the construction of fathering.

On a day when my wife was at work and I was the parent at home, the pediatric nurse practitioner whom we see looked up to inform me that she had diagnosed pneumonia after listening to my then 3-year-old son's chest. Memories of my own childhood asthma were rekindled as I carried my son from the car to the pharmacy and finally to the video store. His cohort affords what may be considered a sort of preschool coffee klatch that possesses a symbolic order that I know a little about. In possession of some common ground, I could decipher that over the past weeks he had been referring to Nemo, and that this was the name of what was then a new movie that had little to do with the captain in *20,000 Leagues Under the Sea* (Verne, 1870/2003) other than sharing a name and the setting of an ocean. A cartoon whose impact has spawned clown fish–decorated beach towels and themed attractions had found its way into my son's psychology, despite his not yet owning any accoutrements or having seen the film.

While renting the film, I remembered a helpless look on my own father's face, signifying isolation that each of us felt some years ago when my pediatrician had difficulty inserting an IV into my then 5-year-old arm during what was to be a 3-day hospital admission for asthma. In this transgenerational moment of remembering as a son while simultaneously acting and feeling as a father, I was not aware that my son and I were to view a film that reviewers have considered a portrait of love in a father–son dyad whose narrative addresses the difficulty found in the tension of holding and letting go (O'Sullivan, 2003). Further, I had no foresight that repeated viewings were to lead to a rekindling of my undergraduate work on gender and a return to conversation with a mentor from that time (i.e., Ducat, Metzl, & Rothschild, 2008).

Nemo's Tale

Following a traumatic opening in which Nemo's father, Marlin, witnesses the death of his wife and the consumption of every fish egg, save the one that will be Nemo, we fast forward to an excited Nemo waking his father on his first day of school. Marlin, the father clown fish, is nervous, and Nemo's excitement is experienced by Marlin as a threat. He suggests that his son put off school for another year. What will be an eventual rupture in their relationship has begun with the father's insecurity related to the recognition that his son is motivated and capable. Marlin cannot situate Nemo's autonomy in a manner that might coexist with dependency needs met by a supportive father. This lack of recognition leaves Nemo in a fatherless situation where being initiated into the structure of the world is in jeopardy as Nemo is asked to sacrifice autonomy in favor of a rigid dependency. Such a precarious position is illustrated throughout the film as Nemo possess a chronic and motivated habit of getting stuck in tubes and requesting help in freeing himself. Repetitive attempts to experience the affirmation of autonomy appear as attempts to complete a second birth in which father provides a holding environment.

As a result of the son rebelling under his father's suffocating inability to constructively support Nemo's autonomy, the angry son is exposed and kidnapped by a hobbyist diver who maintains an extensive saltwater fish tank in his dental office. The surrogate characters Nemo comes into contact with while living in the dentist's fish tank lead him to learn something new about the relation between autonomy and dependency. It so happens that the fish leader of the tank has the same injury as Nemo—a damaged fin. In his identification with this fish, Nemo learns to act on and in the world, injury notwithstanding. Having surmounted his weakness by accepting it, Nemo finds self-assurance in his successful swimming up the intake tube of the tank's filter in order to disable it and initiate an escape plan for the fish. Despite having been formally initiated into his fish tank family, affording a newfound self-assurance, and having an escape plan to return home, Nemo longs for a reunion with his father.

The father on a quest to rescue his son also finds greater self-assurance from his interaction with three characters: first, a potential love interest who alters Marlin's rigid conception of autonomy by teaching that fleeting certainty is an existential truth; second, an enraged shark who bemoans never having known his own father, thus illustrating the danger that too little support of a son's autonomy may create the distorting threat of an angry compensatory exaggeration (cf. Blatt, 2008); and then a sea turtle father who dwells in an extended kinship network that affords an ability to maintain a mutual intergenerational relationship with his own son and father in which autonomy and dependence exist in an affirming dialectic. Eventually, the central father and son clown fish are reunited and encounter a conflict that affords an opportunity for the father and son to recognize and affirm each other as separate, autonomous, and capable of generativity on the one hand and simultaneously connected in mutual love. Their relationship healed, the film ends at the beginning with a significant difference. Again it is the first day of school. This time, a now playful father wakes his son announcing that it is time for school, a reversal illustrating a newfound security and capacity for play.

Analysis

With elements of exposure to danger, rescue, and homecoming, the Nemo story fits the criterion of a folk narrative that embodies oedipal themes (cf. Dundes, 2002; Rank, 1909/1990). The proximal or primary parent who is the source of affection is depicted in a manner in which the parent has no interests other than parenting. This hyperengaged parent who is fantastically idealized may be considered a wish-fulfilling character.

Considered an additional object to mother's primary status, traditional developmental lines favor father as an agent of separation, as fathers are considered to help resolve dyadic conflicts from rapprochement through the oedipal triad (Tyson & Tyson, 1990). However, starting in the 1980s developmental research began to challenge such assumptions due to social change in family patterns (Lamb, 1984, cited in Tyson & Tyson, 1990). For example, in nuclear families in which there is a primary nurturing father and a working mother, father becomes the primary object representation, yet with typical oedipal, read not negative involvement (Pruett, 1984, cited in Tyson & Tyson, 1990).

The challenge depicted in the film is the challenge of finding a voice that speaks with authority, while simultaneously tolerating uncertainty so that another's voice may be affirmed. As Nemo's father is terrified of the vulnerability of uncertain relatedness, there is no room for him to support his son's autonomy. From an attachment theory perspective, father's demand for Nemo's excessive dependence interferes with his son's self-assurance (Fonagy, 2001). Nemo runs the danger of a collapse of self, found throughout most of the film as shown by his frequent utterance of "I can't." This eventually changes to "I can," as assertiveness no longer ushers in the threat of abandonment (cf. Masterson & Rinsley, 1975). For his part, Nemo's father may also be considered to be contending with abandonment fears that retard his ability to appropriately weather his son's developmental process. Such an impediment renders the father unable to see the manner in which his own anxiety has thwarted the affirmative mirroring necessary to forge a mutual relationship. Nemo's rebellious break begins to rework the pathological separation between father and son in a hopeful direction of finding a tolerated and playful separateness. In the externalized separation born of rebellion lies the struggle to negate without sacrificing the other—a threat of destruction as an effort to differentiate in order to be recognized (cf. Benjamin, 1988). The center of narrative gravity then, in *Finding Nemo*, is the struggle for a recognition that facilitates action. To that end, the drama of the film focuses on the questions: Will Nemo or his father be forever separated, destroyed? Will they survive, and if so, might these two selves recognize each other in a supportive fashion? The storyline supports a conception of fathering in which assertion and difference need not lead to abandonment, as by the end of the film, Nemo finds that his father can tolerate and support his assertiveness and knowing this he is able to say, "I don't hate you."

It is striking that at a historical juncture in which fathers may become primary objects in some families, as Nemo's father is depicted in this film, there is a concern regarding fatherlessness—that is, a lack of a holding environment that would be considered a sphere of cultural authority and continuity. It is my contention that the fear of fatherlessness is related to the loss of an idealized father in a postmodern climate. To that end, I would suggest that while indeed a father who is not all knowing is potentially terrifying due to the presence of uncertainty, there exists in this very uncertainty an opening in which a son's difference may be affirmed. Although uncertainty appears necessary for relatedness (Mitchell, 2002), defensive attempts to resurrect the certainty of a strong father appear as ordinary edginess. Within *Finding Nemo* such defensiveness is found to afford a reified certainty. Here, news of Nemo's father's quest reaches Nemo in the dentist's aquarium via a stork with a hysterical character, and father is presented as a superhero who has gone to war to save his son. However, the viewer is situated to know that the father is in fact fallible, and to that end the idealization is fractured and becomes a focus of play within the story.

Finding Nemo is a developmental story for both father and son. It is told from each of their perspectives. In this story of mutual development, mother is not the proximal object of affection, and father's distance is not depicted as a foreign monster or giant to be fought in an edgy standoff of kill or be killed. Father is primary, and the love between father and son cannot satisfactorily be explained as a triadic portrayal of a negative Oedipus complex. The narrative is closer to a hetero-normative relational quest for mutual recognition of one's capacity to be generative (cf. Garfield, 2004, on endeavor excitement for an excellent gender inclusive depiction of the necessity of recognition in regard to generativity).

The narrative thrust for *Finding Nemo* is found in the father's central preoccupation of whether or not he *and* his son are capable of successful action. In my reading of the film as a drama concerning a child coming to terms with the conflict of separateness and connectedness, it is possible to read scenes of the film, such as father being trapped inside a whale while attempting to rescue his missing son, as the fantastic mental representations of a child wishing to be picked up, say from school. However, an alternate interpretation also appears valid. Such a fantasy appears to point to a real moment of parental absence and motivation and could also have arisen in a father's mind. That the film is depicted as a shared developmental journey pulls for such an interpretation.

The contemporary father–son dyad depicted in the film does not embody the hegemonic masculinity found in the classically strong oedipal father–son dyad, but presents the assurance of complete individuation as a distant and uncertain goal for the father as well the son. Father hunger then is understood not only as hunger for father, but is also father's hunger made explicit when males embody a masculinity that is both hard and soft in a culture where softness is often essentialized as feminine.

A developmental theory that explicitly posits that dependency and autonomy coexist in a relational tension across the lifespan (e.g., Blatt, 2008) is congruent with my first interpretation of this film, while watching it with my then preoedipal 3-year-old. At that point, with conviction, I found that the film perfectly depicted development within the subphase of rapprochement as Nemo's developmental tasks concern mastery of intensified separation anxiety, affirmation of basic trust, deflation of symbiotic unity, and firming up a sense of self through increased autonomy (Settlage et al., 1977, in Tyson & Tyson, 1990). That this preoedipal subphase is strikingly similar to the Oedipus milestone has been noted in that both phases grapple with the dangers of engulfment and abandonment (Covitz, 1997). What is unique to the film *Finding Nemo* is that it explicitly depicts a father, who like a child, continues to encounter opportunities to develop and grow.

Although by now it should be clear that there is much about this film that I find appealing, some elements warrant critical commentary. First and foremost, one may find an essentialist portrayal of the irrational as wedded to the feminine in the character that is Nemo's father's love interest in a manner that perpetuates hegemony through misogyny. This central female character suffers a short-term memory loss and finds that she can only think in the presence of Nemo's father. While I prefer to read this as highlighting the need for relational security that is part of the human condition and a playful way of teaching the father that certainty is fleeting, this character may also be understood to represent an old sexist binary of an irrational woman who needs to be tamed by a strong, steady man (Merchant, 1980). This, coupled with the opening of the film entailing the death of the mother, supports a line of thinking that in the quest to find relational security, the feminine, with all of its softness and uncertainty, is disavowed, or that once men obtain a capacity to diminish edginess, women are dismissed. Such a reading suggests that in this film, despite the promise of a father who can mother, masculine security remains an oxymoron. Furthermore, the newfound security of father and son is presented in an everlasting manner. Such an ending suggests a need to vanquish the knowledge that apron strings are reconfigured across the lifespan as fluctuating dependency is encountered throughout a life in which uncertainty exists. This reading suggests that a joyful postmodernism in which ambiguity and uncertainty could be tolerated, if not embraced outright, is fantastic at best. This lack of a tidy embrace of uncertainty certainly fits with everyday clinical experience and the human desire for assurance and continuity.

Clinical Gleanings

In a given day of sitting with clients, one may hear cross-sectional narratives privileging divergent roles and stages across the lifespan. Working with the symptoms that arise when good enough fathers appear lost or to have never existed affords a data source that supports my contention regarding the importance of an engaged father. Threats of a father's engulfment or abandonment appear to lead to a dichotomization of autonomy and dependency based on a rigid belief that these states cannot co-occur in a functional tension in a manner similar to that experienced by Nemo's character and his father in the film. To that end, working on an analysis of this film impacted my capacity to hear themes related to fathering in my clinical work. What follows are two cases that capture this experience and, like the film, situate the psychologies of both father and child.

In my choice to use data from a case of a young woman that I will call Kris, I want to note that although I have focused on the father–son matrix, similar themes of engulfment and abandonment in regard to the mutual recognition of generativity exist in relation with girl children as well. Kris complained of the manner in which her father, in his attempt to be helpful, continually thwarted her autonomy in his need to be needed. She complained of generalized and chronic anxiety and described that her father told her what she would have, never consulting her in regard to what she might want. Mother appeared distant and of little use regarding the renegotiation of this relationship. As a result, artifacts such as her car could become intrusively monstrous sources of engulfing anxiety and rage, marking a relational space in which mutuality could not be found. For example, father would worry when visiting his college-age daughter that she might forget to move her car and would move it for her. Kris would complain that it felt as though her father were being intrusive, as his inability to perceive that she had been able to care for the car in his absence left her feeling as though she had no voice. Further, when she would return home to visit she described a chronic uncertainty regarding if in fact her car would accompany her back to campus. Attempts to improve communication on this front appeared futile. What began to emerge was that her father's intrusive conception that his daughter *might* not be capable of successful action was becoming a self-fulfilling prophecy. In one session, Kris described leaving the driver side window open while the car was parked in a snow storm. She added that upon remembering this, she did not initially act to rectify the situation. We began to focus on a generalized relational pattern in which Kris would either avoid engagement, rebel in the face of potential mutuality, or attempt to tolerate engagement with a dread that things would fall apart. In the wake of such a disturbing relational matrix, a greater capacity for play is a distant goal.

Another client, a man in his 50s whom I will call Jim became tearful when discussing the fact that his own son was about to enter college. While crying Jim informed me that, "It was all over," and that "The apron strings were going to be cut." Although he began to look forward to some additional time with his younger son, across several sessions Jim spoke of his older son's matriculation as a college student with such affective intensity that I began to wonder about the distinction between grief and depression. Prior to this disturbance, Jim and I had addressed that as a child, he had experienced his own father as perfect. Jim further related the uncritically adopted belief that his father's success was not only made possible due to such perfection, but that success in general demanded perfection. For Jim, this idealization was sealed in his father's death and persisted despite his awareness of his father's alcohol abuse. This persistent idealization was accompanied by Jim's devaluing of himself as being an imperfect man who abused alcohol following moments of ego-deflating loss. One memory of Jim's own attempt at boat building as an adolescent was met with a critique by his father that left Jim certain that he was not perfect and therefore prone to failure. While this memory was considered prototypical of his childhood, Jim's associations to feelings of abandonment led to a discussion of his implicit sense that he should be needed, certain, and perfectly steady if he was to be good enough—both as a son and as a father. His insecurity regarding the relational uncertainty sparked by his son's development appeared unyielding. Although the insecurity did not diminish, once his son did in fact start college, Jim began to see that his son continued to seek his advice. This fragile reassurance afforded a temporary reprieve and continued over the following summer when he noted that his son was not yet reliably punctual. Here, Jim's narcissism may be considered to demand that his son persist in being identified as the fallible one in the manner that Jim had sacrificed his own self for his father. Situating this rigid sensitivity in relation to his alcohol misuse became the central axis of our work together. This work included management of the counter-transferential fantasy that we would watch *Finding Nemo* together so that he could see that uncertainty could be part of a healthy masculinity.

Conclusion

Encountered in public space, the changing table may be experienced as an enriching or depleting force for a father as its presence challenges a hegemonic masculinity. If read as a depleting force, one might consciously support the continuity of an idealized and mythic masculinity that devalues softness. Despite neoconservative and hegemonic trends in our culture, the film *Finding Nemo* suggests that there is something normative regarding finding men capable of privileging uncertainty and holding. Simply, the film suggests that it may be possible for heterosexual adult males to tolerate a loss of steadiness without encountering defensive misogyny or homophobia. However, the film suggests that such a plastic conception of masculinity might itself be an idealization, as the film's narrative does not entirely break from a sexist binary. The film ends showing that the leading female character finds security in dependency and the leading male characters find security in separation and individuation. Despite a pluralism found in what some call postmodernity, change appears to exist along a continuum, not a paradigm shifting break. Campbell's (1949/1973) observation that attachment and separation are psychological, not biological, positions has in my opinion yet to be fully assimilated into our lived experience as edginess persists, albeit in changing forms. A psychological theory and methodological frame that afford a perception of masculinities as developing along a spectrum, as opposed to a developmental model that implies the existence of tidy breaks, provides movement away from a reifying hegemony that threatens to thwart play. Such a move might well aid a secure and pluralistic therapeutic action and intergenerational continuity.

Acknowledgment

Earlier versions of this chapter were presented at the Association for the Psychoanalysis of Culture and Society 2006 Annual Conference, Rutgers University, NJ; at the 2007 Division 39 meeting of the American Psychological Association, San Francisco, CA; and at the 2008 Spring Meeting of Division 39, New York, NY.

References

Benjamin, J. (1988). *The Bonds of Love: Psychoanalysis, Feminism, and the Problem of Domination*. New York: Pantheon.

Blatt, S. J. (2008). *Polarities of Experience: Relatedness and Self-definition in Personality, Development, Psychopathology, and the Therapeutic Process*. Washington, DC: American Psychological Association.

Butler, J. (1992). The lesbian phallus and the morphological imaginary. *Differences: A Journal of Feminist Cultural Studies, 4*, 133–171.

Campbell, J. (1973). *The Hero with a Thousand Faces*. Princeton, NJ: Princeton University Press. (Originally published in 1949)

Collodi, C. (2001). *Pinocchio*. Compiled by Cooper Edens. San Francisco: Chronicle Books. (Originally published in 1892)

Connell, R. W. (1990). An iron man: The body and some contradictions of hegemonic masculinity. In M. Messner & D. Sabo (Eds.), *Sport, Men, and the Gender of Order* (pp. 83–96). Champaign, IL: Human Kinetics.

Corliss, R. (2003, May 26). Hook, line and thinker. *Time, 161*(21), 60.

Covitz, H. H. (1997). *Oedipal Paradigms in Collision: A Centennial Emendation of a Piece of the Freudian Canon (1897–1997)*. New York: Peter Lang Publishing.

Diamond, M. J. (1998). Fathers with sons: Psychoanalytic perspectives on "good enough" fathering throughout the lifecycle. *Gender and Psychoanalysis, 3,* 243–299.

Ducat, S. (2004). *The Wimp Factor: Gender Gaps, Holy Wars, and the Politics of Anxious Masculinity*. Boston: Beacon Press.

Ducat, S., Metzl, M., & Rothschild, L. (2008, April). Male fantasies/fantasies of maleness: Psychoanalytic readings of anxious masculinity. Panel presentation at the Division 39 Spring Meeting, New York.

Dundes, A. (2002). *Bloody Mary in the Mirror: Essays in Psychoanalytic Folkloristics*. Jackson: University Press of Mississippi.

Fischer, E. (1963). *The Necessity of Art: A Marxist Approach*. Baltimore: Penguin.

Fonagy, P. (2001). *Attachment Theory and Psychoanalysis*. New York: Other Press.

Freud, S. (1900). The interpretation of dreams. *Standard Edition, 4.*

Garfield, R. (2004). Making a case for father hunger in girls. In S. Akhtar & H. Parens (Eds.), *Real and Imaginary Fathers: Development, Transference, and Healing*. New York: Jason Aronson.

Herzog, J. M. (2001). *Father Hunger: Explorations with Adults and Children*. Hillsdale, NJ: Analytic Press.

Kundera, M. (2007, January 8). Die Weltliteratur: How we read one another. *The New Yorker*, pp. 28–35.

Kupers, T. A. (1993). *Revisioning Men's Lives: Gender, Intimacy, and Power*. New York: Guilford.

Layton, L. (2004a), Working nine to nine: The new women of prime time. *Studies in Gender and Sexuality, 5*(3), 351–369.

Layton, L. (2004b). Relational no more. Defensive autonomy in middle-class women. In J. Winer (Ed.), *Annual of Psychoanalysis*, Vol. 32: *Psychoanalysis and Women* (pp. 29-57). Hillsdale, NJ: Analytic Press.

Marsiglio, W., & Pleck, J. H. (2004). Fatherhood and masculinities. In M. S. Kimmel, J. Hearn, & R. W. Connell (Eds.), *Handbook of Studies on Men and Masculinities*. New York: Sage.

Masterson, J. F., & Rinsely, D. (1975). The borderline syndrome: The role of the mother in the genesis and psychic structure of the borderline personality. *International Journal of Psycho-Analysis, 56,* 63–177.

Merchant, C. (1980). *The Death of Nature: Women, Ecology and the Scientific Revolution*. San Francisco: HarperSanFrancisco.

Mitchell, S. A. (2002). *Can Love Last? The Fate of Romance over Time*. New York: Norton.

Munroe, R. L., & Munroe, R. H. (1994). *Cross-Cultural Human Development*. Prospect Heights, IL: Waveland.

O'Sullivan, M. (2003, May 30). *Finding Nemo*: This story is a keeper. *Washington Post*, p. WE57.

Rank, O. (1990). The myth of the birth of the hero. In *In Quest of the Hero*. Princeton, NJ: Princeton University Press. (Originally published in 1909)

Rothschild, L. (2003). Penis size. In M. Kimmel & A. Aronson (Eds.), *Men and Masculinities: A Social, Cultural, and Historical Encyclopedia*. New York: ABC-CLIO.

Settlage, C. F., Kramer, S., Belmont, H. S., et al. (1977). Child analysis. In *Psychoanalytic Education and Research: The Current Situation and Future Possibilities*.

Stanton, A. (Writer/Director). (2003). *Finding Nemo*. Pixar Studios.

Strenger, C. (2005). *The Designed Self: Pyschoanalysis and Contemporary Identities*. Hillsdale, NJ: Analytic Press.

Trillin, C. (1995, October 2). Turning the tables. *The New Yorker*, p. 108.

Tyson, P., & Tyson, R. (1990). *Psychoanalytic Theories of Development: An Integration*. New Haven, CT: Yale University Press.

Verne, J. (2003). *20,000 Leagues Under the Sea*. New York: Scholastic Paperbacks. (Originally published in 1870)

12

Interiority and Inner Genital Space in Men
What Else Can Be Lost in Castration?

Gerald I. Fogel

It is widely accepted that castration anxiety is a major feature in the psychology of men. Its appearance is traditionally said to be an aspect of the phallic or phallic-oedipal phase of development. Castration anxiety is therefore often characterized as a "higher-level" or triadic fear and is contrasted with the more "primitive" or dyadic fears (and defenses) of earlier, preoedipal phases. Recent advances compel us to expand our perspective on this important subject. We have new and sometimes radically different psychoanalytic views about women, for example, and new knowledge regarding the psychic construction of gender and self and the developmental evolution of psychic structure. We also have new arguments supporting the conceptual primacy of psychic reality, which many contemporary observers consider more appropriate than material reality as a frame of reference for psychoanalysis.

An individual's sexual anatomy is a prime example of a psychologically significant material reality that is impossible to alter or deny—fixed at birth and therefore static. But psychic reality—in this instance the experience of one's body—may nevertheless be the better epistemological ground or "container" for the human mind. The psyche is an entity that is irreducibly bisexual, representational, and symbolic—therefore not static, but dynamic—capable of continual evolution and change through dialogue, deconstruction, and reconstruction. In contemporary usage, it is frequently assumed that when we speak of phallic-oedipal aspirations or powers and how these may be threatened or diminished, we embrace more than the literal anatomical meaning of castration. Narrative complexity and metaphorical profundity enlarge our conception of phallic masculinity and therefore of what may be attacked or thwarted. Put another way, the experience of one's body-mind or embodied, gendered self and of what one has to lose evolves developmentally.

So there is much to take into account in any modern reconsideration of the subject of male castration. A fantasy fear of possible damage to or loss of valued body parts as an aspect of individuation, oedipal empowerment, and higher-level, postambivalent triadic psychic functioning is represented symbolically, almost universally, by a threat of phallic castration. Phallic aspirations and fears are widely observed in both sexes, where they assume an infinite number of unique forms in each individual, overdetermined and condensed from different developmental levels and from a wide variety of situations, fantasies, and body parts. A substantial recent literature on the psychology of women, however, demonstrates that additional strengths and vulnerabilities are observable in adult women that are also genital-oedipal, postambivalent, and triadic, yet conceptually separable and complementary to what we ordinarily call "phallic," as in "phallic-oedipal." These studies show that the developmental evolution of women's experiences of their bodily selves and bodily integrity are linked to an experience of interiority. Such experiences contribute to full psychosexual genitality, selfhood, and capacities for high-level object relating.

As in women, mature male functioning contains similar powers and potentials—ones that are conceptually distinct from and complementary to those we designate as phallic. I refer not to developmentally less mature aspects, such as preoedipal or narcissistic ones, but to additional powers and potentials that flow from inner genital experience—a genital-oedipal conception and experience of the interior of the triadic self rooted in the body. Since such powers are directly analogous to those described in women, I refer to interiority and inner genitality in men, and to their unified appearance in relation to oedipality and separation-individuation. There is no single term, however, comparable to phallic, to represent those too frequently devalued aspects of oedipal and adult development that are primary, "feminine," equally ubiquitous, and essential for psychic mastery, and also therefore threatened or constrained by symbolic castration. In this chapter I will demonstrate inner genitality in men—the developmental evolution and metaphorical elaboration in psychic and psychosexual life of a man's inner genital experience. I will argue that it would be most useful if a simple, universally accepted word existed that referred to a man's "feminine" half, as phallic does to the "masculine" in both sexes. Definitions may prove difficult, but emancipation and integration of such experiences are required for the development of mature mental organizations and realization of full psychic potential. Castration anxiety arises when any crucial part of mature psychic and psychosexual life is exposed or threatened. Without full access to his higher-level interior and more ambiguous continent, a man is castrated, compromised, less than whole.

A Mythic Moment in the Case of Professor M.

In the third year of his analysis, in the aftermath of ending yet another too long sexual affair, Prof. M. met a new woman, one who seemed different from all the rest. The usually articulate professor struggled for words. She was, he said, more competent, more together, there was somehow—well—just more to her. In fact, Prof. M. had been on intimate terms with many apparently competent and attractive women in his life, including the one he had just left and a wife he had divorced years before. Urbane, attractive, and highly successful, he had come of age in the 1960s. Now 49, he was a well-known writer and ran a college department of comparative literature.

Suddenly he recalled a woman he had known in France in his 20s. She had been beautiful and smart—an intellectual equal and true soul mate. Unlike all those before and since (but like the woman he had just met), she had authentic independence and depth, needed no caretaking functions from him; she preferred to hold life and person together herself, thank you. But he had never completely relaxed with her. He now saw that his doubts had been rationalizations—coverups for anxiety about consummating their relationship, making a commitment to this strong, passionate woman. He had felt overwhelmed by her. Memories of several occasions when they took LSD together provided a taste of his inner life at the time. During one acid trip he visually hallucinated the Statue of Liberty—France's gift to America. What a breathtakingly beautiful, awesome figure. Those broad shoulders—and that torch! Another time, however, he had his only bad trip on hallucinogens. He looked between his legs and to his horror saw blackness—his penis was gone! Wait, he said, it was worse. Something awful was there. He had a black hole—a cloaca! Deeply shaken, he was haunted by this terrible image long after.

Webster's New World Dictionary defines cloaca first as a sewer or cesspool, second as the cavity into which both intestinal and genitourinary tracts empty in reptiles, birds, amphibians, and many fish. In psychoanalysis, cloacal fantasies are said to be not uncommon in women, where the proximity of anal, urinary, and vaginal orifices contribute to a conflation and devaluing of these functions anatomically and psychically. Let us consider how psychoanalytic theory prepares us to characterize Prof. M.'s plight. We are impressed by the obvious castration theme, the horror of the missing penis; we frequently also infer an accompanying wish to be filled or penetrated from without. Castration anxiety prompts regressive flight, preoedipal adaptation, and defense—oral, anal, and narcissistic longings, perhaps. Prof. M. wishes and dreads to be a passive and weaker being—possibly a submissive woman. Dreading castration for phallic-oedipal wishes, he needs to be castrated. The symbolically omnipotential image of the phallic woman—Prof. M.'s Statue of Liberty—condenses representations of subject and object, longing and fear.

But should we not also be impressed, as was Prof. M., not by what is missing, but by what is there? I refer to the omnipotential representational power of the cloaca image and the possibility that this fantasy captures not only demonic and disturbing qualities, but profound and empowering ones as well. The primal wish here is to be empowered by a dark hole—empowered, in other words, not from without, but from within. Did Prof. M. desire penetration by or possession of a maternal phallus, or to be empowered by his mother's, father's, French woman friend's, or his own capacity for "cloacal," internal passion and profundity? If he aspires to both, does our theory predispose us to idealize phallic, external qualities at the expense of "cloacal," internal ones? The metaphorical entity "phallic woman" is a useful, universal fantasy construction. Does Prof. M. show us a possible polar partner? Could his awesome, terrifying, mythic ideal be a complementary bisexual prototype, the "cloacal man"?

An Etymological and Theoretical Prelude

Let us for the moment try to ignore the powerfully negative implications of the term cloaca. We shall not analyze Prof. M.'s degraded fantasy about his dark hole, but instead use his hallucination as an example of one of two possible bisexual prototypes. In one—the phallic—powerful, exciting, space-occupying embodied forms compel our attention. In the other—the cloacal—a dark, formless, embodied space stands for all the exciting but scary power and depth Prof. M. saw in his French woman friend. Interestingly, Webster's provides etymological support for the notion of cloacal power and purity. The Latin root is *cluere*, to cleanse; the earlier Indo-European root *klu-*, to rinse or clean; whence the German *lauter*, pure, and English *cataclysm*, deluge, flood, violent upheaval. We are also referred to the English *clyster*, an enema. Although the etymological roots are separate, I am also reminded of the English cloister, from the Latin *claustrum*. These terms refer to a protected, purified, sacred space, or to an arched passageway within such a space. Regarding the cloacal, we find a clear psychodynamic sexist wrinkle. For the dictionary manifestly shows only cesspool and sewer. Sequestered in brackets, like the repressed, are the primal etymological meanings, sources of power that, like nature itself, exist before we can easily label them clean or dirty, good or bad, higher or lower.

These latent but significant etymological roots are ambiguous, and ordinarily cannot overcome the common-sense, devalued meanings. In what follows, I therefore risk offending some readers by going against centuries of degraded (or idealized) usage by sometimes using the terms cloacal or claustral when I refer only to the bisexual prototype of the man with a dark hole. My use of the terms is ironic, however, because of the crucial positive value I assign to this universal prototype. Irony is intended, for example, when I assert that personal or theoretical overevaluation of Prof. M.'s phallic strivings and fears might silently deprive him of, castrate, his claustral or cloacal ones. In such a perspective, outwardness, sharp discrimination, and clarity of boundaries are gained at the expense of inwardness, creativity, and ambiguity born of cleansing and new growth, death and rebirth—the complementary "regression" that accompanies progression, and a possible higher level of integration and integrity. All human beings have hopes and fears of both types of strivings at all developmental levels—for absorption and immersion as well as differentiation and discrimination. All men and women have both inside and outside.

Many aspects of my subject have been known since psychoanalysis began—frequently discussed under the heading of bisexuality. I have already alluded to four topics that comprise the contemporary theoretical context, and a reassessment of bisexuality in light of these newer ideas should prove instructive. Once again, the first subject area is the increasing legitimacy in modern psychoanalysis of the view that psychic reality is both our database and our bedrock frame of reference. Constructionist, representational theories of psychic reality introduce problems that are mighty. Constructionism also frees us, however, from rigid, categorical, or sexist biological and anatomical conceptual constraints. Anatomy and anatomical differences remain real, but how these are experienced, represented, and integrated becomes primary. A second area is our newer notions of how psychic structure evolves. We increasingly measure developmental maturity by assessing the complexity of structural organization and degree of autonomy and integration, as well as capacities for dialogue,

relationship, and personal responsibility. The emphasis is on process variables—representational complexity, multiple perspectives, and symbolic
actualization, not reified psychosexual categories linked reductively to
anatomy, or references to particular psychodynamic contents or simplistic historical stepwise phases. A third area is comprised of hermeneutic,
linguistic, and feminist studies that establish pre- and protosymbolic language and gender templates—categories for the representation, construction, and reconstruction of gender, sex, and self.

The fourth and last subject area is recent psychoanalytic literature,
mostly by women, that argues for a new complexity to our conception of
female genital experience and its developmental evolution, and a small but
significant literature on the inner genital experience of boys. I will briefly
review this last area, follow with a clinical vignette, then revisit all of these
subjects in my closing discussion.

Mayer (1985) argues that women have primary castration anxiety in
relation to their own genital originating in the early experience of the
vulva with its possibility of an opening and an implicit inner space; this
castration fantasy, usually related to oedipal strivings, can be clearly distinguished from the phallic castration complex in women. Both Burton
(1996) and Richards (1992) regard sphincter control and internal physical
sensations related to perineal and pelvic musculature as a possible source
of mastery and control as well as confusion in the young girl. They argue
that such internal bodily experiences ideally contribute to increased genital mastery and psychic integration as development proceeds. Richards
focuses on inner genital sensation and fantasy and states that anything
that threatens or diminishes generativity or sexual pleasure is equivalent
to castration.

Bernstein (1990) describes female genital anxiety and mastery modes
under the categories of access, diffuseness, and penetration. Significantly,
she relates these experiences not only to anatomy, but also to the psychic
representation of complex metaphorical and relational developmental
equivalents. Lacking as easy an access to these vulnerable, but complex
and important bodily experiences, boys can miss out on important areas
of psychic potential. Kaplan (1991a) examines specifically feminine experiential modes characterized by ambiguity, diffuseness, and interiority
in the light of contemporary structural and object relations theory; elsewhere Kaplan (1991b) describes the inner genital experience of boys. In
successful development this omnipotential "feminine" experience should
proceed to a more differentiated and fully integrated oedipal resolution,
where difference and similarity are reconciled in a higher organization.

These authors describe a category of bodily experience that is specifically feminine—primary femininity. As phallic fears refer to the phallus and its symbolic equivalents and transformations, so too these analogous but specifically "female" fears refer to a genital opening and an internal genital space and their symbolic equivalents and transformations. Castration anxiety arises when these spaces or openings are exposed or threatened at the genital-oedipal stage. I wish to apply such conceptions to the psychology of men. In my terms, both men and women have phallic and claustral or cloacal potentialities, and therefore also vulnerabilities, defenses, and adaptive mastery modes. If we no longer think anatomy need be destiny for a woman (or at the least that is not that simple) why must it be so for a man? This idea helps me in countless ways clinically—in every hour of every practice day.

Recently, for example, a woman told me of a vivid new sexual experience. Her lover was on top, tongue in her mouth, penis in her vagina, and exciting anal-rectal sensations accompanied his deep thrusts as well. She felt overwhelmed—too much diffuse sensation—too much going on. Unexpectedly she relaxed, went with it. Amazing, she said, pleased and proud. I considered the contributions of a recent pregnancy to this rich, new experience. I was theoretically well prepared to understand the positive significance of the shame and dread that accompanied the excitement she felt during lovemaking while exposing wet, welcoming, and life-creating, but also scary, destructive, and disgusting inner surfaces, substances, and spaces. I pondered her breastfeeding experiences, her recent, new, empowering memories of childhood maternal attitudes toward brother and father—figures who before only represented a defensively idealized phallic ideal—their capacities for aggression only a source of intimidation and awe. I reflected upon her identification with and regressive pull to engage with a swampy, intrusive mother, and pondered the multiplicity of sources of the accompanying phallic, oral, and anal-sadistic aspects. I noted the interplay among all of these factors, as well as the roles all of them were playing in her increasing generativity and assertiveness in her professional life. I considered additional wrinkles, such as whether in a particular instance her enemies or allies were represented in her psychic reality as masculine or feminine. If both her adult sexual and developmental experiences had an internal, "female," and all-mixed-up or omnipotential aspect, I could also easily see that a differentiated, sublimated, higher-level unity (Loewald, 1988) was already discernible and a fully realizable goal.

The same day I saw a male architect under challenge by events in his professional, relational, and sexual life that were leading to new waves of individuation and success, but also to being overwhelmed. He had smoked pot the night before, a rare and ordinarily prohibited event. He felt an array of highly pleasurable bodily sensations, began to masturbate, and suddenly found himself putting his finger in his anus. It was a most unprecedented and intense experience, but he was also frightened and mortified. He is nowhere near as far along in our work as the woman, but I see a potential analogy to the woman's experience in regard to the spontaneity and multiplicity of his experiences. Must I view his experiences simply as an anxious retreat from sharply discriminated triadic adult phallic masculine triumph and dread? Or can I regard his excitement, shame, and fear as possibly connected to the opening against prior constraints of ambiguously complex and conflated interior spaces as well—inpourings and outpourings that reflect the emergence of new, additional, higher-level components? If so, as with the woman, I can anticipate that his new experiences will complement, not merely be superseded and replaced by, more sharply discriminated phallic-oedipal ones as he continues to grow.

Omnipotentiality in the Analysis of Mr. P.

Prof. M.'s fantasy of himself with a dark hole—the ironic "cloacal man"—supplied us with a possible universal template, a bisexual prototype, like the so-called phallic woman. But to demonstrate how psychosexual complexity and complementarity—the interplay of external and internal genital experience—typically unfolds in actual analytic material requires much more detail. I will present several vignettes from the analysis of Mr. P. He is a businessman in his 40s from a small Pennsylvania steel town who first came to New York to attend college and business school. One day in the fifth year of the analysis he had been excitedly cataloging examples of his newfound freedom, flexibility, and nondriven assertiveness at work, when his thoughts suddenly shifted to his family. He has an older son by his wife's first marriage and a daughter aged 3. He had picked up his little girl at nursery school the day before, and observed with deep satisfaction her exuberant goodbye hug to her teacher and happy play with her classmates. He lingered over an evocative description of her jumping up and down with energy and unmistakable delight. He paused emotionally and said, "She's bright, sensitive, and funny."

After a brief pause, I said, "And it sounds like happy and loving as well."

Tears welled up and he reached for a tissue, but in a somewhat strangulated and conflicted way that was more the old Mr. P. than the new, and was silent. Then he said, "I can't handle that, even though I know it's true. While you were talking I felt a pleasant sensation in my anus, and [hesitating and halting now] I also felt like coughing, which probably means I want your penis in my ass or my mouth."

I said I understood, but that I also wondered if he was possibly getting a little ahead of himself. I went on: "When you were talking about your daughter, you probably were also talking about yourself and about us, something you have or we have together, not just something you want. You were speaking of how much more freely expressive and thoughtful you are with others. So, in a sense, you may be jumping up and down for joy today with me. But when you start to share your happiness and lovingness with me along with your successes, perhaps you can tolerate only so much, then you have to break it off. When you got to sensations in your anus and chest, you jumped quickly to the idea of something coming into you through your anus or mouth. I guess it could be a penis or stool—although it seems much less clear to me about your mouth."

Mr. P.'s response was irritable, but dialogic. "You make the whole thing sound too positive," he said. "You're probably right about the anus, but the cough is negative, bad." But he also revealed that he had had many associations as I spoke. There had been a sudden bad taste in his mouth. He thought of a buddy at work who is helping him negotiate a deal. Of a third man, whom they do not completely trust when the going gets tough, they joked, "He's always willing to hold your coat in a fight." He guessed this was a reference to my alleged prettying up of his experience, downplaying the down and dirty aggressive aspects. Maybe I could not handle the manly stuff.

His friend was the same one who had hiked up a mountain with him on a free afternoon during a sales convention in Denver last year. That event marked a breakthrough in the analytic work, when Mr. P. was conquering lifelong inabilities to take time off, take in new things, take physical and emotional risks, find more flexible and reliable allies. On the mountain he had challenged his prior fear of heights. The height and space were scary but exhilarating. So much air and light! I immediately responded to this vivid imagery and suggested that all this light, height, and air might be part of what was happening to him right now. Might his joyfulness and loving wish to share it with me be exciting but also accompanied by a kind of emotional flooding? Could these flowings be comprised of outpourings, inpourings, sensations that not only were soaring, taking his breath away, but also suffocating or choking him? And might his angry mistrust of me be based on a fear I could not hang in there, fight with him and for him, help him fight me more productively while we also figured out and helped him master these new experiences?

Let us reconsider my exploratory, and sometimes tentative, metaphorical-evocative interventions with Mr. P. First, I suggested that the story about his daughter contained transference feelings. I inferred that he might wish to show me happy and loving feelings like those that his daughter had so unself-consciously displayed at school. His emotional response seemed to confirm this. Then I suggested that he was constrained by various complex and as yet unclear feelings and fantasies concerning "things" moving in and out of various parts of him, but that he might have leaped to phallocentric formulas partly for defensive purposes. I used his mountain climbing associations as an evocative opportunity to articulate more clearly the expansive, but also scarily exhilarating, experience that was actually occurring in him and between us as I attempted to respond to him—his constrained efforts to jump for joy. My construction had additional sources besides the manifest material. Homosexual fantasies and fears had often been prominent in Mr. P.'s analysis, but his idea that he might want my penis in him had struck me as pat in this instance—intellectual, compliant, in a sense too clear, and much too discontinuous with the emotional immediacy of his clear identification with his daughter in his life and the transference just before. In our prior work, issues of idealized male potency, dominance, or submission in an all-male, phallic-macho competitive hierarchy had often screened or defended many other important issues.

Therefore, it was no surprise to me that these too-clear phallic formulas now fell away. New memories immediately emerged, mostly related to his conflicts and identifications with various women—especially his mother, who had flooded him in childhood with hugs, food, and too much exciting attention to anal and other matters. She also had rubbed his chest with Vicks when he had a cough, and frequently had overwhelmed him with "highs" that he became addicted to and often idealized, but that he had no power to get down from. Feelings and fantasies about his daughter, wife, mother, and me emerged, involving nipples, fingers, and hands; milk, saliva, and semen; breath and flatus; bodily smells. The wish for something solid from me was forbidden, exciting, and scary, but also a defensive flight from less clear or more ambiguous bodily experiences. The pleasurable, soothing sense of calm presence inside his anus is one dramatic example. That experience is akin to (although importantly different from) a pleasant scrotal sensation Mr. P. had sometimes noted during soothing moments of containment and affirmation in our work. These experiences struck me as likely possible examples of his newfound capacities to feel centered in his inner manhood, his inner genital space.

Let us note the dominance of mother in the material, but go with the "phallic" aspect for the moment and say that the penis in this instance may partly represent phallic control and mastery in the face of all this letting go and letting in of a flood of feelings and fantasies combining internal and external bodily experiences. Is it not obvious, however, that when Mr. P. states he has no use for an ally who will stand aside and hold his coat while he leaps into the fray, he may wish for more things than a phallus or phallic figure in the conventional sense? For example, might he have wished that his mother's "phallic" probing, exciting fingers, hands, or nipples had been able to hold him more flexibly yet securely, or to insert themselves more firmly but also knowingly and sensitively, or have known when to put him down when he was too high up the mountain that was her flesh, or how to put him in his room to quiet him down when he got overexcited and strung out and did not know it? Or might he have wished she were less intimidated by his aggressive excitement, able to fight with him in a safe and organizing way, thereby making it less necessary to maintain the unrealistic idealization of either her beneficence or the father's rigid and emotionally limited phallic and anal-aggressive dominance patterns?

Following the same logic, in spite of Mr. P.'s manifest, standard ortho-dox-issue wish for an idealized phallic father to "triangulate" his relation to his mother and protect him from her, might he also long for "cloacal" power, absorption, and containment, and for a primary object of any sex to serve as a model and provider in that respect? Might the father have been more useful if he could have jumped for joy, or brought a calmer, "internal" presence to the family, an ability to relax, be spontaneous, and enjoy the rewards of his successes, for example, or to yield control and be a more reassuring and containing presence for both mother and son? Should not an actual ideal parent of either sex be able to "let go" and "go with the flow" as well as "take charge" and maintain secure control? Should not an ideal parent of either sex possess a mental organization that integrates and allows freedom with every psychological mode?

Consider how easily all this omnipotentiality, overdetermination, and creativity could be lost by running too quickly with what seemed to be Mr. P.'s compliant and conventional phallocentric homosexual wish, by contrasting in too either-or a fashion all this interiority and diffuse, body-based emotionality with a pat formulation of phallic excitement, fear, and longing, by assigning one parent or the other the conventional "masculine" or "feminine" role, or by pigeonholing or reducing his chest and mouth experiences to "preoedipal" or more "primitive" experiences with mother. I think Mr. P. wants to combine what I call phallic and cloacal characteristics into a body, including his penis, that has both an inside and an outside. His inner genital space must be able to contain flesh and blood, semen and digestive juices, cavities and channels. There must be a capacity to experience rumblings and eruptions, darkness and light. Not merely penetration power, but volcano, earthquake, and swamp power. Not merely issues of dominance and control, but death and birth, consummation and cataclysm—plus exciting relations with such powers in others.

As Mr. P. continued to expand psychosexual experience beyond conventional masculine or feminine formulas, his sex life with his wife took a new turn—her on top, him on top, anal and scrotal play and sensations; he was a "wrecker" invading her mouth, vagina, rectum; she in turn ravaged him with kisses and pinches to his chest, nipples, and thighs, invading him roughly with demanding fingers, arms, legs. Concurrently in the transference, he could play the "woman" in relation to me, eat and be eaten, invade or be invaded, lead or follow. He became increasingly empowered by his ability, for example, to taunt, control, and turn me on. Seduction, torture, and passionate desire appeared in all combinations and intensities.

Mr. P. was becoming at once more "primitive" and "all-mixed-up," but also more truly "oedipal." "Oedipal" in this instance means triadic, a higher level of structural organization. Oedipal-level, triadic organization reflects a capacity for more complex experiences—that is, more differentiation combined with an ability to "let go" of firm boundaries, "take in" and "open up" to new experiences, be able to put them all together in all their richness and ambiguity. Such mastery, whereby the full vitality and texture of the primary process is rediscovered and liberated as part of the process of attaining a unified and integrated field of higher discriminations, is what Loewald (1988) calls sublimated or discriminated unity. Mr. P. was liberated into new and infinitely complex varieties of experience—in loving and making love, in sex, and at work; in friendships and parenting; in his down time and avocational pursuits.

So Mr. P. demonstrates that authentic "phallic" experience usually contains its "cloacal" counterparts as well—internal spaces, substances, and permeable boundaries—and usually is partly comprised as well of identifications with important women in a man's life. By analogy, not only experiences with women shape a man's inner psychosexual space. Ideal "male bonding" will also transcend simplistic phallic formulas and include the "cloacal" counterparts. Indeed, less boundaried experiences with important male models emerged in Mr. P.'s analysis, powerful experiences that also involved a bodily inner genital self, yet felt entirely masculine.

An example of such man-to-man internality was a time he spoke of having thought about me the night before while watching a television interview of a man who had written a book about mythology. Mr. P. had recently been looking around my office more, entertaining fantasies of bondedness to me in connection with cultural sensibilities we might share: art, literature, music, spirituality. While watching the interview, he had thought, "Fogel would like this." Maybe he would bring me a copy of the book. He fell silent for a bit, then began to run himself down as a "yokel," a hick from the Pennsylvania foothills who never could attain the sophisticated New York cultural and intellectual heights of his analyst. I interpreted this old theme as a retreat, a disavowal. Perhaps, I suggested, he feared he had really "put his finger on something," been touched deeply by something that he could easily imagine might also touch me.

My phrase made him think of putting his finger on his wife's clitoris. After a brief pause, an image of my penis came to his mind. The penis was small, slender, flaccid, but curving up at the end. He guessed he was putting me down by imagining me with this small penis. I asked for associations to this unique and highly specific image. It reminded him of a swan's neck—very beautiful and graceful. The fantasy penis had a small white spot on the end. He imagined lightly touching his finger to it and just then remembered the first girl who had ever touched him. She had a precise touch, could find the most sensitive spot, knew just how to create that exquisite experience. She was great. He described the delicate sensations she had produced with her vaginal lips as well, as the details of this initiation into sexual pleasure flooded back over him. "Maybe you want to be like her," I suggested, "to know what moves me because it moves you, be able to touch me where I live with such precision and grace." Greatly moved by this idea, he was astonished to find himself immediately remembering aspects of his father that seemed entirely new. Mr. P. had always seen his father as swaggeringly powerful, macho, and scary. We had figured out that the father was uptight, insecure, and rigid as well—in other words, not merely strong. But the new memories were unprecedented. His father had used woodworking tools with just such graceful swan-like shapes in a hobby occasionally pursued but only rarely shared with his son as he was growing up. These rare occasions combined "masculine" skill and precision with "feminine" sensitivity and sharing.

Complex and permeably boundaried inner spaces and sensitivities shared by men linked to psychosexuality do not surprise us. But little girls who jump for joy and adolescent sexual companions who happen to be female in this material represent capacities and play roles fully available to Mr. P. (and his father) as an adult, masculine man. In subsequent weeks, Mr. P. became more attuned both to the pleasures and perils in these sorts of male-bonding experiences. There were fantasies of medieval knights and monks, ceremonies of knighthood and consecration, ritualistic swallowing and sharing of blood and semen, for example.

These sorts of combinings of exterior and interior transcendence of the formulistic or commonplace meanings of masculine and feminine are infinite in their uniqueness, variety, and unpredictability in analysis. Brief additional examples from my work with Mr. P. include "hardening" of his heart, essentially a "phallic" defense modeled on his father's personality, to defend himself from the dangers of exposing softer and more tender inner organs and psychical sensibilities. Shortly thereafter, with a sense of excitement and dread, he rented a safety-deposit box. A conventional assumption might have been that the anxious depression that accompanied this highly symbolic action was a defensive regression in response to the oedipal triumph of taking charge of his family finances, a defeat of his father. Of much greater significance, however, was the idea that he could be responsible for his own "security." This meant that he had his own heart and, in a symbolic linking of heart and vagina, his own inner "vault." The symbolic act left him with a cold heart and an empty inner life; individuating from his insecure mother deprived her of her necessary role of being his heart, his inner sanctum, his security. Her depressive hold on him as a child was significantly clarified. On another occasion in connection with new male lustiness in his relationship with his son and myself, male castration rituals were linked to a strengthening of male bonds through shared tribulations and vulnerabilities. Castration could function in ways analogous to pruning plants or trees, for example—necessary to deepen roots, facilitate regeneration, and possibly thereby to facilitate new and more vigorous growth.

Discussion

Freud (1905) once stated:

> observation shows that in human beings pure masculinity or femininity is not to be found either in a psychological or a biological sense. Every individual on the contrary displays a mixture of the character-traits belonging to his own and to the opposite sex; and he shows a combination of activity and passivity whether or not these last character-traits tally with his biological ones. (p. 220, n.)

Freud could grasp and describe human universals at a stroke. But though we might agree that bisexuality is indisputable, few today accept that the terms active and passive adequately capture the polarity for "phallic" and its complementary "feminine" partner. In addition, many of Freud's specific formulations about men and women are now widely regarded as reflecting a severe phallocentric bias. Mr. P.'s clinical material demonstrates how certain Freudian "universals," wrongly construed, may limit a modern psychoanalyst's view. If an inner psychosexual genital self is a good and necessary thing to have, we must try to give it full parity, even if its essential nature makes it difficult to give it "shape" or easy definition. I suggest that all psychic experience combines bodily interior and exterior, less bounded openings and spaces with more clearly defined shapes and forms. Should not the ubiquitous transcendence of the commonly accepted meanings of feminine and masculine in Mr. P.'s analysis also be reflected in psychoanalytic theory?

Grossman and Kaplan (1988) point out that Freud's errors regarding gender were at their most egregious when he was technically not being psychoanalytic. For example, Freud often commented categorically on traits that are characteristic of one sex or the other. Men are active and seek to love, whereas women are passive and seek to be loved. Such static definitional categories are vulnerable to cultural or personal prejudice and are based on observations existing entirely outside a psychoanalytic frame of reference. A psychoanalytic conceptualization of feminine and masculine merely considers the unconscious fantasies and bodily experiences that shape conscious behavior and belief. Such fantasies are always overdetermined, like Mr. P.'s, condensing identifications, wishes, memories, and perceptions, including those of the body and its parts, from different developmental levels and relationships. Categorical errors like Freud's remain commonplace, but ideally need not be a clinical problem. Mr. P. aspired to have a self like a steel-rod phallus, for example, but analysis revealed that sometimes he unconsciously fantasized that he needed such a phallus or must submit to me to get one. But all he actually feared was the experience of uninhibitedly jumping for joy, of unabashedly expressing love, or of being able to move me because he was moved and knew we might be moved by the same things. He had categorically assumed that such experiences were neither safe nor manly.

A second of Freud's errors (Grossman & Kaplan, 1988) was to notice real differences between the sexes and common childhood events and fantasies that predominate in one sex or another, but then to reify them into allegedly "normal" developmental events and narratives. Girls have penis envy and therefore "normally" look to their father or other male surrogates to compensate for the alleged "defect." Men fear the vagina, or envy babymaking, and therefore "normally" climb mountains or fly rocket ships to the moon. Subtle variations of such logic can lead to false assumptions when Mr. P. achieves something like overcoming his fears and climbing a mountain. But I should have no assumptions regarding the unconscious fantasy attainment. How can I know the meaning of the triumph? The celebration may include an expression of a variety of powers—phallic, "claustral," narcissistic, separation-individuation, or relational. The subject or object of that triumph may be construed as male or female, paternal or maternal. The father or mother may be the model or facilitator for his aspirations to become a bold adventurer. Mr. P. had categorically formulated his mountain climbing aspirations as masculine, perhaps even superior to jumping for joy, rather than recognizing that "girlish" jumping for joy was an integral part of the complete mountain-conquering experience.

The lesson is that rigid, content-bound categories or stepwise, concretely defined childhood developmental phases are not psychoanalytic—cannot do justice to the actual ambiguities and complexities of emergent psychosexuality. Such pernicious categorizing, whether done by psychoanalysis or by the culture at large, is usually based on what Kaplan (1991a) calls "exalted gender ideals of infancy." These childhood ideals are preoedipal, fetishistic, sexual caricatures—entrenched infantile fantasies that are played out in identifications and roles that far too often devalue women and the feminine experience. What Freud saw that remains radically true, however, is that adult notions of power and authority within and among responsible individuals and notions about adult genital sexuality are formed in the same prototypical historical time and place—in the cauldron of oedipal triangular family relations. Powerful adults who are desired, envied, and feared must be passionately encountered, struggled with, separated from, and "internalized" for the child to become an individuated center of morality and authority. But our culture has too long supported the ana-tomical illusion that men are haves and women have-nots. That culture has therefore frequently manipulated and distorted these basic psychologi-cal triangular configurations, idealized phallic at the expense of "cloacal" genitality. In fact, however, every child, male or female, individuates in a world dominated by powerful figures of both sexes—loving, hating, fear-ing, envying—shaped by the capacities and limits of whichever parents or surrogates are available, whatever their sex.

Modern Freudian psychology has developed new tools to help surmount the limitations of simplistic sexual stereotyping or anatomical reduction. I have alluded already to the primacy of psychic reality and the construc-tion of gender and self as a core aspect of an individual's representational world. We have, in other words, broken the frequently too rigid bonds that exist between anatomy and its psychic representation or valuation. In addition, as I said earlier, we conceive of developmental maturity in terms of ego integration, object relating, and the flexibility, integrity, and unity of the self. We emphasize structural complexity and intrapsychic process over content—modes of mental organization.

A contemporary perspective on bisexuality might therefore posit not merely inborn bisexual drives, but inborn bisexual ego capacities. Both men and women have the capacity, at higher levels of mental function-ing, to organize psychic reality in phallic and cloacal modes, mediated, of course, through bodily experiences that are also shaped and limited by the particular sexual anatomy one has. Full psychic integration requires mas-tery in both mental modes and integration of the two without reducing one to the terms of the other. Developmentally, we see increasing capaci-ties to embrace multiple perspectives as we progress to higher mental orga-nizations—narrative complexity, not stepwise psychosexual stages rooted in fixed anatomical zones.

Nevertheless, the rooting of psychic reality in psychosexuality, in direct and immediate bodily experience, remains crucial to Freudian thinking. A major problem exists in common usage of the terms phal-lic and phallic-oedipal, which are falsely reified and usually idealized when categorically invoked to represent that which is more normative or advanced. Parens (1990) has addressed this dilemma of terminology, as applied to the psychology of little girls, by referring merely to a first genital rather than a phallic-narcissistic phase. A subtle devaluation occurs if we have no way to speak of what I have termed "claustral" or "cloacal," which implies, as "phallic" does, the presence of higher level organization, of triadic, postambivalent mental functioning, and of full psychosexual genitality.

We must not demote the phallic aspect. We cannot, for example, ignore the legions of little boys who prefer guns and dinosaurs to doll houses. In pioneering studies, Ross (1986) and Mahon (1986) have shown, however, that although such chauvinism may even be necessary in the boyhoods of most men (mediated, of course, through their experiences of their own male sexual anatomy), an integration of the feminine, archaic, and infantile is attainable for men in adult ("oedipal") romantic love. Many others (for example, see Fogel, Lane, & Liebert, 1986) agree that aspects of so-called primitive psychic life—the dyadic, preoedipal, and narcissistic—are frequently attributed to women, and that these factors must be integrated into adult male psychic life. But my emphasis here is not on the so-called primitive.

The particulars (and limitations) of male anatomy have predisposed us to consider male psychosexual interiority as preoedipal because we often see concrete sexual content organized around oral and anal themes. But conceptions of space, spaces, and spatiality are newly available in the oedipal phase and absolutely required for higher-level genital organization. Bell (1964), Kestenberg (1968), Hägglund and Piha (1980), Stein (1988), and others have written important and insufficiently appreciated papers on internal bodily spaces and their representation, referring specifically to inner genital spaces in the male. In a more recent article, Friedman (1996) has built on Bell's and Kestenberg's observations of the significance of testicular, scrotal, and perineal sensations, fantasies, and fears as a frequent (and frequently disavowed or forgotten) organizer for these more tender, ambiguous, and diffuse aspects of male genital bodily experience. Full psychosexual genitality—and therefore what I conceive of as "true" oedipality for both sexes—requires an equally respectable place for both outer (phallic) and inner (cloacal, spatial) genitality.

Freud claimed that the oedipus complex forms the nucleus of everyone's character, and that a castration complex is always a crucial component. We can rescue this important paradigm for modern psychoanalysis if we remember, as Tyson (1996), Loewald (1979), and others have suggested, that the oedipal phase or an oedipal dynamic should not be conflated or confused with a mode of mental organization. A neurotic or triadic organization is characterized by capacities for personal responsibility, flexibility, and autonomy. There is also object constancy, empathy, finer cognitive discriminations, and subtler signal affects. In other words, roughly coincident with the appearance of so-called phallicoedipal dynamics developmentally come many important new ego and relational capacities. These include an emergent new ability to conceive of one's self and others as whole, separate individuals who also have an unseen but vital internal world. Objects may therefore become whole entities in space and thus also contain within them space and spaces—for complex thoughts, feelings, and purposes, as well as anatomical spaces and configurations—real, metaphorical, and illusory. Capacities emerge to see the part in relation to the whole, to experience the symbolic density of the part when representing the whole, and to appreciate the impossibility of ever comprehending and mastering the part when separated from the whole.

Being whole and unified requires such higher-level capacities, and I believe these capacities have the ring of the "feminine" all over them. As Mr. P. shows us, to become a whole person, an individuated man's representations of his masculinity, including his penis, must integrate and transcend masculine and feminine, phallic and cloacal. Subheadings under this oedipal-level psychosexual polarity will include exteriority and interiority, form and substance, discrimination and immersion, part and whole, and a capacity to both desire and arouse desire, for both sexual ardor and sexual surrender. Defining the "feminine" or internal genital aspect of mental life is difficult, but some of its mature characteristics include receptivity, openness, and tolerance of ambiguity, paradox, and multiple perspectives. Somewhat less tangible, but nevertheless crucial for psychic health, are the attainment of experiential groundedness, connectedness to self and others, and wholeness. In sum, interiority and full realization of psychic potential require emancipation of the "feminine," the "cloacal," from the psychic substrate and acknowledgment of its crucial role in higher mental organizations.

Might it be possible to find a term to represent those frequently devalued aspects of adult development that are primary, "feminine," initially organized within oedipal triangular relationships, equally ubiquitous and essential for psychic mastery as phallic aspects, and also threatened by castration? It is easier to begin with the indispensable term "phallic," where one can draw a clear distinction between concrete, material reality—the anatomical penis—and psychic reality—the "phallus." As I have demonstrated in my clinical material, the phallus is a symbolic fantasy construction that exists in psychic reality. Thus "phallic" power is available in varying degrees and symbolic transformations to both sexes. In clinical analysis, I therefore easily say to a woman, where it feels like the right metaphor and the associations support it, that such-and-such action took "balls" or that she felt like a "prick," and felt guilty and dirty as well as penetrating, exciting, and strong. If a woman dreams she has a penis, I try to keep an open mind. If successfully assertive, does she think she needs or already must have a penis? Or does she imagine that exposing her strength as a woman requires a phallic-narcissistic ramrod self to defend the more flesh-and-blood vulnerabilities associated with real muscles and organs, especially the less tangible or visible interior ones? What is envied here is an impossible dream. Men universally share this envy, yearn for a "phallus" big and strong enough to eliminate vulnerabilities of flesh and spirit that are the common lot of both sexes. But elimination of vulnerability also eliminates potential pleasures and powers. For men and women, authentic empowerment must integrate the phallic with other modes, especially if what appears phallic-oedipal is actually functioning defensively as an infantile, formulistic, impossible ideal.

It is difficult to find a single word, however, to represent vital adult "feminine" sexuality, the part that is not phallic, but is its psychic complement. Ordinary usage seems to provide "masculine" words that for most of us signify something vigorous and at least partly positive, words that also say it all and can be saying many things at once. Unfortunately, "feminine" counterparts all seem to lack the easy vernacular ring that "prick" or even "penis" or "phallus" has. Furthermore, the "masculine" words all have an easily visible anatomical reference, a concrete form, which resonates across developmental levels and symbolic capacities—protosymbolic, primary process, and secondary process. Think of the rat penis, the fecal penis, the baby-penis, the breast-penis, the whole-body penis, the phallic mother. For each of these fantasy metaphors we easily intuit links to a formal, phallic prototype. Not so the feminine polarity, which is a space, often an implicit space whose boundaries are diffuse in direct experience, invisible to direct inspection, and some of whose power lies in the intensity that accompanies the letting go of bodily and psychic boundaries and barriers and therefore of formal description or definition.

I have thus far only used the terms claustral and cloacal for the genital psychosexual interior in an ironic sense—claustral or cloacal man—hoping thereby to avoid idealized or devalued connotations imposed on these terms by centuries of common usage. I have also considered "vulvar," "vaginal," or "uterine" man, but intuitively I sense they miss the mark, just as "penile woman" does not seem to work the way that "phallic woman" does. Metaphorical profundity—experiential or psychic reality—is reduced by cleaving too closely to anatomy. The "phallic" and all its fateful symbolic power in human affairs is, I repeat, a fantasy construction: it has one foot in bodily actuality, the other in imagination and symbolic actualization.

The vagina and womb are anatomically "real" but also misleading—not only because of fantasy distortion, but also because of higher-level knowledge, "real" meanings. We "really" know, for example, that the uterus is the site of the gestation process and that nature regularly does cycles of death, cleansing, and regeneration. But although we revere the generativity and creativity of the symbolic "womb," the anatomical "uterus" is not a primary site of early bodily experience in the psychosexual sense. How can a uterus form the nucleus of an embodied, experiential inner genital space?

So, ironically, if a single word is ever to suffice, "claustral" and "cloacal" strike me as the likeliest candidates. The term "claustral" has the advantage, like "phallic," of its classical etymological dignity, and of being something of a blank screen onto which we can project meaning. Unfortunately, the term also lends itself to idealization—to a kind of sanitation or new-age mystification. The term "cloacal," on the other hand, seems to me more grounded in bodily experience, and at least refers explicitly, if only metaphorically, to internal bodily space. Of the available preexisting psychoanalytic conceptions, the Kleinian construct of the mother's insides (Segal, 1964), where all the babies, feces, penises, and breasts exist and come from, may come closest to a common-sense single concept to represent all that it must. It is dark, fantastical, and infinitely powerful, but for me it fails to provide what I seek—a single gritty, exciting, and dangerous enough, sexual enough, word.

This is where the cloaca comes in as primal fantasy representation. It is a universal sexual theory in childhood for both sexes. It metaphorically represents inner psychosexual space—the unboundaried source of fiery eruption, seismic rumbling, and swampy undertow. It stands for the unformed and unseen, for absorption and immersion. It is not pretty and lends itself to easy and frequent devaluation, for it may be conceived as the location in both sexes, as one patient once put it, for the "yuck" factor—the virtually universal disgust with which both sexes regard the inside of the body and its contents at some point in early genital development. So as a means to represent the container of interior psychosexual life, a cloaca may reflect anatomical and psychical correlates of important actualities of human experience. Newly emergent genital sexuality, procreative powers, and authority combine with oral and anal pregenital modes—substances, smells, and textures; contents, processes, and representations—from any place and everywhere, in complicated and always shifting relations to each other, a whole never completely reducible to the sum of its parts. It is gatherer and originator, creator and destroyer, where all things come and go, get all mixed up with each other. Thus, it represents both Pandora's box and cornucopia—a generative space of infinite multiplicity and constant flow, grounded in the dreadful and awesome body, all parts interrelated, borders permeable and shifting, parts submerged in the whole.

Like a phallus, a cloaca can be represented in psychic reality at all levels of psychic maturity. Conceived as static or stereotyped entities, phallus and cloaca may be respectively regarded as exalted or degraded, the phallic as superior to what appears less formed or anatomically locatable. Conceived as modes of experience, however, each may be manifest in more or less archaic or evolved ways. It may be hard to think of psychic "space" as evolving developmentally, but I believe that both psychic representation and psychic space evolve—the contained and the container. Psychic contents—mental discriminations—evolve from the crude, simplistic, and sexualized to the increasingly more precise and subtle. Psychic space becomes less swampy, more lucid. It needs to exclude less to maintain its integrity. It becomes flexible, reliable, and able to flow and go with the flow. Psychic space can also allow more perspectives, have more dimensionality, profundity, and texture.

Elsewhere (Fogel, 1992) I have correlated the appearance of a capacity for imagination, dreaming, and fantasy to Winnicott's transitional or intermediate experience. Might we say that the cloacal evolves from primal cauldron to Winnicottian space? Higher mental organizations ideally free an individual from the reification and sexualization of earlier, more primitive experience. In psychic health, one remains in one's body, but is less a stimulus slave to it. A subtle and less tangible narrative and metaphorical space must transcend one that is more primitive and concrete. For that higher "space" to be vital and alive, however, sublimated or symbolically actualized derivatives of early bodily experience must be present to ground it. A whole and individuated person should contain, integrate, and unify all her constituent parts without sacrificing finer discriminations. It is this containing function that I conceive as the possible essence of the feminine. In its mature and most integrated forms, there must be a transcendence of one's anatomical sex and gender—an acknowledging and containing reconciliation of difference and similarity. Therefore, such experience is equally available to both sexes. As an example, remember Mr. P.'s all-mixed-upness, and the confluence of anal, scrotal, cardiovaginal, perineal, and skin sensitivity contained in certain of his experiences. Also recall the progression contained in successively more differentiated and integrated representations of them, and also the evolution in the quality and consistency of the reflective space he brought to bear upon them.

The female principle contains ambiguity at its core—perhaps a necessary counterpart to so-called masculine reason and necessity. It parallels the right brain functioning that must be added to the left to make a whole mind. But this very ambiguity may make it impossible to find a precise word. Ironically, a fantasy-metaphor cloaca, rather than an anatomically real bodily organ, may provide the more "accurate" word—the better representation for the embodied psychosexual inner genital self. By stressing the metaphorical aspects, we do not necessarily deny anatomical realities and differences, although there will be a danger of such denial. We may, however, do more justice to the essential diffuseness and ambiguity inherent in such powers, the purification and unification hidden in etymological roots, and the enigmas involved in linking the material body to its psychic representations.

If individuation sometimes seems easier for bodies, it is often at the expense of reality, which is not so concrete, dominatable, and obvious as their penis (and the culture) would have them believe. As girls do, boys must eventually learn to cope with what cannot be seen nor easily grasped or controlled—within their bodies, minds, and body-minds. Boys may feel certainty in the obviousness of what they can see or grasp, but therefore mistake what is visible for the whole truth. That which appears anatomically or psychically obvious, clear by comparison to what is enigmatic and invisible, may seem simple but actually be simpleminded. Thus, the apparently easier road to separation-individuation for a boy may actually lead to psychological constriction.

An Interesting New Literature

Naturally, any complete human being unites both "principles," the masculine and the feminine. In Hindu mythology, Shiva and Shakti (known also respectively as the "avenger" and the "destroyer") are the deities that objectify male and female. It is also said in that tradition that the lingam, the phallus, is a symbol, a representation of Shiva's power, but that it cannot exist without the vulva surrounding it. Shakti supplies the energy without which the male is merely form, without vital substance or ground. Thus, the masculine-feminine polarity wants to reach, I think, even beyond these complex, endlessly overdetermined primal representations, such as phallus and cloaca, to something that defies easy representation. The I Ching contrasts heaven and earth. Buddhism contrasts the sharp sword of discriminating wisdom with all-embracing compassion.

But can psychoanalysts contribute to what in the past have been primarily regarded as philosophical or theological issues—issues such as the relationship between doing and being, effable and ineffable, figure and ground? I think so, because there are many similarities in our own clinical and theoretical struggle to understand the relationship between material (including bodily) and psychical reality. There is, in fact, an exciting new psychoanalytic literature that plays on the differences and relationships between material and psychical reality. Schafer (1992) considers them in relation to unconscious narrative. Laplanche (1987) considers the universal mixture of actuality and illusion in psychic reality and notes that although the primal parental objects are always actual and historical, they also inevitably have enigmatic qualities in psychic reality, are "enigmatic signifiers." Butler (1993) tries to demonstrate that materiality itself ("body," "sex") can only "appear" or "endure," can "only live within the productive constraints of certain highly gendered regulatory schemas" (p. xi). Laqueur (1990) demonstrates that the notion of anatomical differences between the sexes is relatively modern, although powerful gender differences have existed since antiquity. These modern scholars believe that matter and space, boundaries and surfaces—entities—are only known to us through gendered representations. Materiality itself, in other words, its actual texture and vitality, appears in psychic experience only through such discriminated forms, inevitably powerfully contributed to by unconscious, archaic ones—in other words, by infantile sexual theories.

Thus, as Freud (1900) first discovered, all psychic experience that is alive must be grounded in the archaic, the unconscious "core of our being." In more traditional psychoanalytic terms, psychic health combines the intensities and qualities of primary process, the cognitive discriminations of secondary process, and perhaps the ambiguous and paradoxical, higher-level qualities of Winnicottian transitional space as well, into a more unified and fully integrated mental organization. Thus, a core ingredient of all higher-level mental function may be this enigmatic, "feminine" mental space. These are merely glimpses of a vast new literature that offers the promise of an eventual integration of the findings of modern hermeneutic, linguistic, and feminist studies with classic psychoanalytic psychosexuality and object relations theory.*

A Last Look at Professor M.

I hope you have not forgotten Prof. M. I began this chapter with his terrifying hallucination that he had a cloaca and begged your indulgence that I borrow his fantasy for a word to represent a prototype, the male with a dark and unseen psychosexual inner space. Intending irony, I called this prototype cloacal man, despite the possibly imprecise and degrading connotations. Now we have come full circle, and I have reluctantly concluded that although we need the omnipotential prototype to complement the universal prototype of the phallic woman, we probably cannot use Prof. M.'s word. The actual analysis I used for my example, that of Mr. P., showed that neither patient nor analyst need have in mind a specific cloacal fantasy to search out and liberate a man's inner genital self from the fear, distortion, and devaluation that so commonly limits it. Few men have an explicit fantasy of having a cloaca. I believe that all may have a fantasy construction of an inner genital space, however, and I made the best case I could that a cloaca might be more suitable than it appears at first glance to serve as a primal organizing concept to represent such a space. Before we dismiss the word entirely, however, and before I conclude, let me share a bit more of what we eventually learned about Prof. M.'s cloaca.

Later in his analysis, while talking about cigarettes, Prof. M. rediscovered a significant screen memory. He had once been a heavy smoker and suddenly recalled walking as a child—perhaps he was 6 or 7—into the

---

* I confined my review of contemporary views of the psychology of women to the traditional psychoanalytic literature. This literature draws on, but usually does not systematically cover the enormously diverse and productive larger body of work from many disciplines loosely organized under the label of psychoanalytic feminism. For an excellent review of this area, see Chodorow (1989). She distinguishes psychoanalysts who think about women from psychoanalytic feminists (mostly academics), reviews this diverse literature in detail, attempts synthesis where possible, and delineates many of the current unsettled questions requiring further dialogue. Benjamin (1996), in a paper that appeared only after my own was completed, also does an excellent literature review. Her ideas on gender ambiguity would have been quite useful to me while writing my paper. She speaks, for example, of transcending the concrete complementarity of oedipal dimorphism—the "simple logic of oedipal opposites"—with the gender ambiguity which is "everywhere present in concrete life." What she calls an integrated postoedipal position I call "true" oedipality, but I believe that many of our ideas are compatible, particularly in our call for transcending various reductionistic polarities without denying the inevitability that these polarities exist nor of their probable developmental necessity.

bathroom where his father was sitting naked on the toilet reading the newspaper and smoking a cigarette. The dense smoke and feces created a smell that was utterly overwhelming and indelibly imprinted—powerful, pungent, unpleasant, awesome. He described visual details as well: the open pack of cigarettes, book of matches, and other newspaper sections lying on the floor. But his dominant vision was of his father's body—large and swarthy, his trunk covered with dense, black hair.

Prof. M. favors his mother's family, and, like her, he is fair; he always imagined himself to be rather delicate and physically vulnerable, although this is not actually the case. His father had affectionately kibbitzed him a bit, Prof. M. thought, although he could not bring back any of the banter. He vividly recalled, however, following with his eyes the dark hair of his father's chest and belly down into the darkness framed by the rustling newspaper and his father's thighs, all converging into a blackness between his legs that was comprised of thick pubic hair merging into the invisible inside of the toilet that looked like an inky cave below. Neither his father's penis nor his scrotum were visible in the blackness, although maybe, now that he thought about it, there could have been a soft suggestion of those shapes somewhere in there. So here, the astonished Prof. M. reflected, was his father's black hole—the dark interior, the source—the breathing, pulsating heart and belly of the whale. Here was the dragon's cave, the source of fire, smoke, and fierce, terrifying, and wondrous sounds and smells.

The discussion of smoking had begun with the mention of an old movie starring Humphrey Bogart and Lauren Bacall. He and his no-longer-new woman friend had watched it together the night before the session. They were getting more deeply involved, talking about living together. The movie referred, interestingly, almost precisely to the time of the childhood memory. Images of smoking represented dramatically for Prof. M. the sexual authority, potency, and cool sophistication of these larger-than-life screen personalities. Bogie and Bacall were like a magnificent childhood vision of his parents—their clothes, their moves; the curving lip, the finger picking a piece of tobacco off the tongue; the languorous looks, the thrilling seductive potency. It was Dionysian, said Prof. M., androgynous, this power—like a serpent or snake. Both parents had had these qualities for him at times, but clearly his father was in the foreground today, his possibly overstimulating but clearly affectionate banter with his young son, the centerpiece and also the key to the real life and intense feelings contained in this entire sequence.

Here were the dragons of the childhood stories that had thrilled and frightened him—the knowing, mesmerizing bright eyes, fierce jaws, nostrils, and mouth come newly alive as he talked. His mother had French inhaled, his father had blown smoke rings. Both parents were heavy smokers, and Prof. M. followed precociously in their footsteps in his youth. They were young when he was born, loved night-life, jazz. They sometimes took him to jazz clubs in his teens—memories also full of excitement, apprehension, dense cigarette smoke, musky and pungent body smells, and black people. Black musicians were heroes to his father. Music, nighttime or "dark" knowledge and power—being "cool" or "hip"—all these things suddenly stood for depths in his father's inner life for which Prof. M. had new, profound, unrequited longings. Other associations included Blake's tyger, Goya's Saturn devouring his children, and the black hole in deep space that irresistibly pulls the whole universe into it.

There was more, but I wish only to make one point. This memory of Prof. M.'s father is not a screen that defends against or a displacement from his observation of his mother's "castrated" genital. There is nothing missing, but rather something there. Just as his mother's sharp tongue, probing cotton swab in his ears, and long fingernails had phallic attributes that actually combined strands from many objects, developmental levels, and historical moments, so too this experience of his father. Despite its composite nature and relation to both parents, I offer it as evidence that in this material it is the father's psychosexual interior that dominates this important fragment of Prof. M.'s past and present experience. Although oral and anal themes abound, placing these too concretely in the foreground would seriously reduce the power and full developmental attainments contained in Prof. M.'s newly recovered oedipal-level experiences. This memory screens, both expresses and defends, his awe, dread, excitement, longings, aspirations, envy, competition, identification, and identity with—all of his feelings regarding his own and his father's inner genitality, his cloacal power.

Now we have more data to answer the very first question I raised regarding whose cloaca, whose dark hole it was that Prof. M. hallucinated in longing, dread, and envy back in his 20s when he suddenly felt so overwhelmed by his beautiful, sophisticated French woman friend. But we probably cannot conclude that the term is suitable for wide or general use on the basis of the evocativeness or precision of Prof. M.'s fantasy. Especially in light of the extreme negative connotations of the term cloaca, it seems neither safe nor common-sensical to shout it from the rooftops. Without a word, achieving full legitimacy and parity for what I have referred to as cloacal will be more difficult. But word or no word, deprived of his "feminine" parts, a man is castrated, compromised, less than whole.

So if a man aspires to be all that he can, he must admit he has more to lose in castration than his phallic powers, and certainly much more than his penis.

Acknowledgment

This chapter originally appeared in *Psychoanalytic Quarterly, 67*(4), 1998, pp. 662–697. © The Psychoanalytic Quarterly. Reprinted with permission.

References

Bell, A. I. (1964). Bowel training difficulties in boys: Prephallic and phallic considerations. *Journal of the American Academy of Child Psychiatry, 3,* 577–590.

Benjamin, J. (1996). In defense of gender ambiguity. *Gender and Psychoanalysis, 1,* 27–43.

Bernstein, D. (1990). Female genital anxieties, conflicts and typical mastery modes. *International Journal of Psycho-Analysis, 71,* 151–165.

Burton, A. (1996). The meaning of perineal activity to women: An inner sphinx. *Journal of the American Psychoanalytic Association, 44*(Suppl.), 241–259.

Butler, J. P. (1993). *Bodies that Matter.* New York: Routledge.

Chodorow, N. J. (1989). Psychoanalytic feminism and the psychoanalytic psychology of women. In *Feminism and Psychoanalytic Theory* (pp. 178–198). New Haven, CT: Yale University Press.

Fogel, G. I. (1992). Winnicott's antitheory and Winnicott's art: His significance for adult analysis. *Psychoanalytic Study of the Child, 47,* 205–222.

Fogel, G. I., Lane, F., & Liebert, R. (Eds.). (1986). *The Psychology of Men: New Psychoanalytic Perspectives.* New York: Basic Books.

Friedman, R. M. (1996). The role of the testicles in male psychological development. *Journal of the American Psychoanalytic Association, 44,* 201–253.

Freud, S. (1900). The interpretation of dreams. *Standard Edition, 4–5.*

Freud, S. (1905). Three essays on the theory of sexuality. *Standard Edition, 7.*

Grossman, W. I., & Kaplan, D. (1988). Three commentaries on gender in Freud's thought: A prologue on the psychoanalytic theory of sexuality. In H. P. Blum, Y. Kramer, A. K. Richards, & A. D. Richards (Eds.), *Fantasy, Myth, and Reality: Essays in Honor of Jacob A. Arlow* (pp. 179-181). Madison, CT: International Universities Press.

Hägglund, T.-B., & Piha, H. (1980). The inner space of the body image. *Psychoanalytic Quarterly, 49,* 256–283.

Kaplan, L. J. (1991a). *Castration anxiety and the female perversions.* Unpublished manuscript.

Kaplan, L. J. (1991b). *Female Perversions: The Temptations of Emma Bovary*. New York/London: Doubleday.

Kestenberg, J. S. (1968). Outside and inside, male and female. *Journal of the American Psychoanalytic Association, 16*, 457–520.

Laplanche, J. (1987). *New Foundations for Psychoanalysis*. Cambridge, MA/Oxford, UK: Blackwell, 1989.

Laqueur, T. (1990). *Making Sex*. Cambridge, MA/London: Harvard University Press.

Loewald, H.W. (1979) The Waning of the Oedipus Complex. *Journal of the American Psychoanalytic Association, 27*:751-775.

Loewald, H. W. (1988). *Sublimation: Inquiries into Theoretical Psychoanalysis*. New Haven, CT/London: Yale University Press.

Mahon, E. (1986). The contribution of adolescence to male psychology. In G. I. Fogel, F. Lane, & R. Liebert (Eds.), *The Psychology of Men: New Psychoanalytic Perspectives* (pp. 229–241). New York: Basic Books.

Mayer, E. L. (1985). "Everybody must be just like me": Observations on female castration anxiety. *International Journal of Psycho-Analysis, 66*, 331–347.

Parens, H. (1990). On the girl's psychosexual development: Reconsiderations suggested from direct observation. *Journal of the American Psychoanalytic Association, 38*, 743–772.

Richards, A. K. (1992). The influence of sphincter control and genital sensation on body image and gender identity in women. *Psychoanalytic Quarterly, 61*, 331–351.

Ross, J. M. (1986). Beyond the phallic illusion: Notes on man's heterosexuality. In G. I. Fogel, F. Lane, & R. Liebert (Eds.), T*he Psychology of Men: New Psychoanalytic Perspectives* (pp. 49–70). New York: Basic Books.

Schafer, R. (1992). *Retelling a Life: Narration and Dialogue in Psychoanalysis*. New York: Basic Books.

Segal, H. (1964). *Introduction to the Works of Melanie Klein*. New York: Basic Books.

Stein, Y. (1988). Some reflections on the inner space and its contents. *Psychoanalytic Studies of the Child, 43*, 291–304.

Tyson, P. (1996). Neurosis in childhood and in psychoanalysis: A developmental reformulation. *Journal of the American Psychoanalytic Association, 44*, 143–165.

Index